AMERICAN GANGBANG

AMERICAN GANGBANG

a love story

SAM BENJAMIN

Gallery Books

New York   London   Toronto   Sydney   New Delhi

Certain names and identifying characteristics have been changed.

G

Gallery Books
A Division of Simon & Schuster, Inc.
1230 Avenue of the Americas
New York, NY 10020

First Gallery Books hardcover edition October 2011

GALLERY BOOKS and colophon are registered trademarks of Simon & Schuster, Inc.

For information about special discounts for bulk purchases, please contact Simon & Schuster Special Sales at 1-866-506-1949 or business@simonandschuster.com.

The Simon & Schuster Speakers Bureau can bring authors to your live event. For more information or to book an event contact the Simon & Schuster Speakers Bureau at 1-866-248-3049 or visit our website at www.simonspeakers.com.

Designed by Joy O'Meara

Manufactured in the United States of America

1   3   5   7   9   10   8   6   4   2

Library of Congress Cataloging-in-Publication Data
Benjamin, Sam.
American gangbang : a love story / Sam Benjamin.
1st Gallery Books hardcover ed.
p. cm.
1. Pornography. I. Title.
HQ471.B455 2011
306.77—dc22
[B]   2011010873

ISBN 978-1-4516-2778-7
ISBN 978-1-4516-2779-4 (ebook)

For my family, who stood by me loyally—
no matter what

ONE

Once upon a time, I was twenty-two and fresh out of college, with a heart young and open and free, and I had but one dream: to move to California.

My father seemed rather unwilling to grasp this concept. "Are we really *that* bad? You can't even consider staying on the east *coast*?"

"David, calm down." My mom nodded at me apologetically. "He really doesn't mind the idea so much."

"I don't like New York," I said. "In fact, I *hate* New York. I can't even stand to be there for two days. You know that."

"I have never met anyone who honestly *hates* New York. It just doesn't happen very often. Quite likely you are the only Jewish person in the whole *world* who *hates* New York."

It was hard to win an argument with my dad—being a psychoanalyst, he did this kind of thing for a living—but in this case, I didn't have to win. All I had to do was leave. So I did. I took my graduation money and I bought a 1980 diesel Volvo, and I drove it to California. To a place called Santa Cruz.

A funky ad tacked up on a health food store bulletin board led me straight to a two-man bungalow on the east side of town, inhabited by a forty-year-old vegan named Periwinkle. He was a spiritual gardener hailing from Berkeley, California, with an enormous experimental music collection, impeccable aesthetic taste, and a passion for social justice. He also had about twelve cents in the bank. Periwinkle refused to buy any new articles of clothing, a policy that extended to underwear.

"You can find *great* underwear at the Salvation Army," he scoffed. "There are too many wonderful pairs of underwear out there in the world today to justify spending seven dollars on new ones."

Periwinkle was forever out in the front yard, laboring with grand enthusiasm and perfectionist fervor on his small, beautiful garden, when he really should have been working at someone else's place, for money.

"I don't care, Sam, that's the thing," he explained to me. "I'm so *happy* gardening—so much happier than I used to be. Do you know what I used to do?"

"No," I said. "What?"

"I used to be a *traveling salesman*! I'm dead serious. I'd go from town to town, selling life insurance policies for some company that I'd never even visited, making tons of money, flushing it all down the drain. It's *incredible*—incredible that it took me so long to wake up. Incredible that I finally did wake up."

One evening, Periwinkle and I rocked back and forth in a salvaged chair on our tiny front porch, listening to the Pacific Ocean. "Tell me, Sam," Periwinkle said, "what really motivates you?"

"Ah . . ." I hesitated, hoping to come up with an answer that would suitably impress my new friend. "Civil libertarianism?"

"I would have guessed girls," Periwinkle said, smiling.

"Well, that's probably a little closer to the truth," I admitted. "*Art's* really my bag, though."

"Art!" Periwinkle said, approvingly. "How'd you get into that?"

"College. It was my major."

"Very cool. What's your medium?"

"Well, I used to be into comics. But I was pretty terrible at drawing, as it turned out. So then I tried writing short stories. But that got boring. It was like, just me and my computer, you know?"

"Sure," Periwinkle said, toking on his bowl. Like most other Cruzians, Periwinkle had a real fondness for marijuana, but the difference was, he smoked leaf. No buds: just leaf. An eighth of chopped marijuana leaf went for around ten bucks in those days. He was dirt poor, Periwinkle, but he really loved to smoke. All the time.

"And now?"

"Well, now, nothing, I guess. I'm still trying to figure out what I'm good at."

"You know what I like?" Peri said, the weed sparking his enthusiasm. "You know what *I* think is art? *Cable access.* That stuff is brilliant! We had a station in Berkeley when I was growing up."

"Well, sure, cable access is cool."

"Do you want to start your own show, then?" Periwinkle asked, hopefully. "Santa Cruz could use a really smart, strange cable access show."

"I don't know. I don't think I would make much money at it."

"Of course you wouldn't," Periwinkle said, eyeing me distrustfully. "No one makes money from cable access television."

"Well, I don't know."

"Consider it. Follow your *passion*." He bit off the last word with surprising spitefulness, as if he'd spent a regrettably long stretch of his own life doing just the opposite.

The truth is, I wanted to be an artist. I wanted it bad. Precisely how I was to accomplish this was unclear, since I was not proficient at drawing, painting, sculpting, or any other artistic pursuit; nonetheless, art is what I had my sights set on. Thank God for postmodernism.

My alma mater, Brown—like most American liberal arts institutions operating in the latter part of the twentieth century—had adopted the postmodern way of thought as a virtual religion. The upshot was that you no longer had to be able to *draw* to be good at art. Take, for instance, Conceptual Art: Sherrie Levine photographed other people's photographs. No skill needed there—just a good idea. Piero Manzoni sold his own breath (in balloons). Robert Rauschenberg *erased* a Willem de Kooning drawing. And how about Found Art? What else was there to say about Found Art besides acknowledgment of its basic genius? You found a piece of crap on the street and called it Art. *Yes.*

Goofy-ass Video Art, for instance, was one of the greatest things I'd ever seen. In my History of Contemporary Art class, I'd watched a guy named Chris Burden purchase ad time on a Los Angeles station, then run a freakish, disturbing thirty-second clip that showed him dragging his naked body through piles of crushed glass. Inspired, I decided to give Video Art a whirl myself. Using the postmodern technique known as "recontexualization," I simply "re-presented" an old videotape of the 1983 Miss Teen USA Pageant to my class. I admit, I did so with some trepidation: my peers could become intellectual bullies at the drop of a hat, especially amid impassioned classroom critiques. Best friends had cut each other to ribbons over minor cultural missteps in the past. But, to my delight, my classmates adored the bold move.

Clearly, I had found a formula. I began to run with it. For my next project, I took a mysterious German porn flick that I'd found in a sad New York City smut shop and completely reedited it, inserting English subtitles, removing every trace of sex. What remained was an unfunny, cheaply produced, highly degraded specimen of sub-cinematic dogshit. A classmate declared that while watching, you were confronted by the *absence* of porn. Inside, I beamed.

From that moment on, there was no question in my mind. I could go pro; I could use my brain to make a buck. It was just a matter of figuring out how.

It was a slow month in Santa Cruz. I haunted the local cafés, sad-eyed, pouring dark coffee down my throat, waiting for some sort of inspiration. But nothing was coming, and I was floundering. When my twenty-third birthday rolled around, I decided to take advantage of the occasion. I headed out on the town for a night of debauchery.

There was a downtown bar that I'd had my eye on for some time—the Asti. A lot of mean boozers hung out there, which didn't bode well for me, but the only known pub alternatives were the Drop Inn, which was equally full of dangerous shitheads, and Rosie McCann's, a pseudo-Irish joint full of assholes watching ESPN. But none of that mattered to me that night. It was my birthday, and I couldn't stand the idea of spending it alone. So I headed for the Asti.

Half an hour after entering, I got lucky. A girl named Charlie—an inebriated but sexy waitress, fresh off the evening shift at a nearby seafood restaurant—approached me at the bar and started talking to me. Hot tonsil-breath beat against my face, but I nodded earnestly. Charlie's well-proportioned body was beckoning to me.

An hour later, we were back at her little beachfront apartment, licking each other's faces hungrily. She moaned inside my mouth. I seized a hank of the hair at the base of her skull and pushed her up against the living room wall.

"Don't wake my sister," Charlie whispered, chewing on my neck, her nails digging into the flesh of my upper arms, making tiny cuts. "She's sleepin'."

"Don't worry, I won't," I promised.

"She's pregnant," Charlie added, struggling out of her shirt.

"That's great," I breathed, staring at her enormous, amazing tits for one long moment. "Boy or girl?"

"Who cares?" Charlie shot back, angrily, covering her chest with thin, dishpan hands. "Who are you with, me or her?"

"You, babe," I assured her. "You!"

"That's better," Charlie said, smiling a child's contented smile. "C'mon, let's *do* it already! I'm probably gonna pass out soon, so we better get started."

But neither of us had a condom. It didn't matter much to Charlie, who was straight up *ordering* me to fuck her, but I was hesitant. As eager as I was to create a child who had her perfect tits and my gigantic nose, I realized that, for the moment, I was unfit to raise a child. So I had sex with her leg, and ejaculated onto the arm of their couch.

Charlie hardly noticed. She was drifting badly. I gave her face a small, unobtrusive nudge with my thumb, then a gentle slap. When there was no response, I pried open her mouth, separating her jaw with both hands, and took a look inside. Everything was okay in there: no vomit, no obstructions to the airway. I was still peering into the depths of Charlie's oral cavity with curious, drunken fascination when her pregnant sister unceremoniously appeared on the scene. She fixed me a hard look.

"Who are you?"

"Friend of Charlie's," I said awkwardly. I removed my hand from her mouth, letting her jaws snap shut. I looked down at myself, at the small pool of semen drying on the couch. "I was going to clean that up."

"Right," Charlie's sister said.

She was a fraternal twin, I could see, but a twin nonetheless: a fatter but still-alluring version of the groggy vixen by my side. The rim of her fertile belly protruded from the bottom of her T-shirt. She poured herself a grapefruit juice over ice, offering me nothing.

We stared at each other for a long, weird moment.

"So, are you just gonna stay like that all night?" the sister said.

"What do you mean?" I asked, confused. "Oh, naked. Sorry." I covered myself with Charlie's leg.

"Not that I mind, especially. You have a pretty decent body."

"Oh. Well. That's very . . . kind of you."

She gazed at me sidelong, caressing her placental lump in a bizarre fashion I couldn't decode. Finally, she said, "Listen. Why don't you stick around for a while? Get *freaky*."

Frightened, I gathered up my belongings and ran. Streaking home, the mean California wind in my face, I felt a stab of childish despair. With no real income to speak of, I was clearly doomed to assume the life of a degenerate. What was my next move—how could I make a *buck*?

TWO

I remembered that Santa Cruz held a flea market every weekend, in the parking lot of an old drive-in. I knew a little bit about beat-up movie cameras, used stereos, and kooky magazines. Maybe there was a buck to be made in scavenging old stuff, giving it a polish, and reselling it at sky-high profits.

I set out for the Skyview Flea Market, keeping an eye out for cool vinyl, Super 8 cameras, and slide projectors that still had their bulbs intact. I cruised the aisles amid armies of big-breasted rockabilly chicks, their Elvis-haired boyfriends, and thin-bearded antiques store owners who came early and fought dirty and wore terribly sad taut corduroy pants that had little indentations where their balls had rubbed up against the wales so very endlessly.

I sped around the massive market, trying to focus on making an investment in my future. A naïve vendor sold me a stack of "naturist"

magazines from the early 1960s—*Eden, Sun, Jaybird,* and so on—
and I found a functioning Polaroid SX-70 Land Camera that I was
certain I could sell for more than a hundred bucks. Then my eyes
fell on a table crowded with beautiful, beat-up microphones.

"Any of these work?" I asked the guy behind the table.

"*Many* of these work," the guy said, with a smile that was incredibly warm, almost inappropriately kind. "My bro," he added. He was
a ragged-looking old mountain hippie, disheveled and most certainly unshowered, but he emanated this rather extraordinary aura
of serenity. I found it pleasant just to be in his presence. "Are you
interested in any particular one?"

"I'm interested in one that *works,*" I said, laughing.

"Are you thinking of recording something?"

"Well, I might do that," I said evasively. "Actually, yeah! Show
me something a musician might use."

"Well, here's a nice Shure. It's a real beauty, isn't it? It's a con-
denser mic, but of course you already knew that. It's *super*flexible:
good for both acoustic and electric, hardly any distortion to speak
of. It's basically your totally cool, all-around magical, do-it-yourself
studio microphone."

"Yeah, I guess I could take a chance on that," I said. "How much
are you asking?"

"Twenty bucks."

"I'll give you three."

He laughed. "You strike a hard bargain, sir. Perhaps I could show
you something more in your price range."

"Do you *have* anything else?"

"Now that you mention it," he said, "I do. Come and take a look
at Dusty's back room."

I stepped behind the table. Dusty took a look over his shoulder and then slid open the rusty side door of his van. Inside, a stack of about thirty ancient VHS tapes, some in boxes, some bare, lay sprawled out on a blanket.

"These are *adult videos*," Dusty announced, regally.

"From the 1920s?" I asked, inspecting a tape dubiously. The yellowing, hand-printed label read: *Her Welcum Waggin'*.

"No, mid-eighties," Dusty said, seriously. "The guy who owns the land up in Boulder Creek where I've been parking my van has decided it's time to divest himself of his own personal collection. These are *vintage*, bro—a real slice of erotic history. Not much use to me, though. I cater to a more musically oriented clientele, as you've noticed. With that in mind, I'd let you have 'em all for three bucks apiece."

"Two."

"That's what I said. Two." Dusty grinned, producing a wrinkled paper sack from somewhere within the recesses of his musty van. "Now then. May I wrap these up for you?"

I couldn't wait to get home and try out my new pornos. Like most reasonable people, I had a real soft spot in my heart for sex videos. To me, they were kind of like a specialized wing of Video Art, reserved especially for degenerates. Happily, Dusty's tapes appeared to reflect a serious and dedicated porn aficionado. They represented a wide range of erotic interests: there was big-studio stuff, displayed in oversized boxes, like VCA's *Whore of the Worlds*, and guy-on-the-street porn, like early Buttman and Ed Powers. But the greater part of his collection consisted of amateur tapes. They boasted generic titles like *Cheaters* and *California Dreamin'*, and bore labels that had been stamped out in small batches by dot matrix printers, proclaiming copyrights to companies by now doubtlessly defunct

("Power Productions, Ltd."). I imagined all manner of sex acts, performed by anonymous fuck machines, recorded on clunky Betas by bumbling videographers who'd landed inside the world of adult film by accident. With a sense of childlike joy, anticipating hours of doltish fun bracketed by short, meditative bursts of whacking, I sat down to begin my pornographic education.

Dusty's tapes didn't disappoint. They were deliciously obscene, and almost deliriously cheap. A few of the rawest weren't even really *movies*, in the strictest sense of the word: they had no dialogue, no plotline, and no discernable characters. Essentially, all they had was rutting. Some, though, made a rudimentary pass at maintaining a through-line. *California Dreamin'*, for instance, was about an aging surfer who rents his house out to a procession of young blond girls — not real creative, and yet, the tape was fairly packed with gems.

The clothes that the *Dreamin'* performers wore, for example, brought back a rush of vivid memories. A left-ear earring, a banana clip, and a pair of stonewashed jeans all hit me within the context of one blowjob scene. I loved how the '80s-style pornos *looked*, too — they'd been shot on cameras that were predigital, but postfilmic, produced at some historical moment that fell between the Portapak and the Handycam. Adding insult, the sound was invariably subpar — uniformly tinny and almost always underlined by an unflappable background hum. More than anything else, they reminded me of cable access programming, with their charmingly degraded production values and their dolt-as-auteur authorial signature.

I snuggled deeper into my cozy nest of blankets, popping in tape after tape. The porn kept serving up the genius of accidental art. *Her Welcum Waggin'*, for example, videotaped in a dilapidated trailer home by a director who kept reminding his starlet, "remember, don't think about the camera, darlin'," took great care in according to the most basic rule of progressive video art; that is, it avoided all narrative trajectory whatsoever. The film began with about half a minute of meaningless, perverted silence, after which a guy with a blond mustache who looked exactly like Matthew McConaughey (but for a tattoo of what appeared to be a leper on his right forearm) entered and immediately mounted the woman. They fucked on the kitchen floor, in exactly the same position and without saying a single word or changing so much as a facial expression for so long that, after a while, I was sure I was watching a "happening," or some new endurance piece dreamed up by a disciple of Andy Warhol. But I wasn't. This was just *porn*—incredibly ill-conceived, poorly executed, amateurish porn—and it contained a remarkable, unique beauty all its own, uncodified by, and unimaginable within, the context of contemporary art.

Greedily, I grabbed another tape, and then another. The Ed Powers stuff was creepy and reeked of sleaze, but I enjoyed that. Ed played himself, a shy nebbish in his mid-thirties who'd begun to invite pretty girls that he found on the street or located through channels in LA's adult industry to come over to his house and fuck him on camera. Two charismatic adult film stars, Jamie Gillis and Randy West, both of whom were just beginning to show the first signs of aging, joined him; together, they were the Nasty Brothers. Jamie and Randy were in good physical shape, Ed not so much, but all three of them took turns interviewing and then sloppily porking the girls. It wasn't very erotic, but it was *real*.

Amateur porn tossed you some regular girls—waitresses, substitute teachers, teenage fuck-starlets at the very beginning of their careers—and the frank, uncomplicated format of the videos left them unencumbered by unrealistic plotlines and idiotic costumes. The girls answered the prosaic questions about their lives more or less honestly, it seemed, as if they were participating in some odd anthropological film project about a highly specific subset of people, those drawn to fucking on stained couches for the entertainment of strangers. And even when Ed and his buddies quit the interviews and began pandering to a more prurient set of interests, the video was still documentary-like: you could learn a lot about someone by the way that they bucked when experiencing an ecstatic moment. To my bleary, late-night eyes, even the fakest orgasms seemed somehow confessional.

I sampled from almost all of the tapes that night. It was early morning before I pried myself away from my VCR. An expansive warmth had begun to emanate from the center of my chest, spreading outward to all reaches of my body. I threw on a hooded sweatshirt and wandered dreamily out to the porch with a bowlful of Periwinkle's leaf, intent on catching the sunrise.

It was as if I had discovered a whole new universe, one that reflected back to a period of time that I'd long forgotten, or never experienced in the first place. What was it that Dusty had said—erotic history? These fuck videos were packed with intimate glimpses of real people, naked not just in dress but in action—momentarily unguarded, weirdly free.

Toking happily, I rocked back in my chair, imagining for a moment that I was *there* with them, starring in the worst movies of all time, playfully humping around with fun-loving, impulsive chicks, and earning a big paycheck at the same time. Or no, even better, *filming* the whole thing! I envisioned myself sitting in a big director's chair, with a megaphone and a beret, a trustworthy underling taking dictation as I dreamed up the next retarded "scene" for a movie that no one expected anything of, a film everyone imagined would be utterly inconsequential. But I would show them all. I would pull off a *surprise*—a sex film that had heart, one that had soul. I'd make a porno that was actually *good* . . .

I stopped, mid-puff. My mouth hung open, and the lighter loosened from my grip, threatening to fall. A chill flashed through my body. Every hair stood on end.

Of course, I thought. My God, it was all right there in front of me.

Thousands of adult movies were produced each year. The majority of them were thoughtless garbage. And yet, they *sold*. They sold like crazy.

I could do that, I thought, wildly. *I could do that . . . but better.*

It was so beautiful—so incredibly *simple*—that I wanted to smack myself for not thinking of this sooner. I had no pretensions about becoming a "fine" artist. I sucked at drawing, painting, sculpture, graphic design, photography, and acting—and I knew it. But in truth, I didn't want to be part of the contemporary art world at all. It felt phony and unreal to me, a playground for rich kids. Porn, on the other hand—that was *relevant*. People didn't wax poetic about porn; they *used* it. And yes, maybe they often regretted doing so: maybe porn was junk food, a quick fix that left you somehow unnourished. But it didn't have to be that way.

All you needed was a little *ingenuity*! If you were going to make an adult video, you had to include a little nudity, a little intercourse, and a few bodily fluids. That's *all*. Once you took care of those totally basic requirements, the field was wide open. I mean, if you wanted to, you could make a serious courtroom drama, as long as the last ten minutes featured a dildo scene between the DA and the defendant. If you did that, you were set; if you did that, you had just made a *porno*. And people were naturally curious about pornos. They would want to watch.

People would watch. The words rang in my head as I sat there on the porch, the sun now beginning to rise and swell in the sky. An *audience*! If I made a porno, I wouldn't have to beg my friends to watch it—they'd be begging *me*. And strangers would *pay* me. I could sell my tapes on eBay. They had a Mature Audiences section, tucked away at the very bottom corner of their Category page. I'd peeked there before. Amateur porno tapes, VHS dubs with hand-printed labels, were doing serious dollars.

I could *do* this. I knew it in my gut: I could make this happen.

I began fantasizing about scenarios. I wasn't sure what direction I wanted to go in, but I was certain that it had to be different than the rest of the stuff out there. Pornographers operated on that assembly-line mentality, but not me. I would edit my tapes carefully. What's more, I'd make sure to record faithfully what went on during the making of the scene. If someone farted in front of my camera, that was going in the final cut. If a guy used Viagra to give himself an erection, then I was going to show him swallowing the pill.

I rocked back and forth in my chair, growing progressively more excited. Yes—*the honesty trip!* I'd include the rough edges, stuff that no one else would think to keep in. I'd pay my actresses on camera, but not before sitting them down to have an open discussion about their reasons for making such a terrible career move in the first place. I'd make pornography that deliberately left room for sponta-neity. I'd find interesting people, put them in weird situations, and go forward from there. My life would become strange and spectacu-lar. I would make movies, and plenty of cash, but more importantly, I would have *experiences*.

I knew what I was going to do with my life. I was going to be-come a pornographer. An *artistic* pornographer.

THREE

In the meantime, though, I was broke. I had to latch on to some kind of employment, and quick.

I managed to finagle a job at the local health food store, where, to my delight, they stuck me behind the juice bar. It was perfect: while I squeezed beets and slung wheatgrass, I kept an eye out for possible coconspirators. Casually, I began to bring up genitalia more and more often in everyday conversation, eyeing my customers to see if they betrayed any abnormal interest. The plan worked like a charm: within days, I met a mellow, middle-aged pervert named Dennis who mentioned quite shamelessly, as if it were the most natural thing in the world, that he liked getting pissed on. Immediately I knew I had found a kindred spirit.

Motioning to my manager that I was going on break, I whipped off my apron and signaled for Dennis to follow me to a corner table, where we could speak more privately.

"I'm liking what you're saying," I whispered.

"I can *tell*," Dennis murmured, excitedly. "Are you thinking of arranging a . . . 'party'?"

"Something like that," I said. I eyed him intensely. "How would you feel about taking a 'shower' in a more *public* forum?"

"What've you got in mind?" Dennis asked, coloring slightly.

"Let me put it like this," I said quietly, my eyes locked into his. "How would you like to star in your very own porno movie?"

Dennis looked at me, his mouth slightly agape, seemingly stunned at his good fortune. "That sounds *amazing*," he whispered.

"I'm thinking of becoming a pornographer," I explained. "Maybe you can be my first real star."

"But who are you going to get to perform *with* me?"

"Who do you want?"

"A really bitchy, dominatrix type would be *great*," breathed Dennis.

"I'll find you one," I promised. "That shouldn't be very difficult at all. Now, how much are you asking, Dennis?"

"Why, I'd do it for free," he announced, smiling. "It'd be my pleasure."

"Good *man*," I said, my eyes filling with unexpected tears. "Thank you, Dennis. This is going to be just terrific. Oh, wow—I think it'll be a lot of fun, don't you? Something to remember, a real *experience*."

"I eat shit, too," Dennis said, helpfully.

Momentarily stunned, I slowly swiveled my head to see if anyone had overheard us. No one seemed to be looking in our direction with a horrified expression, so I assumed we were okay.

"You eat . . . *what*?"

"Oh, I eat shit. I prefer it to drinking piss."

"*Drinking* piss?"

"Well, bathing in it, drinking it. Whatever. I probably like drinking it better. And of course I prefer eating shit to either of those."

I looked at him. "Are you fucking with me?"

"No, not at all," Dennis said. He shook his head earnestly. "Nope."

"Well, listen, Dennis, I just don't know about all this. I don't know if I could *shoot* that."

"Oh no. You can't make a sex tape that shows defecation," Dennis said, authoritatively. "Not to sell, at least. It's very illegal."

"Oh," I breathed, relieved. "Well, that takes care of that."

"I'd be up for it if you wanted to set something up privately, though."

"Right." I stared at him for a long second. "I think I'm going to pass, Dennis."

"Great. No problem. Let's do this peeing thing. I'm really excited about it."

Finding a partner for Dennis proved to be easier than I imagined. All I had to do was visit a few BDSM websites and shoot off a bunch of emails; within a week, I'd received a phone call from Janay, a tall, muscular blonde from San Jose who was totally enthusiastic about my proposition. For $300, she'd not only humiliate Dennis, she'd also sit down for an hour-long interview with me on the day of the shoot.

"Obviously, I'd like to punish him a little bit, too, if that's all right."

"That sounds just fine," I said. "I'll run that by Dennis the next time I talk to him."

"Best part of my job," she said wistfully. "I have a thick, leather whip . . ."

"I bet you do," I said. "Do you work in a dungeon?"

"I actually don't, Sam," Janay said, brightly. "I'm lucky enough to be able to make my living almost exclusively as a video-dom. I've done lots of work for a San Francisco–based company called Redboard. Are you familiar with them? The guy in charge is named Duck Dumont. He's actually quite well known in pornographic circles—as the legend goes, he shot Traci Lords's first film, back in the early eighties. Anyway, Duck's sort of fallen in love with what I bring to the screen. He's given me my own series."

"What's it called?"

"*Debbie Does Whip-Ass*," Janay said, proudly. "He lets me really thrash those fuckers."

"O-kayyy," I said. "Let's just say, though, that, for instance, Dennis doesn't really want to get hurt?"

"Then I'll just totally humiliate him," Janay said, shortly. "I really couldn't give a fuck one way or the other, just so long as I get to make him cry."

Not long after I settled on a date with Janay and gave her directions to my house (Periwinkle had given me permission to use the living room as our set), I called Dennis.

"Sam!" he said eagerly. "What's the good word?"

"Got some great news for you, Dennis."

"You're *kidding*! You found somebody?"

"I sure did. And she's gorgeous, too."

"Oh my God. Oh, my God. Do you have pictures?"

"Absolutely. They're on the Internet, I'll give you the Web address in a second. She's a beautiful blonde, about thirty-two years old, sexy as hell. Her legs go all the way up to her neck, Dennis."

"This is incredible," Dennis whispered, breathlessly. "I can't believe this is happening to me. And is she a bitch?"

"Possibly . . . though she was very polite on the phone. Here's the thing, though: it sounds like she wants to do you some physical damage."

"Well, I'm not really into *pain*," Dennis said, doubtfully.

"Yeah, that's what I figured. Listen, don't worry about it. She still wants to do the video. Are you busy this Saturday?"

"This Saturday? Wow, that's soon. Are you serious, Sam?"

"Of course I am, Dennis. This is important to me, too, you know. Now, can I count on you to be there?"

"Yes," Dennis said, after a brief pause. "You can count on me."

Dennis called me on Friday evening, wondering what he should wear.

"Do you think I should try to look . . . cool?"

"I don't think that's necessary. You're gonna get pissed on, you know?"

"You're right, you're right. Sorry, Sam. I just wish I were in better shape, though. I'm usually pretty good about going jogging, but lately, with work and all . . ."

"Dennis," I interrupted gently. "Please stop worrying. You'll look great, I promise. Now, try to get some sleep."

But I was having trouble sleeping myself. On Saturday, I awoke with a tight, nervous stomach, and I couldn't help wondering if it might be best to call the whole thing off. Things had moved so fast, after all—there was still time to turn back. But I squelched the urge. When afternoon rolled around, Janay showed right on time, toting a pink canvas bag so large and bulky that it looked as if it might contain a dead child. "Costumes," she explained cheerily. "And a few of my instruments. In case your friend changes his mind."

"Great," I said, weakly. I flipped my camera on. "Do you mind if I start the interview?"

"Not at all," Janay said, settling comfortably onto Periwinkle's low-slung couch. "I love your aesthetic, by the way. *So* Northern California."

"Thanks," I said. "Most of the stuff is my housemate's."

"Even so," she said, generously, "you show good taste simply by choosing to live with him."

"Thanks," I said again. "So . . ."

"I'm sorry. Please go on."

"How'd you ever get the idea to be a fetish-film actress?"

"Well, you might not believe this, Sam," Janay said, leaning toward me and my camera, "but I used to be quite shy. I hated to draw attention to myself. I never wore revealing clothing—never even wore a bikini to the beach. I wouldn't have sex with the lights on. I was very boring."

Indeed, I wouldn't have believed it. She was quite sexy by anyone's standards. "What happened?"

"About three years ago, I was in a motorcycle accident," Janay said. "I sustained considerable trauma to my head. When I got out of the hospital, the strangest thing started happening. Suddenly, I wanted everybody to look at me. Apparently the injury to my head had the effect of making me an extreme extrovert. Particularly in the sexual arena."

"That's wild."

"Isn't it? Straightaway, I started dancing at clubs. Within a very short time, I landed in front of the camera. And that's where I've been ever since." She smiled. "I guess you could say that I'm making up for lost time."

"Do you do hardcore, too?" I asked.

"Oh, I'll do a solo masturbation every once in a while, if someone asks me. And I'll happily do a nude photo shoot with a guy, as long as there's no actual penetration. The idea of having sex on camera just doesn't appeal to me. I'm more drawn to the fetishy stuff. It's . . . richer."

"Psychologically richer?"

"Yes," Janay said, beaming. "That's it exactly. Fetish is like a . . . game. There's lots of talking, lots of banter. And since I'm always a top, I always win."

"Why do you always have to be a top?" I asked. "Don't you ever want to submit to anyone else?"

Janay paused for a moment. "I spent the whole first half of my life submitting," she said. "I used to get beat a lot. So, I'm not really into getting dominated much anymore."

"Oh," I said, rather unsure as to how to respond. "Okay."

"You know, Sam," she said, "I'm not *stupid*. I know that every time I go out there and start playing the dom, I'm dealing with my history, with my personal demons. But when I think back to how I used to be, how I used to live? I was totally in denial. I was scared of my own pain. When I take a moment to think back on how it was, I'm actually kind of pleased to be doing it this way now."

Janay and I finished talking, and then she asked for a few minutes alone, to "get into character." I picked up the phone and dialed Dennis.

"Dennis Seltzer."

"Dennis. It's time."

I think now might be as good a time as any other for me to mention that I had absolutely no clue as to what I was doing. I had basically zero experience shooting "action." My video efforts in college had been limited almost exclusively to long tripod takes, where, as often as not, I'd be filming myself, goofing for the camera, usually while wearing a wig. There'd been considerable leeway for mistakes and do-overs. If I wanted to take all night to get one shot, I could. Here, I'd have one chance to make it look good, and that would be it.

I also had no real idea what I wanted to happen in the scene. Dennis was going to be "humiliated"—but how? Did we hash out an attack plan beforehand? I was at least nominally the director; did that mean I was supposed to tell them what to do? I had no idea what they should do. In fact, how was I even going to know when the scene was *over*? As Janay stepped out of the bathroom, clad in black spiked boots and leather chaps, hoisting a riding crop menacingly in her right hand, I was suddenly frightened out of my mind.

Janay motioned disgustedly at Dennis, who grinned up at her. I noticed he'd gotten a haircut, the poor schmuck.

"Is this him?"

I turned my camera on. "Yep, that's him."

"Well, hello, mister. What's your name?"

"Dennis."

"I heard you're 'not into pain,' Dennis."

"Yes, that's right." He looked up at her dreamily. Totally in love.

"Well, even though I'm very disappointed in you, I'm going to respect that. Got it? I'll respect you, as long as you respect me."

"Yes."

"Yes, what?"

"I . . . I don't know."

"Yes, *mistress*."

"Yes, mistress," said Dennis, obediently.

I zoomed in on him, framing his face inexpertly. I prayed that the light in the living room was good enough. I prayed for the ability to hold the camera steady.

"I want you to get those clothes off. Get on the floor, little doggy."

Dennis took off his clothes and went down on all fours. He didn't have too bad a body for a forty-five-year-old guy. A little paunchy, but there were signs of health there.

"Hump my leg, doggy. Hump it good." Dennis humped. "Now stop. I want you to stand up. Turn around. That's right: turn around. Now turn around again. Keep doing it, Dennis. Don't stop."

In my Californian living room, a totally nude middle-aged man was on his feet, revolving slowly, his eyes closed.

"I feel sick," said Dennis, after a few moments.

"You spoke incorrectly, Dennis. Keep going." She folded her arms. "I feel sick, what?"

"I feel sick, mistress," mumbled Dennis. "Please . . . I really want to stop."

"Oh, stop then," Janay said, irritably. "You're a very *weak* little boy, aren't you, Dennis?"

"Yes, mistress," agreed Dennis, wobbling unsteadily. "May I sit down, please, mistress?"

"Of course, Dennis," Janay purred. "Sit down, weak little boy. Sit down and watch me, and I'll let you do what little boys *love* to do." Janay stretched sexily and removed her top. "Look at my tits, Dennis. Look at my tits and play with yourself." She bent over and began running her hands gently over her tanned body, alternating her sensuous glances between Dennis and my camera. I panned across her breasts shakily, hoping against hope that I was covering this monumental occasion competently.

Janay checked Dennis's groin for signs of life, but there were none.

"What's the *matter*, Dennis? Don't I turn you on?"

"Your body turns me on immensely," whispered Dennis.

"Then what's wrong? Why aren't you getting hard?"

"I don't know," mumbled Dennis. He looked up at the camera, and I knew somehow that he was going to apologize to me, so I held up my hand and motioned that it was fine, that he was to soldier on. We weren't going to stop.

"I have a *surprise* for you, Dennis," Janay said sweetly. She tromped off into the kitchen. When she returned, she was wearing a strap-on: a nine-inch plastic penis advancing from her crotch. "I had a feeling this might appeal to you."

Dennis looked as excited as a child on Christmas morning. *"Yes!"* he whispered.

"Then come here and suck my cock," Janay said, smiling. Her boy obeyed, gagging happily. I approached them cautiously, taking a seat on the floor next to Dennis, filming his face and his hot breath in the air around me. Some of his drool got on one of Periwinkle's plants. It was a little disgusting.

"Now," Janay said, removing her plastic penis from Dennis's mouth (it made a small *pop*), giving his head a small shove with the back of her hand, "let's see how you're doing." But his penis was still limp.

"What is your *deal?*" Janay yelled. "Do I not *do* it for you?"

"No, you're *perfect*," whispered Dennis. "I *swear*."

"Then why is your *dick* soft? Get it hard, Dennis, or our game is over."

"I will," he promised. "Mistress. Let me . . . let me watch you some more."

Janay sighed, frustrated, but she took off her leather chaps, revealing black g-string underwear and an ass so perfect it looked like it had been drawn by Marvel comics. I checked it out expectantly on my LCD screen. It photographed very nicely.

Lying on his back, Dennis massaged his knob, trying desperately to bring it back to life. Janay squatted next to him, running her riding crop delicately through Dennis's graying chest hair.

"Dennis?" she said softly.

"Yes, mistress?"

"Do you know how much self-control it's taking me not to use this on you?"

Dennis laughed nervously. He glanced toward me for support, but I only hovered silently behind my camera, recording all.

"Usually, sweetie," Janay continued, "if a man insults me, the way that you're insulting me right now, he *pays* for it. But not Dennis. No, he doesn't *like* pain. But guess what? *I* like pain, Dennis. That's what turns *me* on."

She looked down at him for a reaction, but Dennis was speechless. His penis was as limp and shriveled as a dishrag.

"*Fine!*" she yelled. "*Be* that way! I'll give you what you want. You pathetic little *cocksucker*! Here, doggy! Open your fucking mouth. Open your mouth, you little fucking dog bastard."

She pulled off her g-string and squatted over Dennis's face. For a wild moment, I was sure she was going to crap on his head.

But instead, she began to urinate in a drinking glass. It was a strong stream; a gusher. It felt like it would never end. She collected it all and then handed it to Dennis with a flourish.

He swallowed as much piss as he could handle. But some ran down his face, out the sides of his mouth, finding a home in his gray-streaked goatee. A cluster of droplets freckled Periwinkle's couch.

"Lo-ok," Janay sang, and both Dennis and I followed her index finger. "It's *wor*-king."

Dennis's cock now stood at full attention.

"Now *do it*," Janay ordered. She stood up, completely naked save her stilettos, pointing the riding crop down at Dennis's face with crazed gusto. "*Come*, Dennis. Come *now*."

"I'm trying," pleaded Dennis, jacking his penis miserably. He licked his mustache, in search of erstwhile drops, but already he had begun to wilt. He worked vainly for a while, but it was over, and we all knew it. He shortened his strokes, then abandoned the job altogether. Dennis lay back and closed his eyes, defeated. Janay knelt down next to his supine body; I followed suit. For a long moment, the three of us huddled there, exhausted, the slow, patient hum of my video camera the only audible sound.

FOUR

Periwinkle had his doubts about the whole thing.

"This is . . . very brave," he said, reviewing the raw footage with me that night. "With a little effort, you might be able to edit this down to something halfway compelling. That Dennis is a *freak*."

"You don't know the half of it."

"But really, Sam, let's think rationally. Would anyone actually choose this to jerk off to?"

"Everybody likes something different," I said defensively. "That's the inherent beauty of sexual cinema."

"Well, that's very open-minded of you," Periwinkle said. "I wish you the best of luck trying to sell it."

In the end, he was right. I pruned the footage down to a compact twenty minutes, alternating action shots with interview snippets from both Janay and Dennis, and felt rather pleased with my efforts. But when I put it up for a "Dutch" auction on eBay (meaning that multiple buyers could bid successfully on the tape), priced to move at $6.99, only four people bit. I should have known. The true urine aficionado is notoriously difficult to please.

For the first time, I felt discouraged; more, I was confused. Was I a pornographer, or wasn't I? My identity was in a terrible state of limbo.

I couldn't stop fretting about my film. Nervously, I sent copies off to friends. One prompt reply, via email, told me all I needed to know.

"Bro," it read, "I couldn't beat off to that if my life *depended* on it."

I'd done even worse than I had imagined, then.

I decided to call my dad.

"Sam! Great to hear from you! How are you?"

"Really good, Dad. How's Chapel Hill? How's the house?"

"We can't complain. Spring is in the air. The daffodils are out. They look spectacular. What's wrong? What do you need?"

"Just a little bit of money. Just a touch."

"No problem. What do you need, a hundred bucks? How about a hundred and fifty? Tell you what: I'll send off a check in the next couple of days. You get it back to me at your leisure."

"I was thinking more like a thousand."

"Sorry, I think the connection went out for a second. I must not have heard you correctly. What'd you say?"

"A thousand?"

"There it goes again. You see, I thought you said 'a thousand.' But you couldn't have said that—right, Sam?"

"I'll pay you back, Dad. I'm dead serious. And just so you know, this isn't going towards the rent. I've got a whole business plan in the works here."

"Which is *what*, may I ask?"

"Dad, I'm almost in the position to fill you in on it. Be patient with me for just a short while longer. I want to be able to present this vision to you in its fullest flower."

"That sounds highly suspicious. Why don't you take a couple extra shifts at the juice bar? A little hard work never killed anyone. Or come out here for a month or two. We've got *plenty* to do, I promise you that. The kudzu is *completely* out of control, for example."

"Dad, I live out here now. Come on, what do you say? It's just a grand. I'll pay it back in sixty days, promise. If not, you can start tacking on five percent interest."

"Compounded daily. Listen, I'll talk it over with your mother, and we'll let you know. In the meantime, I'll be waiting to hear about that 'business plan' of yours. It sounds extremely dubious."

My dad was right, of course—it *was* a rather dubious plan. Clearly, I had only the most basic sense of what appealed to the contemporary porn connoisseur. And to make matters worse, I had no leads on actors. My future hinged, I realized suddenly, on my ability to procure some true porno headliners.

The next weekend, hoping to do some research, I hitched a ride up to San Francisco. There was one place that I especially wanted to check out: "The Lusty Lady." From what I'd heard, it was a forward-thinking sort of joint, a workers' cooperative owned by the women who danced there. Progressive strippers, I thought—what better candidates for New Millennium porn could there be?

But the place had a decidedly sad, fucked-up vibe to it. You cashed in $10 worth of quarters, then entered a tiny booth, where you fed the coins into arcade-like slots in order to open a small sliding window. The temporary peephole gave you a view of a dimly lit room that contained two or three semi-punk chicks—essentially Suicide Girls with a little more meat on their bones—who were walking around very, very slowly with "sexy" looks on their faces like masks. They had lit the viewing booths up, so the strippers could see you just as clearly as you could see them. If you beckoned to one, she'd saunter over, biting her lip provocatively, treating you to some profoundly aggressive eye contact. Either that, or she'd just bend over and put her ass up in the air. That was your cue to start beating off.

Sooner or later, your window would come down; when that happened, you put in more quarters. It was a weird place. I suppose that if you wanted to put in the time, and the money, the possibility for an erotic connection was there. Certainly, there was this odd sensation that the girls were casing you just as closely as you were casing them, and that produced a few moments of unexpected vulnerability, which I found interesting, if not exactly pleasurable. Overall, though, it wasn't really what you'd call a "feel-good" environment. I still felt the familiar strip club sensations of loneliness and mutual disrespect. It made me feel like a john, and I wasn't into it, so I beat off quickly into a wad of paper towels, and disgusted with myself, made for the door.

My next stop was in the Mission, a sex shop called Good Vibrations. The worker-owned store boasted a huge collection of silicon dildos and adjustable cock rings, but it also sported a "sex-positive" floor vibe that was decidedly nonsleazy, without being totally antiseptic. I skulked around for a little while, then finally got up the nerve to approach one of the store employees, a sexy fat Mexican woman in her mid-thirties whose name tag read Felice Amador— Happy Lover.

"Can I help you with anything?"

"Well, I don't know," I said. "That kind of depends."

"On what?"

"On whether you know anybody who will fuck on film for me. See," I said, smiling shyly, "I'm sort of a pornographer."

Felice listened to my pitch patiently, then, surprisingly, voiced a concern quite resembling my own.

"There's so much room for *growth* in the genre, it's true. I've always felt that way."

"Porn doesn't have to be shitty!" I cried, desperately relieved to find somebody else who saw it my way.

"I know, right? But our culture is so ashamed of having non-retractable genitals that we punish ourselves for feeling horny by producing the worst sexual aids imaginable."

"And that's where Good Vibrations comes in?"

"Right. It's like, we all want to *do* it . . . why not just admit it? Be proud of being carnal. It means you're still alive."

"Have you guys ever considered making movies?" I asked.

"It's funny that you mention it, because we've actually just started to have some serious talks. We're thinking about putting together a good bisexual movie. They're in really short supply."

"Sounds great," I said. "But do you think anybody who works in the store—or even shops here—would be up to making some porn, now?"

"It's definitely worth a try," Felice said. "Why don't you make up some sort of flier, and I'll put it in the dressing room. That way, everybody'll see it."

I wandered around the city for the rest of the afternoon in an agitated state. My pavement pounding had paid off; I was making important connections. The dream was progressing, that much was undeniable.

I stripped naked, facing myself in the bathroom mirror.

"You serious about this?" I asked, roughly.

"As serious as I've ever been about anything in my life," I answered.

"Are you willing to make sacrifices?" I demanded.

"Yes, I am," I vowed. "I'll do whatever it takes."

"Are you willing to go that extra mile?"

"Yes, *sir!*" I barked. "I'll bare it all. *Someone's* got to do it."

"That's the spirit. *Bare it all.* In the gay section of eBay."

". . . Sir?"

"No need to hire a bunch of actors. Get oiled up, and masturbate yourself on camera. Make a jack-off film. The best that's ever been made. Be a star."

The idea wasn't without its own rakish appeal. I could bring it back to basics. And I had to admit, jack-off tapes were really moving. Maybe I could even make enough money to pay my dad back. Make the guy proud.

I laid out a cursory shot list, stuff designed to get your contemporary gay hot. First I figured I'd go out to the local schoolyard and shoot some hoops in my underwear. There was a water fountain there—I could get wet, real wet. Then back to Chez Periwinkle for a quick erotic weight-lifting session and a brief rubdown. Then maybe some light stretching and shoving grapes up my ass.

I didn't have to shoot it all by myself, either. I called up my friend Spinach Brown, who agreed to come over and help, even though she was weak from a month-long colon-cleansing fast where all she could eat was red berries and pickles.

"I once made a porn," she remarked, absentmindedly.

"You *did?*" I frowned. "What are you talking about?"

"It was for a guy named Casey," she explained. "'Casey's Cumshots.' His thing was huge, fake cum shots. He had this big dildo that he'd hollowed out, with a turkey baster inside it. He'd just *blast* me with about a gallon of piña colada mix! It was *gigantic*! Covered my whole face, my tits, got in my hair, everything."

"And that's supposed to be sexy?" I muttered, jealous.

"I'm sure whatever you have planned is far sexier."

She filmed me digging in Periwinkle's garden, zooming in, I could sense, on my strong biceps, my rock-hard calves. I flexed everything that I could, willingly abetting the fetishization process. I could see it on slo-mo already.

Everything was going great until I peeled an organic banana and used its browning skin to wank myself off. Spinach filmed in awkward silence for two or three minutes, then left without a word. Sighing, embarrassed, I fished around in my closet for my trusty tripod. I'd be finishing this mission alone. Halfheartedly, I lay upside down in my bathtub and came on my own face.

To my surprise, the tape sold like crazy. Its success convinced me that I was now a "performance artist." I announced to myself, unable to hide the pride in my trembling voice, that I was going to keep on following this trail—that no matter how rough it got or how lonely I felt, I was going to keep on the path. The path of the righteous pornographer.

To extend the conceptual scope of the project, I began to include a bonus item along with the videotapes I was sending through the mail, for a small additional fee: used pairs of my own underwear that I'd jizzed into and then sealed in Ziploc bags. At last, I was a success.

FIVE

For inspiration, I returned to the flea market and picked up as many adult videos as I could. This time around, though, I made it my business to try to get my hands on some newer releases, so as to see what today's pornographer was up to. Expensive features like *The House on Chasey Lane* were always good fun, if only to remind you of the competency gap that existed between Hollywood screenwriters and Hollywood pornwriters. But on the whole, I found that I preferred the gonzo videos.

Gonzo, a movement in porn that began in the late 1980s, is immediately recognizable by its informal attitudes, low production values, and improvised scripts. In gonzo, the director, who is almost always also the cameraman, enacts the role of a first-person narrator who is on a type of sexual "quest"—usually, to see as many attractive women naked as possible. The director, serving as a kind of sexual surrogate for the viewer, is always bold enough to peek up the skirts and down the shirts of his pleased female victims. While John "Butt-man" Stagliano is generally considered the godfather and master of gonzo, scores of copycats have done it quite competently, and to the great enjoyment of their viewership. Joey Silvera is a gonzo genius. So is Jamie Gillis—his *On the Prowl* series, where he'd drive around and pick up "real" girls, was the basis for Burt Reynolds's limousine scene in *Boogie Nights*.

Over the years, the genre evolved and broadened, to where *gonzo* now refers to almost any porno that's shot handheld and lacks a plot. Though these videos don't deliver much in terms of story, their slapdash, improvisational character, and perverted authorial signature often allow for an unintentional but pleasant fissure in cinema's traditionally tight narrative weave. In gonzo, one *knows* the performer. Granted, the guys don't usually get much screen time—sometimes they're never even filmed above the waist—but the women are often treated to a brief (and usually lewd, but still) interview before the scene begins. After viewing three or four movies that the same actress has appeared in, it's often possible to cobble together a basic sense of who she actually is.

Through these films, I grew more and more curious about the "pro" scene. When you got lucky, things got interesting out here in the Santa Cruz sticks, but everybody knew that down south was where it was really happening. Los Angeles was where the *stars* were—the *porn* stars. That's where you did this job professionally. Not as a weekend thing, not between shifts at the Reddi Mart or a juice bar, and not as an experiment. LA was where the *lifers* were.

I envisioned them as an elite pack of misfits with nice asses who had made the commitment to go ultrapublic with their cum grunts. Few were well known by the masses—really only Ron Jeremy and Jenna Jameson could boast of true name recognition—but every girl who'd made it onto the box cover of one of Anabolic's *Initiations* was a luminary in her own right. Every greasehead director who'd released six titles of his own *Cherry Poppers* rip-off was getting play in thousands of darkened rooms every evening. And every newbie starlet was *somebody's* favorite, had at least one guy totally excited, daydreaming at work, thinking, *what if I really met her?*

It was a minor and manageable kind of fame. These were small-time, makeshift celebrities, and they honestly fascinated me. I wanted baseball cards of all of them, so I could memorize their stats. *Led the league in DPs in 1995 . . . Signed with Vivid right out of high school . . . Traveled for half the '92 season . . . Set Los Angeles Metro area record for most on-set Vicodins swallowed in a single afternoon, 14 . . . Spent much of the 1998 season at Oak Tree Rehabilitation Center for Drug and Alcohol Dependence . . . Returned in 1999 with surgically enhanced breasts and husband-manager, director Leon Gucci . . . Still holds single-season record for most anal gangbangs, 8 . . .*

And what about the guys? Some of them put up crazy numbers. Janay said that she had done a photo shoot with a guy who had been in over two thousand movies. That was Lou Gehrig–like. And some of the workhorses who had been going for twenty years, like Peter North and Tom Byron—well, they had probably done like five thousand films. Maybe more. I'd had sex with ten women in my life. It boggled my mind a little. These people were special.

My porn proficiency leaped when I found an Internet site called LukeFord.com, a gold mine of porn star gossip and history, run by the son of famous Seventh-day Adventist preacher Desmond Ford. Luke, genuinely fascinated by the performers and their chaotic personal lives, had spent several years of his life establishing himself as the industry's most dedicated journalist. The extensive, fairly literate star profiles that he published on his site were generally fair-minded and impartial (he would often transcribe entire interviews verbatim), but in an industry where tempers flared easily, he soon acquired a reputation as a muckraker and gossip hound. Especially vexing to some was his habit of printing the real names and birthplaces of performers.

Luke was a bit of a character in his own right. In the summer of 2000, when I started to read him, he had already converted to Orthodox Judaism, and his rabbi was threatening to excommunicate him if he didn't sever his well-known association with the adult industry. Eventually, after several months of public vacillation, the guy ended up selling his site, quitting the business, and then, in true porno fashion, staging a comeback. It was excellent drama. And though some found his writing fantastical, I felt like I had gained a great deal from Luke.

Take, for instance, Tony Eveready, one of my new favorite gang-bang guys. How could I have thought, without Luke, that he had been romantically involved for two years with the actress known as Porsha? Never mind that I wasn't exactly sure who Porsha was; I could hunt around, do some detective work, find out. And Chasey Lain: the Wicked Pictures contract star had two implants in *each tit*. That was *interesting* to me.

And there was more, too. *Plenty* more according to Luke:

Tori Welles, star of *The Chameleon*, had been a teenage runaway prostitute. Felecia, the hottest Latina in the business, had a crush on Jodie Foster—she wanted to kiss her "beautiful little hips."

T.T. Boy's favorite movie was *Gone With the Wind*. Larry Flynt lost his virginity to a chicken. Dave Hardman got paid a dollar a pound to have sex with obese starlets in films like *Heavyweight Cumtenders*. Dynamite devirginized High Pitch Erik on the Howard Stern show for five grand. On Steve Hatcher's first shoot, Nina Hartley sauntered over to him, stroked him twice, and said, "That's a fine, fuckable dick you've got there. You'll go far in this business."

Keri Windsor grew up in Saudi Arabia. Vince Voyeur hated to get his balls wet. Kelly Nichols appeared in the movie *C.H.U.D.—Cannibalistic Humanoid Underground Dwellers*. Black porn queen Midori was singer Jody Watley's little sister. Rocco Siffredi used to go by "Tito."

Soon I'd generated a list of favorite stars, and I'd look for them in video stores—Misti Rain, Krysti Myst, Belladonna, Mirage. I checked out the American Cocksucking Championship series for Adriana Sage, and came away a huge Alexandra Quinn fan. *She* had a good entry on Luke Ford: she'd pulled "a Traci Lords" and performed while underage for two years, then, after being deported to her native Canada, returned to LA and hit the scene with renewed determination and heightened freakishness. I talked about her with Periwinkle, who seemed for some reason to think that at one point she'd been a man. A huge homeless guy who strolled around downtown Santa Cruz with a radio wrapped in a garbage bag agreed. Online, one fan wrote, "Quinn likes to get fucked with a loaded gun held to her head." I believed it.

I began to contemplate mingling among this exotic band of outcasts. What would they think of me? Would they accept me as one of their own, welcome me into the fold? Perhaps they'd see right through my charade instantly, recognizing me as weak and privileged. I spent whole nights mapping out intricate, imaginary conversations in laborious detail.

With July dying, I brought a copy of my first video to a film forum in San Francisco and screened it for a small audience. Sandy Spago, the curator, an attractive twenty-four-year-old blonde with a wry smile and a big ass, said she'd found it "intriguing." I heard something in her voice that told me to push further.

"Like porn, do ya?"

"Oh, yes."

"Ever thought about giving it a whirl?"

She grinned at me teasingly. "Maybe I already have."

Immediately, I whisked her away to North Beach to drink wine and talk smut.

"It was a spanking video," she related. "*Candy Asses*, or something like that. I wanted to do something *wild*, you know?"

"Sure."

"But he made me cry, the bastard. Just kept going and going until I broke, even though I said my safe word. I *said* my safe word." She glared at me over the top of her wineglass. "Those fuckers just wanted to see a real reaction."

"Looks better on camera," I explained.

"Yeah, great." She scowled darkly. "I never even got a copy of the film."

"Maybe you could buy one," I suggested.

Sandy stared at me balefully for a moment and then just shook her head. "I want to do it again. Do it *right* this time."

"Why?"

"I like the attention," she said seriously.

I grinned. "Well, I'm not real interested in making a spanking video."

"Oh, fuck spanking. I want to get fucked. I think it could be really hot. Why are you *laughing*?"

"I'm not laughing," I said, laughing.

"Do you think I'm like, coming on to you? I'm not. You're cute, but you're not my type, at all. I'm into older guys. I like a guy who I can feel comfortable calling Daddy."

"O-kay! Don't hold anything back, by the way."

"I'd be very interested to fuck a whole *bunch* of guys," Sandy said, frankly. "It seems so ornate, don't you think? So excessive."

"But a *gangbang*? Surely you're kidding."

"What? Don't you think I'm tough enough for it? I'd *love* to see how many guys I could get off at the same time. Don't you think that'd be *riveting*?"

"Listen," I said. "Calm down for a second. Gangbangs are chaotic. Messy. And they're packed with undesirables. What if they decided to rise up as one and overthrow us? It'd be disastrous."

"They wouldn't do that, silly. We'd find a bunch of really sweet guys who're totally cute. Or at least," she amended, more realistically, "not totally disgusting."

"I'm *telling* you," I said, "it might look good on paper, but in reality it'd be freaking disgusting. Imagine all those sweaty sacks in one room."

"Hmm," Sandy said. She twisted her mouth and wrinkled her eyebrows, thinking. A young guy sitting across the room recognized her and waved happily.

"Hi, Sandy!"

"Hi, Brian! I can't talk right now. I'm discussing porn."

"There's no hurry," I said. "I'm sure that if we both think about it for a couple of weeks, sooner or later . . ."

"I get really turned on when guys stalk me," she interjected.

"Listen, Sandy, seriously, that's super interesting, but it'd be a little difficult to capture that on film, don't you think?"

"You don't want to work with me," Sandy said. She stared at me.

"What are you talking about?"

"You heard me. You don't want me in your films. You're intimidated by me."

"*Intimidated?*" I snorted. "Come now."

"It's true," Sandy said. "You don't know what to do with a girl who's just as smart as you and has her own fully developed, unconventional sense of sexuality. Do you?"

"Please. That's totally ridiculous."

"Is it? I think that in your heart of hearts, you're really holding out for some Barbie doll who'll bob her head all pretty-like and then suck all the cum down her throat without saying a word, right?"

"Hey," I protested, "you got me all wrong."

"I think I got you all *right*," Sandy said, smiling. She crossed her arms. "You want to see me suck that kid's cock for you? Hey, *Brian!*"

"No," I said firmly. "Please, don't."

"I want to make a *porno*," Sandy announced. "A really good one. You can ask me questions, and then, when I'm getting fucked, you can play my interview back in a tiny box in the upper-left-hand corner of the screen. You know how to do that, right?"

"Sure, but . . ."

"And instead of a gangbang, I'll just do a couple of guys, okay? First one, and then when he's all done, I'll do the other. Two guys— you can handle that, right?"

"Well, all right, but how are we going to . . ."

"We'll place an ad in the paper. The SF *Weekly* has a 'Wild Side' section, and that should be perfect for us. We'll get tons of responses, and then we'll hold tryouts. You can videotape everybody, and I'll pick the winners, and we can put that in the film, too. It'll be like *reality porn*." She looked at me expectantly. "Now, what do you say?"

I shook my head in amazement. "Why me?"

"I like you," Sandy said, simply. "I liked your film. It was honest. Let's do something honest."

"Well, all right," I said weakly. "You win."

SIX

I placed an ad in the paper, sending out an SOS for guys in their mid-thirties who wanted to fuck a "submissive 24 year-old blonde bitch with a towering IQ." Predictably, we got a lot of riffraff, which was sort of fascinating (I taped all the phone conversations), but I managed to filter out most of the more dangerous psychos before Sandy and I met our "candidates" in person. We played God for an afternoon, cross-examining a gaggle of hapless cranks, like Lonnie, a red-faced male nurse who didn't mind "dressing up . . . you know . . . wearing a wig," and Karl, a pubic-bearded Rollerblading enthusiast who glided up to his interview wearing spandex short shorts, Terminator wraparound shades, and a fluorescent yellow safety vest.

Then there was Black Dave, a genial Gulf War vet–gone–substance abuse counselor, who made it clear that, if chosen, he was going to "leave the boots on"; Chuck, a golden-haired elevator repairman who referred to his dick as "Elvis" (Sandy thought that was cute; I found it repugnant); Ron, a slim, dark-skinned business-man who, it turned out, had actually seen *Candy Asses*; and Dohvid, a short, bespectacled Jerry Garcia enthusiast who was an articulate speaker on all matters sexual. I would have voted for Dohvid, but he foolishly admitted to having a small wiener, and Sandy tossed him. (When he held up his hands a few inches apart to describe his length, Sandy's straight-faced, hardhearted reply was "Are you into anal?")

She chose Black Dave and Chuck, and they both went to the free clinic on Haight Street to get HIV tested. I sensed that we were on the verge of something really special here, maybe even impor-tant. The suspicion was reconfirmed a thousand times over when Black Dave showed up to Sandy's apartment on the day of the shoot and pulled down his pants to reveal the most monstrous dong I had ever seen. It was eleven inches and thick. The thing was like a Prin-gles can.

But Dave was a sweetheart. "I was thinkin'," he confessed ner-vously, as we rolled pregame film on him and his snakeskin cowboy boots, "no matter what happens, *just let me eat her*. Please, Lord, all I'm saying—*let me eat her.*" Dave, curiously enough, had gotten his porno feet wet already; in February of the previous year, he'd taken a trip down to Los Angeles to participate in *The Houston 500*, the gangbang to end all gangbangs. Houston had fairly annihilated Jasmin St. Claire's previous record of 300, set in *The World's Biggest Gang Bang 2*. The previous "champ" was Annabel Chong, who, in January 1995, serviced 251 men in an eight-hour stretch.

I was actually surprised they let Black Dave *leave*—he was a natural. He was so into Sandy's snatch that I don't even think he remembered I was in the room, much less videotaping him. He lapped her up, and I tried to frame it just so. In a way, that was sort of artistically fulfilling. But when Dave started power-fucking Sandy on her tiny corduroy couch, I was somehow let down. It was so . . . ordinary. I watched his huge elephant penis go in and out of its mudhole. Wasn't this supposed to be somehow *different*? Wasn't there something more *original* they could do?

And Sandy looked sort of sad down there, getting whaled on. Sweat beaded up on her pale skin; she gripped the couch hard with her left hand, to keep from falling off. I don't know, maybe she was having a good time. It was impossible for me to tell.

Chuck was next up, but he was late. After an hour, I called him, and we were met with bad news: Chuck had come down with a case of the porn jitters. He was bailing.

"Please, bro," I said. "I'm depending on you."

"Yeah, well," he said, unconvinced.

"And Sandy really wants to meet Elvis," I reminded him. He relented and said hell, I guess I can come on over, give it my best shot. And he did. But it was a terrible thing to watch.

So confident and full of life in tryouts, Chuck-the-elevator-guy had completely psyched himself out before we even started rolling, and no matter what we did to entice him, Elvis simply wouldn't come out to play. I offered Chuck half a Viagra, tried to explain that penises get scared, too, but he just sat there and shook all that golden hair miserably. Sandy kissed him sweetly all over every inch of his body, but it was no use, and so we wrapped.

As he was leaving, Chuck remarked with a nervous laugh, "I guess you'll have to edit all that stuff out."

"Oh, no," I said, clapping him cheerfully on the shoulder. "That's going *in*. It's great human drama."

"Human drama?" he said, a horrified look dawning on his face.

I ushered him gently but firmly out the door. "Keep in touch," I said. "I may want to use you for future projects." I closed the door in his face.

I went back to Sandy's room, where she lay sprawled out on the couch, wrapped up in a big blue bath towel, staring up at the ceiling. "*That* was agonizing."

"I'm so sorry," I said.

"Not your fault," Sandy murmured. She hoisted herself up to a sitting position. "I always feel guilty when a guy can't get it up—like somehow I wasn't good enough, you know?"

"Ah, the guy was just spooked. It wasn't you."

She shot me a dirty look. "I know it wasn't *me*, Sam."

We stared at each other.

"Well, listen, here's some money." I handed her $400 in cash.

"Stop it," she said. "I don't want you to pay me."

"Don't be a fool," I said. "I'm going to exploit your image all over the Internet." I was only partially kidding, and probably we both knew it. Her living room got very quiet. I sat down on the floor and gazed at my sneakers stupidly.

"Let me take you out for a drink, then," said Sandy. "We'll celebrate. Do you want to go to the Lusty Lady? It's right down the street."

I laughed. "Yeah, sure."

We walked down to Kearney in our flip-flops and got $100 in change and pumped quarters into the slots. You weren't allowed to get into the same booth, but we did it anyway. Sandy knocked on the Plexiglas window and waved at the strippers like they were lions in the zoo. Then she went behind me and pretended to be buttbanging me, and I winked at the girls who were walking around in their typical loping, unhurried way. Sandy took off her shirt and pressed her titties up against the glass, nodding enthusiastically and pointing at herself: *pretty good, huh?* Eventually, one of the girls told on us, and we were made to leave. We went to another dirty hole up on Broadway. A dark-haired stripper with small, hard tits and a lean, fuckable torso danced up on top of the bar in platform heels. I stared up at her hungrily, unable to disguise my desire.

"You like that, huh, Sammy?" Sandy said.

"She's okay," I lied. In truth, I wanted to insert my tongue up her ass so bad that it hurt.

Sandy kept on buying me shots, but I wasn't in the right mood. I had to drive all the way back to Santa Cruz anyway. Somehow, on the way out of the city, I got lost.

The film did lousy.

It didn't even clear a hundred bucks the first week. I started waking up every morning right before my alarm clock, with an increasing sense of anxiety and hopelessness. My home, which had seemed so vibrant and unique only months before, suddenly felt covered with mold. A bumper sticker that I kept seeing around town on this decrepit brown Honda summed it up pretty well: "Santa Cruz is an Irony-Free Zone." One day, I saw the car parked outside a bakery and waited around until the owner showed up. He was a cheerful-looking, craggy-faced guy with black nerd glasses who was wearing a pair of small red devil's horns on top of his head.

"Got your Halloween costume yet?" he asked, tweaking the horns.

"Uh . . . it's like a month and a half away."

"Never too early. Never too early. I'm James T. Martin. Who are you?"

"I'm Sam. I was just admiring your bumper sticker."

"Thank you kindly. I made it myself. Could I interest you in one?"

"No, that's all right . . ."

"Well, how about some kitty-cat ears?" He dangled a pair of black ceramic triangles from an elastic thread. "Granted, they usually look a lot smarter on the ladies, but maybe for your girlfriend?"

"Don't have one. Look, I was just . . ."

"Hey, do you need a job? High season's just starting for me. I need someone to help me sell these handmade devil horns and kitty-cat ears, even though they really sell themselves. Move 'em for ten and I'll let you keep five. Fifty percent commission, best deal in town. What do you say?"

For the hell of it, I agreed. James was the best salesman I had ever seen. It was astounding to watch him in action. He could walk into a gas station, buy a Mars bar, and just sort of offhandedly unload a jumbo pair of green glitter horns onto the cashier. Everything that came out of his mouth seemed to make this weird kind of sense. He had that gift.

"I do carpentry, too, when it's absolutely necessary. But that's only in the lean months, when I haven't sold enough horns, or abstract paintings. I have some pretty nice abstract paintings over at the house, I could let you have one dirt cheap. What do you do?"

"I make porn."

"I love porn. I've always wanted to make a porn, actually. Not be in it, of course—I'm far too unattractive for that. Just create one. How do you like it so far?"

"It's a weird road."

James and I started driving up to San Jose and San Francisco most weekends. I was the worst salesman who had ever lived. One time James and I split up, and I went to Haight Street, where for three hours I stood by myself in pathetic silence, waiting for someone to notice the black devil horns strapped to my head and ask me where they could get some, too. When James came back, I asked him how he'd done.

"Not so good, not so good. Just sold thirty pairs or so, that's hardly the kind of numbers I should be doing this time of year. How about yourself?"

"Zero. Listen, I'd like to not do this, if that's all right with you."

"Nonsense. You just haven't hit your stride yet. We have to get you into a more freewheeling type of atmosphere."

We headed down to the Castro, where James made me go into gay bars and tell people I was selling the horns to put myself through junior college. I made some dough, and that made me happy, for a time.

But things weren't all right at home. Santa Cruz was growing smaller and smaller. I was treading the finest possible line between sexual pride and sleazery, and I knew it. Some guys could preach the free-love gospel and make it sound proper, but I lacked the confidence, that gift of gab. I figured it was only a matter of time before the hippies discovered the real me, and denounced me in the town square.

My temper spiraled into blackness. More and more often, I'd sit at the kitchen table with a cup of cold coffee, staring at nothing. I wondered if I was having a nervous breakdown. I took on more shifts at the juice bar, just because they were there. A quirky nineteen-year-old girl who worked in the store's vitamin section announced that she had a crush on me, and I promised her the moon, but she wouldn't even let me eat her pussy. It hurt.

But I kept pushing. My dream depended on it. Desperate for action, I called up Spinach Brown.

"What's the occasion?" she said brusquely. We hadn't spoken for months.

I was too ashamed to speak for a second. "I need to talk to Casey," I said finally.

"Casey who?"

"Casey's Cumshots."

She hooked me up with his cell. In the middle of the day, on a Tuesday, I screwed up the courage to call the guy. To my surprise, he sounded overjoyed to hear from me.

"There's somebody else making porn in Santa Cruz? Well, no shit. I'll drink to that!"

"Maybe we should get together sometime," I suggested casually. "Work on some ideas."

"Christ, let's hook up right now! I'm at the Drop Inn. *Drop on in!*" He laughed uproariously. "Hey, would you mind doing me a favor? Could you bring me over a sandwich or something?"

"Sure," I said. "What do you want?"

"Anything. Just get here soon. I'm really hungry."

I went by a place called Zoccoli's and got him a roast beef sandwich. Casey seemed like a roast beef kind of guy. I walked into the Drop Inn with my paper bag. The bar was totally deserted except for one overweight guy with long hair who had two Michelob bottles in front of him, both empty.

"Casey?"

He extended his hand. "My friends call me Rich. Casey's just my porn name. What's yours?"

"I don't have one."

"Well, that's a hell of a gutsy move. I guess your parents are dead?"

I laughed stiffly. "No . . . Here, I brought you a sandwich." I held up the paper bag.

"That's great. Put it right there on the bar." He stifled a tiny burp, holding two fingers to his purplish lips. "Listen, you didn't happen to bring any beers, did you?"

I looked around, confused. "Isn't this a bar?"

"Yeah. They'll only serve me so many here. They know me too well." He belched again, covering his mouth in this ladylike way, and paused thoughtfully for a moment. "Look, I know this isn't the best timing or anything, but I think I should go throw up for a little while. Don't worry, this always happens. I'll be good to go in like, twenty minutes."

I sat there in the dim bar by myself in the middle of the day and listened to the muffled sounds of Casey vomiting explosively in the men's room.

"What'll you have, guy?" said the bartender.

I pointed toward the bathroom. "I'll have what he's having." When he turned his back to get me a Michelob, I left.

It was time to get out of these bush leagues. I was ready for a shot in the bigs. I was heading to Los Angeles.

SEVEN

Life was good again. The shroud fell away from my eyes, and I got my smile back. My stomach felt excitable and nervous, but my mind was alert, my thoughts impassioned. I started packing my bags.

I rented a U-Haul and crammed my life into it. I disconnected my phone, said good-bye to a few people. On New Year's Eve, as a going-away present to myself, I called up Peri's dealer, Bryce, and asked him if he had any cocaine.

"Sure," he said. "How much do you want?"

"I don't know," I answered, thoughtfully. "How about twenty bucks' worth?"

"Twenty *bucks*?" Bryce sneered. "You must be fucking kidding. Do you know how much twenty bucks' worth of quality cocaine is? That's like, a *line*."

"Well, pardon me," I said, offended. "All my money's tied up in the stock market."

"Best I can do you for twenty, bro, is some *rocks*."

"So give me the rocks," I shot back.

"Ha," said Bryce. He waited and so did I. "Are you serious?"

"Yes."

"You're white, right?"

"Yep."

"Well . . . ," said Bryce. I could feel him smiling on the other end of the phone, like the fucking irritating, condescending Northern California drug dealer that he was. "O-*kayyy* . . ."

He showed up about half an hour later with a small baggie of crack and a little pipe, the kind that you can buy in a gas station as a "vase," with a tiny rose in it. "I took the liberty of picking up a smoking utensil for you—two bucks extra," said Bryce. He grinned widely. "Of course, you probably already have one, right? Seriously bro, do you even know how to *do* this?"

"I think I'll be able to figure it out," I said smartly, grabbing the rose-pipe and baggie from him, handing him twenty-one dollars and four quarters. "Thanks, Bryce. You've been a huge help."

Crack turned out to be a cinch. All you had to do was double-lock your bedroom door and cover the gap at the bottom with a beach towel so no one can smell that weird scent of chemicals burning, and pull the blinds down, pull 'em tight. Then all you really had to do after that was get totally naked except for some love beads and put a piece of a Brillo pad in the end of the pipette (after taking the little rose out and placing it in your wallet as a keepsake) then pack the rock and torch it. You'd suck in the sweet, thick smoke, and within seconds you'd feel better and be able to think more clearly and more joyously than you ever had in your entire life. You'd be full of love for the universe and all of its inhabitants, and every inch of your skin would tingle. You'd massage your testicles and be filled with tender love for each separate ball. Your breath would get short and you'd tremble, but it wouldn't be over, no, not yet; because your beautiful hands would stray to your incredibly tender and suddenly plump nipples, caressing them with a delicate, measured elation that would send cold delightful tremors up your spinal column, making you suddenly shake your head involuntarily from side to side so rapidly that your eyes would blur and all of a sudden you'd have to fall over and lay on your stomach in a nakedly blissful agony, running both hands over your face, perceiving every whisker in bas-relief, feeling them like they were quills.

Then, quite suddenly, you'd be down. Plummeting precipitously from the cliff of genius into a depression of such monstrous intensity that the idea of taking a sharpened jackknife to your face and disfiguring it horribly would seem the wisest thing to do. But then, of course, you'd arrive at a compromise: slip another rock into the pipe. And that was easy, too. All you had to do was pick up your lighter and drop it immediately, because your hands are trembling and there's so much sweat on your forehead and upper lip that it's running into your eyes and blinding you, and your tongue is involuntarily lapping up the droplets like salty wine. Then you'd scamper over to the blinds and take the stealthiest peek out onto the street, quite casually, of course—really only to pass the time while you're chewing on your lower lip and swallowing over and over again, mindlessly. Then it's over to the already disconnected phone to pick up the receiver and listen intently to see if you can hear the sound of your line being tapped; that should only take about ten to fifteen minutes, after which you're free to stare down at your penis, which has retreated into your body with such seriousness of force that it's basically just a tiny nubbin, more of a vestigial *trace* of a penis than anything else. *Then* you can smoke. *Then* you can take a deep breath, grasp the lighter tightly, put the pipe between your teeth like a glass cigarette, and torch the rock. Ascend the summit. Then careen off. And so on.

I played the game until around 3 A.M., when, to my immense relief, the cocaine ran out. At that point, I collapsed onto my back, my heart pounding, and tried to jerk off, which was really hilarious. My prick was about half an inch long and the width of the pipette. Next I tried to sleep, which was equally funny. It just wasn't going to happen. I pulled up the blinds, watched it get light out.

A few hours later, I was headed down to LA.

The trip from the Bay to LA generally takes anywhere from five to seven hours, depending on what route you take and how many times you stop to eat. But I was pushing one of those long U-Hauls, with the Volvo dragging behind on a hitch, and my general uneasiness driving the big truck coalesced with an unwelcome but nonetheless totally persistent messianic crack dementia, and in the end I was unable to make the trip in less than a grueling, cursing, self-pitying, involuntarily-catnapping-at-the-wheel-for-five-to-ten-seconds-and-then-shrieking-in-pure-terror eleven hours.

My new housemate, Bob, was there to greet me when I pulled up that evening in Silver Lake, exhausted. Bob was an openhearted, freckle-faced fellow in his early thirties, whom I'd located on the Internet only a few weeks prior. He fairly crackled with pep.

"Hey, pardner! Welcome to your new *home!*"

I stepped out of the cab gingerly, my back aching from the long drive, and extended my hand in greeting.

"Screw all *that*, dude—you're givin' me a *hug!*" Bob jumped me, squeezing me in a tigerish embrace, then jokingly lay his head on my shoulder. He giggled happily, until my road aroma enveloped him.

"Oh my *lord!* Sam!" Bob doubled over with laughter, covering his nose and mouth with his tank top. "There's a *shower* inside, first door on the right. You *must* hose yourself down, pronto!"

I followed his orders, exercising a brief ablution on my stinking body. There was a massive tub of blue body wash in the shower, and I sampled from it cautiously. When I emerged from the bathroom, somewhat refreshed from the long journey, I discovered my new roommate luxuriating in the comforts of home. Bob lay stretched out on the living room couch, feet up, a Fresca in hand.

"I am *so* glad to have you living here, Sam. I don't know you *that* well yet, but I can tell already that you're a freakin' *cool* guy."

"Thank you, Bob." I toasted him with an imaginary glass.

"The last guy who lived here was a real *psycho*." Bob chuckled happily, remembering. "What about you—you live with any real *nutcases* recently?"

"Not really," I said. "My roommate in Santa Cruz was probably the best friend I had up there."

Bob sat up, sobering quickly. "I hope that one day you'll say the same thing about me, bro," he intoned seriously.

"I'm . . . sure I will, Bob."

"Yeah *right* you will!" Bob giggled. He reclined again. "You'll be all, 'my first roommate in Los Angeles was a *mental* case!' You'll be all, 'I wanted to *commit* him!'"

I laughed awkwardly. "No."

"'He was gay as a maypole!'"

"Of course I wouldn't say that," I said.

"'*As gay as a thermos of white wine!*'" yelped Bob.

I just shook my head, helplessly.

"I *am* a big fag, of course," said Bob, thoughtfully, settling deeper into his couch, which seemed to already bear the imprint of his body. He whirled around suddenly to stare at me. "Could you guess?"

"Um . . . I think so?" I said, hesitatingly.

"*Lis-ten* to this guy!" He clapped, delightedly. "'I *think* so.' How *polite* you are, Sam! And what a little liar, too. Shee-it." He sneered, putting his hands behind his head. "You were all, 'Um, *guys*? I *think* I found the lead for *Paris Is Burning 2*. Come *on*, Sam! 'Fess up! You were all, '*Guys! Found one!* I *think* he wears a kimono to bed!' '"

"But I'm not like that," I said, confused. "I'm . . . fine with you being gay. It doesn't bother me at all."

"Good thing," observed Bob, nodding seriously. "Not everyone can hang with it." Then he grinned at me pleasantly, and held up his fizzy drink. "Fresca?"

Bob was a little out of his mind, but he was friendly and generous. He showed me the hot spots in our neighborhood, like Smog Cutter, a weird, windowless watering hole with an appealingly ugly clientele and a decent pool table, and the Busy "B" *supermercado*, where you could buy six pounds of raw pork butt for a dollar. As a team, we moved with cat-quick agility through the city streets. In due time, Bob proved his mettle by establishing himself as an informative and indefatigable repository of gay star gossip.

I spent a couple of days walking around my neighborhood alone, trying to get a sense of what I was up against. South of Sunset, Silver Lake was safe but run-down, boasting a score of ninety-seven-cent stores, cheap pawnshops, and dilapidated storefront churches. We did have a nice view of the Hollywood sign, though, and when I would trudge up the street early in the morning to go pick up a newspaper, the huge white letters would loom over me, grand and mythic. I caught myself imagining all the youngsters who, like me, had come to Los Angeles on a *mission*. Had anyone else dreamed a little porno dream?

"You want me to see if there's an opening down at the warehouse?" Bob inquired one evening, evidently having noticed that I was jobless. He operated a forklift in a carpet warehouse in Montebello. "It's not bad work, once you get used to it."

"No, thanks," I said, noncommittally.

"Looking for something closer to home, huh? Well, I can't say that I blame you, the commute's a bitch and a half." He narrowed his eyes, studying me, then pounced. "If you don't mind me asking, what exactly is it that you *do*, Sam?"

"Well," I said, "I guess you could say I'm sort of an artist."

"An *artist*! Hey, that's *great*! Listen, do you think you could draw a funny picture of me with like, a giant cock? There's a guy at work who's just been *eyeballing* me. I think he needs just the *tiniest* bit of encouragement."

"I'm not much good at drawing."

"Oh," said Bob, agreeably. "Then you . . . paint?"

"Don't paint," I said, smiling slightly. My eyes twinkled mischievously.

Bob inched closer to me, his eyes alight with undisguised curiosity. I should have known better than to try to slip anything by him; he had a keen sense of sexual perversion. "Oooh, you do something *juicy*! What *is* it? Tell Bobby all about it."

"Well, Bob," I said, grinning, happy to have someone new to confide in, "as it just so happens, I am in the business of making pornos."

"*I knew it!*" he exploded gleefully, throwing his arms up in jubilation. "Oh, I *so* called this one!"

"Bob, I . . ."

"I was *tellin'* the guys at work," he continued, his voice rising excitedly, "I've got this new roommate, he is *hot*, man! I mean, he is *smokin'*. That kid's got a *ten-inch dick*, I can just *feel* it—"

"Bob," I interrupted. "Wait. I'm not a porn star. I said, I *make* pornos."

He looked at me, crestfallen. "Is there a difference?"

"There's a difference," I said soberly.

"You . . . don't have a ten-inch dick?"

"No," I said, gently. "I *shoot* the movies, Bob. I'm sorry."

"Aw, hell!" said Bob. "What a *tease!*" He socked me playfully on the shoulder, but it actually hurt. There was some anger in that punch. Bob sulked in silence for a moment, considering what might have been. Then his mood appeared to shift. "Aw, heck, what am I thinking: filming's almost as good! *Porno?* That's *hot*, bro, *super hot.* And listen, don't be sorry that you have a small dick. *Plenty* of guys do. Now, tell me more about this; tell me *everything*, Sam!"

I soon fell in love with LA's dirty banana trees, her anorexic palms. They sprouted with persistent vitality, swelling up through the concrete, towering monuments to a demented brand of hope. But still I was nervous. The specter of imminent financial disaster loomed nearby. My well had finally run dry. I was broke.

For a few days, I tossed around the idea of applying for a job at Nature Mart, the health food store in neighboring Los Feliz, but then quickly reconsidered. After all, I hadn't come down to LA to work at a *grocery store.* I'd come to get into the sex industry, *period.* To feel it from the inside.

I began to consider stripping, and then, more reasonably, go-go dancing. Apparently, it was a pretty sweet gig: I'd had a friend in college, Dale, who'd supported himself senior year almost solely by dancing in gay bars. You just got up onstage, he said, drunk and in your underwear. Go wild and let it move on from there naturally. I pictured bottles of beer upturned playfully over Dale's head, bathing his cherubic blond curls in festive suds. I saw his graceful heels mapping an ancient rhythm on a rugged, wooden stage. The toast of the town.

Dale also mentioned, somewhat offhandedly, that sometimes he let customers jack him off in the bathroom for forty bucks. "It's like that," he said, by way of explanation.

If I was frightened at the prospect of making the scene at an all-male sock hop, however, I was far more frightened of the alternative, which was the job at Nature Mart, so one day I picked up the *LA Weekly* and began to hunt.

Before long, my eyes settled on an ad for "Club Hump." *Beefy Go-Go Boys Drive Mixed Crowds Crazy!* After a brief internal struggle, I summoned up the nerve to call the promoter, if only to find out what was what. Seeming friendly enough, he invited me to come by on Wednesday. Amateur Night.

Club Hump was on Crenshaw, not in South Central, but up in Hollywood; still, it was a mostly black club. The head dancer met me at the door. His real name was William, but at the club, he went by Daredevil. He broke it down for me.

"You get two songs. Either you pick 'em, or the DJ does it for you. I'd pick 'em if I were you. Slip him a dollar. He'll play your shit for sure, then." He took a moment to look me over, a concerned look on his tough face. "You ever done this before?"

"No," I admitted. "Not really."

Daredevil put a protective hand on my shoulder, lowering his voice to a whisper. "Just don't show no fear out there. They will mothafuckin' *rip you to shreds* if they smell fear. You got that?"

I nodded. Daredevil patted me on the back and walked away, shaking his head, as if he knew something I didn't.

There was no changing room at the Hump—just a "VIP" room upstairs, which housed a pool table, some hangers-on, and another dancer, an effeminate black kid named Jason. He seemed quiet, but when I said to him, smiling, "You nervous?" he shook his head, seriously.

"I just love to *dance*."

As I dressed, the club started to fill up. The crowd included vaguely menacing "thug" types, there with their straight-billed baseball caps; a number of quiet, masculine, clearly gay black men, conspicuously *not* on the DL; a sprinkling of strong-legged, rowdy transsexuals; and quite a few big, fat black mamas. Assembled together, they vibrated with a terrible potency. I feared the worst.

The DJ began to warm up the crowd. "We know that y'all come out here on a Wednesday night for *juuuuust one* thang, right? To see a little *ass*!"

The crowd roared in approval. I saw one of the trannies at the bar pick up her glass, as if toasting the idea.

The DJ continued: "Club Hump, as usual, is bringing you its best. We got some hot young brothas here tonight; scooped 'em up right off the street! *Y'all ready for some ass?*"

They answered with another roar, with animal intensity.

"*Y'ALL READY FOR SOME ASS??*"

They throbbed together like hungry dogs, starving for meat.

"*THEN LET'S DO THIS!*" He threw on the first record of the night, and Daredevil bounded down the steps to greet the mass of wild flesh. He was wearing a trench coat, which he quickly discarded to reveal only a black pair of bikini briefs. The crowd went totally berserk. Especially the big girls.

Daredevil rippled his muscles and fucked the air. He wagged his crotch up and down, in a sort of dorsal double time that white mortals could only dream of imitating. The man had a huge cock. You could see it straining against the black nylon of his underwear. He was cut, sculptural, and they were lining up to go stuff money into his g-string. Men elbowed one another with degenerate abandon, bodies swaying as they jockeyed for position. The ladies bared their claws, hissing viciously. All to be near that awesomely articulated midsection. The 'Devil cleaned up. He made something like $200 in five minutes.

I (most unfortunately; *most* pitiably) was next.

Picture it, if you will: cheap leopard-skin-print briefs, secured at the ninety-nine-cent store, hugged my genital region. A pair of light blue Skechers that my mother had bought me in San Jose, months before. No socks. My little yoga body didn't feel so hot, compared to Black Panther, king of the Crenshaw jungle. *Who am I fooling here?* I thought wildly. *I have wide hips and minor scoliosis.*

And then, to top it all off, the DJ put on a Prince song.

I'll never forget that feeling of walking down those stairs. The look on the crowd was one of utter blankness. Gone instantly was the collective, shared desire. It had disappeared, vaporized. There wasn't even a "root for the underdog" undercurrent in the room. Just an impassiveness—and hostility, wanting to explode.

Like an ass, I began dancing wildly, enacting a pathetic burlesque of sexual abandon. *Color you peach and black. Color me taken aback. Ba-by.* But no. Absolutely not. Dangerously intimidated, I decided to shift gears: asserting myself in reverse, I brandished my bikinied buttocks at the hostile mob. I waggled them from side to side, looking back hopefully over my left shoulder. The hateful faces staring back at me told me all I needed to know. I was bombing as only a pasty-white Jewish boy adrift in a new city, showcasing a flaccid, five-inch wiener suctioned by polyester fabric dangerously close to his naked left thigh, could bomb.

A few people gave me pity dollars—*handed* them to me—and when I attempted to dance close to them, in some form of gratitude, they smiled, looked embarrassed, and focused on the wall behind me.

Mercifully, my time ended, and I stumbled offstage, up the ignominious stairs, where I retrieved a towel from my bag. As I wiped the sweat off my body, my breath returning to its normal rate, I observed the rest of the show. Jason, the young kid, had followed me, and he was wearing knee pads, for some reason. If memory serves, he was dancing to Janet Jackson. He seemed quite acrobatic, doing weird hip-hop push-ups, maintaining absolutely no eye contact with anyone, gazing at the far wall. He lacked only the Madonna microphone to complete his sad, superstar image. No one really tipped him, either, which cheered me enormously.

I took my six dollars that I'd earned and approached the bar, where I bought a beer. I drank from it, my energy spent.

"You want to fuck me up the ass?" asked one of the transvestites, leering.

"Huh?" I said. But before she could repeat herself, the words registered, and I shuffled back upstairs to change.

EIGHT

My parents and I had a little thing going where we spoke on the phone every Sunday. A couple of weeks after I'd gotten settled in LA, I decided to come clean to my old man. It had been a long time coming.

"Dad? You know how you're always talking about how you want to know what I'm doing with my life, but I never tell you anything?"

"Yes. You guard your privacy jealously. Like a jackal. You haven't told us a single thing about Los Angeles since you moved there."

"Well, I decided you were right. It's not good, and I owe you an apology."

"Accepted," he said. "Thank you for saying that."

"Would you like to know what I'm doing with my life?"

"Please, mystery man."

"I'm producing porn."

There was a moment of silence on the other end of the line.

". . . Excuse me?"

"I said, I'm producing porn."

"And what do you *mean* by that?"

"Exactly what I said. You wanted to know what I'm doing with my life. Well, against all odds, I've managed to insinuate myself into the porn industry. Pretty cool, huh?"

He cleared his throat. "Ellen, get on the line." He waited until my mom clicked on. "How long have you been doing this?"

"To be honest, I've sort of been 'in the business' for about half a year now. Hi, Mom."

"Hi, Sam," she said. "What's this nonsense?"

"Oh, I make porn," I explained.

"But what about the juice bar?" snapped my father.

"I worked there. Part-time. But now I make porn."

My father's temper had held remarkably well to this point, but now he exploded. "But this is *nonsense*! Ellen, say something, please! What has our son gotten himself into this time?"

"Dad," I said calmly, "there's no need to get all riled up. I'm part of a very well-established, historically sound industry. Stood the test of time. In fact, you could sort of say it's the second-oldest profession."

"That thousand dollars I lent you," he mumbled, remembering. "*This* was your business plan?"

My mother spoke up. "This is some kind of elaborate joke, right?"

"Look," I continued, "I can understand your reaction. Heck, if I had a son who went to work in the porn business, I might be a tad bit disturbed, too. But what you don't get yet is that I'm out to produce a different kind of porn. A *progressive* kind."

"What does that mean?" he snapped. "Porn is *porn*. Our son, the pornographer."

"Sam, you're not 'acting,' are you?" pleaded my mom. "I don't care what you do, just tell me you're not 'acting.'"

"Our son, the *pornographer*?" repeated my father. "Holy God. I can't believe I'm saying this out loud."

"But don't you see? All porn isn't cut from the same cloth. My mission," I proclaimed proudly, "is to change the game. From the inside out. I am going to make porn that's *art*."

"Ellen, did you *know* about this? Have you two been keeping this from me?"

"Have you lost your mind?" said my mom. "*What* are you *implying*?"

"Jesus," I said, annoyed. "Will you two listen? I'm making movies that are actually *movies*. I'm trying to make videos that help you know the people *inside* the bodies. You know, their personalities and stuff. Their motivations." I paused, then took a small chance. "It's very Freudian."

"Don't you dare try to hook me!" yelled my dad.

"Seriously, Dad?" I said. "You might like them. Listen, I have an idea. I'm going to send you one of my movies. Would that be all right with you? Would you watch it? It's about domination. And urination."

"Oh, wonderful," he said, exasperated. "We'll screen that very soon. Then we'll both wheel ourselves over to the hospital and have a brain aneurysm."

"You guys," I said, "I have to go now. I have to go make porn. For the record, I think you were right: I haven't let you in on my life enough recently. From here on out, it's all about truth, openness, and honesty. Talk to you later."

My new life was full of promise, but my wallet was still thin. I had never really been a broke person before, and to be honest, I wasn't very good at it. I spent a lot of time hanging around the house, just sort of fretting over unknowns.

Bob had nabbed a new boyfriend, a close-mouthed, long-banged musk ox of a guy, just off the bus from rural Michigan, and he liked to fuss over him, preparing plates of fatty, pinkish hamburgers topped with melted Kraft singles, sweet neon pickle discs, and Pepsi-Cola. I was always invited to share in the cheap-meat festivities, though my own contributions to the table (rice cakes, for example) were politely ignored.

One night, after a few teacups of Captain Morgan, Chester, the boyfriend, revealed to us that he knew how to make McDonald's special sauce. And he set out to prove his word. "It's just ketchup, mayonnaise, and mustard," he said proudly, mixing a taster's plate. "Why should I go out and pay for it, when I can get it at home for free?"

Bob nodded his head, smiling in an agreement that was probably lust influenced. It had to be. Special sauce? Was this my *life*?

One day they invited me to the beach, and although the idea of being a "gang" with them depressed me terribly, I decided it would be impolite to refuse. Chester drove us down Highway 1 in his tiny green hatchback, and we found a beach, spread out our ragged towels in the hazy sun. Bob played solitaire and smoked cigarettes while I paged slowly through an old *Artforum*; Chester ate three bologna sandwiches in a row. Then the wind came. On the way home, I fell asleep in the backseat, waking up in a Food 4 Less parking lot to the sound of "One More Time" playing on someone else's car stereo. I was thoroughly sad.

Poor, man! I wasn't *used* to this. The month was coming to a close, and I hadn't even made rent yet. Situations such as these coiled my innocent stomach into a tight peptic knot. I envisioned calling my dad, but quickly I realized that would never do. I was twenty-four years old and an aspiring *pornographer*. Calling *Daddy* was no longer an option.

No, I would have to handle this myself. There were a million ways to make money in LA. I settled on answering a couple of the ads in the back of the *LA Weekly*—the ones that call for "Hot Guys! X-rated Photo Modeling! Earn 1,000's daily!!!" I wanted $1,000s daily.

The first lead took me to a totally regular-looking living room in West Hollywood, where a sloppily dressed guy with a beard and a Polaroid camera told me to get naked on his couch and make myself full-sized. He stood there, waiting patiently. When I failed, he fished around in his smut stacks and found a straight porno magazine. "Try these puppies on for size," he said, and folded his arms, hovering over me. I spat on my palm and took a good look at the pages of *Tight*. There was something oddly tranquil about beating off in a total stranger's living room in the middle of the day, listening to the faint buzz of the noisy streets. Soon I would be out there, fighting traffic. But not just yet.

Fifteen minutes passed. Finally, I managed a small, uncertain boner. The photographer asked me if I would consider sucking his dick. I said that wasn't really my scene. He showed me the door.

The second ad led me to a large building on the Sunset Strip, just a block east of the Whisky a Go Go, where a very old man took a look at me with my shirt off and said, hesitant to overcommit, "You look decent." Then he put me to the Polaroid test, which I failed resoundingly. When he mentioned offhandedly that he usually did his shoots "in the woods," I exited quietly, that old desperate feeling making its slow creep up my stomach.

They had me up against the wall. But I wasn't beaten yet. I was a

young man in a strange city; yet somehow, Los Angeles felt right. Up
north, they'd called LA "plastic," but they were wrong—dead wrong.
LA was better than that. It was *stranger* than that. LA was a sudden
blowjob in the cheap seats at a Dodgers game. LA was watching your
sister do yoga in fuckable heels. Los Angeles was a traffic jam at midnight; a six-year-old wearing lingerie; a famous newscaster nude on
a mauve beach towel, examining his testicles for cancerous lumps.

Everyone here was flashy and evil and alluringly fit. The homeless had the best tans of anyone, and don't think they didn't know it.
A thick, Calvinistic sense of ambition pumped quietly through the
city streets: *This is gonna be my year,* you could hear each struggling
screenwriter, each terrorized backup dancer, each would-be real es-
tate developer whispering to themselves, *and I'll gut the first bastard
who gets in my way.*

My intuition told me to follow their example. If I could stick
with porn, if I could withstand the heat, I stood to make enormous
gains. After all, our society needed someone like me, a guy willing
to venture out into the muck in order to record careful, diligent
notes about this quintessentially American subculture. We needed
a courageous cultural anthropologist—someone unafraid to don the
loser's mask, to enact the total douche bag, so as to ingratiate himself
into this gaggle of pimps and whores and crooks and retards, in the
process educating the populace at large.

I could be that douche.

Hunger remained the only truly egregious thorn in my side. Santa
Cruz had attuned my palate to biodynamic produce and nitrate-free
meats, but those days were long gone. More often than not, lunch
was a sixty-nine-cent can of Goya kidney beans, washed down with a
cloudy glass of tap water. Still, I survived. Maybe fried beans weren't

the most delicious meal you ever heard of, but doused in hot sauce, salted to hell, and served with a side of raw banana, they became something unusual, almost memorable. Secretly, I kind of relished my pennilessness.

Not that being broke wasn't without its disadvantages. One day, out of nowhere, my Volvo stopped working. Just wouldn't start. I couldn't afford to get it to a mechanic, so, drawing upon my severely limited automotive knowledge base, I figured it was the U-joint acting up; either that, or the transmission pipe needed fluid. I couldn't decide. In either case, the dilemma was academic, because I didn't have the money to fix so much as a burned-out taillight. I abandoned my car on a corner of Heliotrope Avenue, and took up Bob's purple Schwinn.

Bicycling in Los Angeles County is extraordinarily dangerous. Many drivers have never seen these strange bicycle machines before, and, mistaking you for a dangerous alien spacecraft bent on Earth's destruction, will try to ram you off the road. Thus one must always don a thick white helmet before weaving through heavy traffic. The Styrofoam kind, made for epileptic fourth graders and available at most thrift shops, will do just the trick.

I cruised through Hollywood, pumping proudly, ignoring the rage of the impotent drivers all around me. Finding a lunchtime snack shop, I sat down for a quick Coca-Cola and a soothing doughnut. I received a pleasantly wide berth; people do not bother you if you leave your epilepsy helmet on. Yet something felt very wrong. My *look* was wrong. The hot porn chicks of this world didn't fall in love with sensitive retards riding purple bicycles to doughnut shops. They went in for rock star types: chance takers. I needed a new image. Something that said, I'm a *bad* boy. I'm not afraid to get wild.

My opportunity came sooner than I expected. The next evening, I received a phone call from Felice Amador, the sex shop clerk I'd met in San Francisco the previous summer. Good Vibrations was making its first porno movie, and she'd been tapped to direct.

"Are you still 'in the business'?" she asked.

"Baby, I *am* the business."

Felice laughed. "Well, how would you feel about getting in front of the camera?"

"I'd love to," I said. Finally, someone who recognized my unique gifts. "What do you need me to do?"

Felice explained: they were making a porn rarity—a legitimately bisexual video. Hot guys, hot girls, hot gender confusion. The whole nine.

"Where do I fit in?" I asked, suspiciously.

"Depends on what you're willing to do," said Felice. A pause ensued. "What are you up for?"

"Don't know. What are you paying?"

"Flat rate," said Felice. "Four hundred and ninety-nine dollars, across the board. For everybody."

"Very democratic," I breathed, somehow relieved. "Can I be the lead?"

"Absolutely!" said Felice, giggling. "You'll have to take it up the ass, of course."

After a few moments of my flustered stammering, she explained that she meant strap-on sex with a woman. I'd be topped, made to submit.

I considered briefly. *Why not?* It seemed a gutsy move, somehow. Courageous, in its utter disregard for my future.

"I'll do it," I announced, mostly to myself. "I'll do it."

They made plans to pick me up in LA two weeks later. Good thing, too: I didn't have the money for a bus ticket to San Francisco. I was eating beans and scrambled eggs for breakfast, lunch, and dinner. Bob was just as bad off: he'd lost his job at the carpet warehouse for hitting on a reclusive but hunky janitor who turned out to be harboring some serious rage issues. Bob took a wrench to the groin for his troubles, and when he came to, he found out that he'd been canned. Now he lounged around the house all day, watching NASCAR and babbling about how Chester and he were going to get married.

"I want that man to have my *children*," Bob declared, picking at the adhesive bandage that covered his left cheek.

"But what about the janitor you were so hot for?"

"Pity the janitor!" said Bob. "He had his chance."

"So, you're ready to start a family with Chester?" I asked skeptically. "Be faithful, all that stuff?"

Bob raised himself up on one indignant elbow. "I'm speaking *metaphorically*, dude." He shook his head. "Some people."

It was a tense time. With Bob no longer bringing in any income, nerves frayed quickly. Soon he informed me that he was very sorry, but he was going to have to ask me to leave.

"Leave? What the hell did I do?"

"Not a thing," said Bob cryptically. "Not a damn thing. Look. I'm not worried about you. You'll land on your feet."

The timing wasn't ideal, considering my own lack of funds, but a friend of a friend hipped me to a dingy storefront in Echo Park that was renting for pennies. I arranged for a meeting with the Mexican slumlord who owned the place. All of his tenants slept in their stores, from the so-called "pet shop" to the "hair salon" to the "incense factory," but he pretended not to know about it. Of greatest importance, it seemed, was the clear understanding that he would never, ever pay for a single repair or improvement. Under any circumstances. The place had no gas and only a rancid stall shower. But none of that mattered to me. It would be a roof over my head. And I was one strap-on scene away from being able to afford it.

"We're calling it *Slide Bi Me*," Felice announced, when they came to pick me up.

"Why?" I asked, cautiously. I hugged a paper bag's worth of costumes closely to my chest. There were two cans of vegetarian chili in there, too, just in case. I had literally twelve dollars to my name. I felt insane.

"We have a Slip 'N Slide theme going in the movie. It's gonna be silly, you know? Fun, playful. Don't worry, Sam. We're making a different sort of porn."

So there was someone else who believed in my mission. I relaxed. I was with friends now.

We made the ride up Interstate 5 with little problem. Felice bought me lunch at McDonald's, and as she drove, I balanced a large black sketchbook on my lap and drew, like a contented little child. As we made our way up the Central Valley, we passed Cowschwitz, the giant cattle ranch. It was a frightening sight—all of those spooky beasts pushed up against one another, murmuring a secret language, gently shitting onto their own legs.

We arrived at our set, a wooded spa retreat, located an hour outside the city. It was dusty and dry, but suffused with Northern California calm. I was the only member of the cast who was from LA—all the rest were art students and friends of Felice's from San Francisco. Of course, I thought them amateurs. I found Sarah, the film's producer, more exotic, though: she was a beautiful, sensitive, dreadlocked lesbian in her late twenties, with quiet charisma and a poetic Ani DiFranco–style secret rage locked up inside her. She had the Good Vibes, women-empowered vibe written all over her. She was a grown-up, mostly, and I wanted her to like me.

A script found its way into my hands. Though written by members of the so-called creative class, *Slide Bi Me* boasted a typically threadbare porno plot revolving around a company picnic, some dynamite potato salad, and a host of randy trust-building exercises. Clearly, I was going to have to improvise at length in order to give my character sufficient depth.

Ten years of teen drama angst came gushing out of me in rehearsal as I hammed up every single word. "That's not necessary, Sam," Felice snapped. "Just do the line and let the other people talk." But I couldn't stop. I delivered each line as if it were a Shakespearean soliloquy, and the crew, fledgling film students tickled to be shooting "erotica," giggled to one another. It was a wonderful experience.

Though I was aiming to play it cool, I had to admit the prospect of being on film was making me excited. Down in LA, I was the rookie, the kid, but here, no one had ever been in a dirty movie before. *I* was the pro here. *I* knew porn. Porn was my middle name. Finally, I was the rock star.

"*Where's the guy who's taking it up the ass for the first time?*" yelled Hiroshi, the costume designer.

"Oh, that'd be me," I coughed, raising my hand at half-mast.

He held out a pair of chinos. "We got these for you special. Please try not to bleed on them."

"Of course." I laughed weakly. "No . . . no bleeding."

He smiled. "You're gay, right?"

"No. Straight."

"Yeah," he said. "Straight to bed."

Oh, what was the use? I wasn't going to prove my masculinity to anybody on this set. The main thing was, I was getting some attention. Now I could understand how all the porn girls felt. Sometimes you just needed to be looked at, no matter how dumb the project. You just wanted to be *acknowledged*.

Soon I was introduced to my partner-to-be, Lysette, a hefty Cuban mulatto power dyke with freckles on her brown skin and strong softball player's forearms. I'd seen her type before, roaming the Mission, shooting confident glances all over the place, manufacturing sizzling sexual connections with everything in her path. At twenty-two years of age, she looked like a young Condoleezza Rice, with bigger tits.

"Ever take it from a girl?" asked Lysette.

"No," I admitted.

"Then I'll probably have to go easy on you," she said, reluctantly. "But let's warm you up anyway. Follow me."

We found a bathroom and locked its door. Lysette stripped me naked and lay me on my stomach in the bathtub. "This is lube. It'll feel all juicy. That's a good thing." She administered the liquid gel to my asshole, like a mother bird feeding her children's hungry mouth. It was a profound experience, like a rebirthing or something.

"Now let me start with this *baby* dildo." She took a pink vibrator, about the size of her thumb, and began shoving it up my anal canal. "What's *that* feel like?"

"Feels like . . . I gotta poop?"

"Exactly. That's exactly right. But you're not pooping. Don't worry. No poop."

Slowly, she increased the size of her instruments, stroking my hair and whispering gently to me the whole time. After some time, I could handle a respectable girth.

"I never thought it'd come to this," I mumbled.

"Sorry?"

"Nothing. I'm ready."

We walked out into the great outdoors. Limping slightly, I nodded to Felice. We were standing by.

Sensing drama, the mob of camera operators surrounded us,

locked us in a tight clinch. Lysette pointed to the ground; I un-
dressed hastily, intimidated. My dreadlocked lover kissed me on
the head, then pushed me toward a pink blanket. In the summer
breezes, sequoia trees towered above me hundreds of feet high.

I was powerless. It was very exciting, in a way, to be so *not* in control. Lysette penetrated me from behind, and I rode the wave of her
desire. Then she flipped me over and fucked me on my back, my
knees around my ears. "You okay down there?" she asked. I nodded
weakly. I could barely speak. She tried to go easy on me, but by the
end, her natural rhythm took over, and she fucked me down into the
ground hard, no apologies offered.

Postcoitus, my insides coiled, hot and glowing, the rough fucking
perhaps dislodging some ancient trauma. Sarah, my producer-crush,
spied me, naked, carrying my crumpled clothes in a bundle. "Way
to *go*, Sam!" I rushed past her to go weep in the woods.

Later, feeling more stable, I scored half a joint and smoked it by
a creek. Deep breathing helped me get myself back together. Without a doubt, I was mortally embarrassed. But there was no sense in
waffling now—the die had been cast. And the more I thought about
it, the better I felt. *It took guts to do what I did.* I was up on my hind
legs, now. Crying to be heard.

Feeling stoned, slightly mystic, I stumbled up the path toward
the house. Felice was directing an orgy scene. Two guys and two
girls rolled on top of one another like suckling puppies, popping
members both real and prosthetic into every available orifice via
methods God had never foreseen. A mangled Slip 'N Slide lay beside them, a telltale marker of Good Clean Fun.

I watched them play for a while, reflecting privately that in LA,
porn had never really looked like this. Down there, the players
looked more like cartoon superheroes, with their synthetic vaginas,
their double-wide cocks. These people were all sorts of imperfect,

and some of them quite hairy, but they were having fun. And they were having real sex. It sort of blew my mind.

Suddenly, out of the corner of my eye, I saw a figure waving at me. It was Sarah. *Oh*, I thought. *I'm in the camera's line of vision. How embarrassing.* I moved a few steps over.

She continued to wave at me. I frowned, pointed at myself. *Me?*

She nodded, beckoning me toward her again. I walked over, obediently, and she put a finger to her lips, motioned toward the house.

The producer led me into the kitchen, stood inches away from my face. I trembled, amazed at our closeness. "I saw you watching that scene, Sam."

I nodded, hypnotized by her strong beauty. Her perfect lips.

"You want to *be* in that scene. *Don't* you, Sam?"

I nodded again, this time in wonder. A wave of gratitude crashed over me, and without warning, I felt a strong urge to cry. *Sarah was like me.* She understood. Sometimes, you just wanted to be *looked at.*

Without warning, she jerked open a large Frigidaire freezer. A blast of cool air pressed against my body, and I shivered uncontrollably. I watched dumbly as Sarah, backlit, in slow motion, retrieved from within the freezer's depths one of our picnic props: a Jell-O mold shaped like the United States.

Then something broke in me and I seized the Jell-O from her grasp like a fumbled football. I sprinted back to the scene, stripping the clothes from my body along the way.

"Felice!" I whispered. "Look!" I laid the Jell-O on the ground directly in front of the orgy and began lapping at it happily, like a dog.

Felice grimaced, annoyed. The performers raised their heads and glanced toward me with curiosity. I performed a few more showy licks for their benefit. Then, very carefully, I removed the

America-shaped gelatin from its mold and placed it, quivering and cold, onto my naked chest.

"Watch this," I whispered. I held up a finger, breathless. "Just watch."

I fell into Urdhva Dhanurasana, the yogic backbend. The cold sweet fruit jiggled atop my abdomen, traversing my pectorals, covering my heart.

"What in the fuck is he doing?" Felice mumbled sadly.

"No idea," said her cameraman. But he tiptoed closer to me, to get a better shot.

I arched my back farther, my head nearly brushing the ground. The United States of Jell-O wobbled, nearly toppling from my chest. But it quieted, evening out, and I closed my eyes, ecstatic, breathing in deep.

For one brief moment, it was as if the world had imploded. All was quiet; all eyes laid on me. My hands shivered in the late-afternoon chill; my shoulders quaked, begging for surrender. But I held my ground. And it sounds so stupid, but looking back, it was truly one of the ecstatic moments of my life. My pelvis rocketed toward the sky; my heart pushed forward, almost out of my chest. And my flaccid, tiny penis waved bravely in the Northern California wind.

NINE

I cashed my entire *Slide Bi Me* check in order to move into my new little roach den. The grimy Echo Park storefront space boasted plenty of character, in the form of dangling electrical sockets, no gas, and deranged neighbors. To my immediate right, a mean, bulky woman ran a pet shop that contained basically no animals. She owned an iguana that was two hundred years old, a rabbit that was covered in what looked like human shit, and that was it. Her menacing scowl warned me not to investigate further. To my left lived a tiny, dapper Mexican *artiste* named Tenzeno, who spent his days smashing up painting after painting. He seemed to throw a new one together almost every afternoon. They stacked up against the wall in depressing heaps.

Though I found Tenzeno's paintings striking, he never sold one, ever—a fact that caused the little fellow about an equal amount of pique and pride. "I'm left out of the gallery system, Sam," he announced to me one day, extinguishing a wretched cigarette into one of his huge jade ashtrays, a stylish orange jersey draped across his chest. "Socioculturally, I'm a *desaparecido*." He glared at me pointedly, knowing that I had just graduated from college, that my parents had spent the bank on me. "The system is really corrupt, which I don't have to tell you."

We struck up a modest friendship, Tenzeno and I. We would meet in early mornings for homemade coffee filtered through paper towels. After ten minutes or so, Tenzeno would produce a rolled cigarette clogged with brown bits of marijuana. Riding the wave of a small buzz, we'd debate art, or porn. To his mind, excessive focus on human genitalia elicited deep waves of sadness in the viewer. Whereas I believed a full frontal of a shining, shaved labia could, given the right context, provoke euphoria. We discussed.

But when Tenzeno's water pressure went on the fritz, he began sneaking through my back door and washing his crusty dishes in my sink. I found that upsetting. We got into a screaming match, during which he called me a "voyeur." Later he apologized and presented me with a scavenged electric wok. We dined on hot red beans that night.

Poverty was back, stronger than ever. My parents sent me some raisin cookies in the mail; they got me through a tight spot. My friend Michael arrived in town one day, desperate to make porn. Instead we squandered his budget watching live nude oil wrestling. Defeated, I rode the bus to Venice Beach and tried my hand at staring glumly at waves. Wasn't too bad at it. Then an old pair of blue jeans washed up onshore next to me.

I took to the boardwalk, where Rollerbladers whizzed by and fat bums removed wet Camels from their mouths to throw up gently into paper bags. I kept walking, head down. What did I care? All around me, the smell of cheap pizza and baby oil.

Various leads came and went. A Manhattan fashion photographer who loved porn dangled a photo retouching job in front of me, and I bit. But he got cold feet, reneged on our deal. I sank further into depression. When I couldn't justify spending my cash on yoga anymore, I begged a skinny woman who ran a local studio to let me clean up her place after hours in exchange for free classes. She loved the idea and handed me a mop.

It wasn't so bad, being a yoga janitor. I swabbed the wooden floors of the shala with a monk's precision, a little black stereo floating late-night soft rock treasures into the air. Spiritual work is easy work, men. Not to mention, some of those rubber mats smelled pretty good. The funk of honest sweat clung to them. It felt sort of vicious, in fact, to spray them down with my alcohol solution. As if the bacteria were doing cool little headstands and things.

I ate more broccoli. I sold half my CD collection. I found change in pay phones and claimed it.

Finally, one night, everything changed. I'd been trolling the Web for an hour or so (purely research purposes, you understand) when I came across an "interracial" website, one in which hordes of black men frolicked among the montes pubis of tiny white girls, to the perverted delight of the site's paying members. Recalling that I, too, had an "interracial" in my vault—Black Dave vs. Sandy Spago—I contacted the site's administrator, a man named Pitts, and offered to sell him my scene.

Pitts responded quickly, offering that he'd actually been hoping to create some videos of his own for some time now, but had been stumped, due to being based in Seattle. His talent pool there was limited. How would I feel about trying my hand at producing a scene for him? I told him I'd consider it. I quoted him my rate—a very reasonable four hundred dollars—and told him to give me a week.

My first responsibility, of course, would be to procure the actors.

Finding fellas would be simple. A quick post to any online adult message board would spawn hundreds of drooling responses in one day. Getting a girl? That would require the help of professionals. Following a lead and my best intuition, I headed over to the second-largest porn agency in Los Angeles: Reb's PGI, which stood for Pretty Girl, International.

But if Reb's agency was indeed international, then it spoke overwhelmingly of the third world. Stark tobacco nests had been ground into the yellowing fibers of his stairwell carpeting by the tread of one thousand boot heels. The walls fairly cringed, wanting for a fresh coat of paint, or at least a wipe down. And that old familiar porn aroma, *eau du blowjob*, followed you like a grim virus, all the way up the stairwell, right in through the flimsy front door.

I was greeted at the front desk by Clarence, a wiry, cheerful fifty-year-old hophead with a gleaming shaved dome and a Newport cigarette. Clarence's job was to deal with walk-ins like me.

"Can I help you?"

"I certainly hope so," I said, somewhat haltingly. New to this sort of thing, I wasn't quite sure how it all operated. Maybe this would be like trying to buy a bong at a head shop, where they threw you out if you didn't ask for the thing with the right term: *water pipe*. "I'm looking for . . . a white girl."

"Oh, we have that."

I scratched my head and searched for the proper terminology. "A white girl, who's into the concept of black guys."

"The *concept*?"

"She'll be sleeping with them," I clarified. "I want to do an interracial."

Clarence considered. "You going to need A?"

"Who's A?"

He hooted. "A's *anal*, man! Do you want it up the pooper?"

"No," I said, flushing. "I don't think that'll be necessary."

"Then it's eight hundred bucks," said Clarence, happily. He lit his smoke, rubbing his bald dome with the meat of his palm, still holding the red lighter. "Plus seventy-five dollars to the office. That's our referral fee."

"Sounds fair," I said, cheered that the whole process had been so simple. I'd had more trouble getting gym memberships. "Agreed."

He grinned at me. "Lemme show you the Book."

Pretty Girl's Book was legendary. Each girl the agency represented had the right to two crude Polaroids and a list of dos and don'ts. The heavy, overstuffed directory contained the rap sheets on literally hundreds of working porn actresses. Porn producers in good favor with the office were allowed to spend whole afternoons thumbing through the catalog, drooling over the photos, which always featured one full-body shot from the front and one from the rear, doggy-style, looking back over one shoulder.

I shuffled through the pages rapidly, observing the toned, often heavily tattooed young bodies before me. Many of the actresses were surprisingly hard-looking, as if they were fresh from murdering somebody with a hammer claw, or on some sort of leave from hooker's prison. More than a handful sported disappointing names: *Butter, California, Charity.* That was a bad career move, to my mind. One-namers didn't last. One-namers ended up slogging away in mediocre leather dungeons in San Bernardino, toiling away in eternal obscurity to atone for their lack of creativity.

"How about her?" I asked, pointing to a small, frowning girl with kinky brown hair, who went by the slightly more inventive "Amber Ways." I supposed she had based her name on the character Amber Waves in *Boogie Nights*—a weird sort of twist. She glared up at me nakedly, almost angrily, but someone had scrawled "Interracial" next to her Polaroid.

"Great choice. Amber's one of our best girls. You'll love her."

So we set it up. Easy as that. I found my guys just as smoothly—they were two best friends named Bert and Vance, and both were plugged into the SoCal swinger scene. They were willing to do the job for $50 each. Bert was a touch old for public nudity—he was at least forty, with a small, somehow muscular belly extending roundly over the belt of his jeans. But he moved with the confident intensity of a former professional athlete: agitated, jumpy, ready to bang.

"I do this kind of thing *all the time*," he insisted. "We both do."

"I can come four or five times in an hour," Vance interjected.

"Oh, me, too," Bert assured me. "None of this one-nut business!" He and Vance cracked up, slapping hands.

"Let me explain to you guys how this is going to work," I said. "Vance, you'll . . ."

"I want my porno name to be Darth," Vance interrupted. "Darth Callous."

"He's into all that *Star Wars* shit," Bert said.

The pair were headed to a swing party in Granada Hills that very weekend; they assured me that if we arrived early enough, the owner of the house was sure to let us shoot there for free. "Just let him watch, if he asks. That's good swing manners."

I packed my bowling bag full of provisions: towels, douches, model releases, lube, baby wipes. The Volvo, now back in working order, rumbled deep across the Valley. It was a fine, warm night. I wore my porn director's outfit: a short-sleeved orange polyester Izod and tight bell-bottom corduroy slacks. Greed rumbled excitedly in my stomach. I was going to be rich.

The shoot went even better than I had imagined. Bert and Darth, though amateurs, attacked their prey with passion and intensity.

"No Viagra or nothin'," Darth bragged.

"We just love pussy," Bert explained, breathing hard.

I got plenty of footage. It was totally plotless nonsense, of course, reminiscent of the 8mm anonymous hardcore "loops" that first drew raincoaters to New York City bookstores—but so what? It wasn't in my contract to be creative. I was a hired gun. Now it was time for *me* to get gonzo.

If there was a letdown to the night, it was only that, postscene, Amber just sort of accepted her paycheck and disappeared. She had been a very quiet and reserved sort of porn actress. I was mildly disappointed that we didn't get to know each other better, but, having been in her shoes myself in the recent past, I acknowledged the psychic demands of giving your all to the camera. Afterward, you need your space. Perhaps we would have other opportunities to socialize.

I sent the tapes off to Seattle, pocketing four hundred bucks for my efforts. Immediately, Pitts ordered another shoot. We settled into a steady rhythm: he would front me cash, and I would run to Pretty Girl, scouring the Book for new names and new bodies. I spent entire days in Reb's cramped antechamber, watching the new arrivals complete their forms. Each morning, Clarence would interview and catalog a score of half-pretty brats looking to score: sad Portland punks with dead dads and milky, exquisite legs; weird MILFs with drum-tight abs and tattoos of Lucky Charms on their asses; and black girls named Shakesphere who hoped they were getting a head start on their singing careers by shitting into a moist towelette for a bearded photographer in a rumpled explorer vest.

Soon I met Gus, a cynical guy in his early thirties who lurked in a musty, unused corner of the building. His sole responsibility at PGI seemed to be taking the nude Polaroids of the aspiring actresses.

"I guess lots of guys would think I'm lucky to do this," he grumbled. "But I'll be honest, I can't stand it. These chicks are downright revolting. I don't even want *blowjobs* from them anymore. I tell you, I'm done with it."

Apart from snapping pics at Reb's, Gus also worked with Mike Hott Video, probably the most debased mail-order porn company in the history of the universe. Their bestselling line was something called "Party Pigs"—Gus's doing. "It's disgusting," he bragged. "No one could *possibly* enjoy this."

Gus, who had done ten long years in the business, took a certain choleric pleasure in educating the raw newbie who stood before him.

"Hey, listen. You know that fucker, Randall, who works the desk for World Modeling? Well, he *performs*, did you know that? *I* shot him once. He's got the biggest dick you ever saw. But he can't get hard. *Twelve inches*, and it can't get hard. It's like a big, floppy hose."

And then Gus would laugh. He had the awful hee-hawing bray of a donkey, the kind you never hear out loud except in a darkened movie theater—or while discussing anal sex in broad daylight.

"Hey—you ever shot a tweaker? You ever wonder, like, why is this chick wearing like ten coats of pancake? Well, I got a secret: her *pores* are too big. Meth turns your pores into these massive *craters*. They're like big, wet, black freckles."

Gus knew everyone and had sympathy for none, least of all the girls, many of whom carried intense personal struggles with them on their journey.

"Look, I know they've been abused, I know they've got eating disorders like a motherfucker. But that actually *helps* them, if you think about it. Say you've been puking after every meal for a year. Chances are, you can deep-throat with the best of them. You've got no gag reflex. None."

———

Bert and Darth, newer than I to the adult film industry, likely gave not a damn about these issues. They were in it for the sex, period, and the sociology was secondary. Bert, in particular, was addicted to pussy. Chubby women the world over had found their way into his damp bed, felt the rub of his sheets. An amateur videographer, Bert often documented his adventures; I was made to watch the disturbing footage more than once. "I know this isn't *professional*, like yours, bro. But I figured you'd want to see me take *this* chick on! Wow! Not bad, huh?" But it *was* bad. Bert fucked large, sloppy asses hungrily, snuffling the rapacious, thirsty grunts of a pleased dog. This was a man who would sleep with any woman, anytime, no questions asked. A purist.

Darth was more complex, harder to pin down. He was much younger than Bert, but far more silent, as if guarding a trove of hard-earned secret knowledge and life experience. A veteran of four years of military service, he held a black belt in Kempo karate and exuded a thrilling air of potential violence. Yet he was kind, even delicate, with me, showcasing with quiet pride his immaculate collection of vampire hardbacks (he was an Anne Rice man), gently stroking the dorsal scales of Baby, the enormous adult boa constrictor with whom he shared his life. Baby made her home in his bathroom, sliding threateningly across the tiled linoleum floors, flicking her tongue coquettishly and swallowing the occasional rat whole.

Fearing the recriminations of my neighbors, I began to stage most of my shoots at Darth's apartment in Long Beach. Those first few shoots were *so bad*. This is not an exaggeration. A single 500-watt bulb dangling from Darth's popcorn ceiling illuminated our set with shocking baldness. Because I didn't know how to white-balance my camera, an uneven yellowish hue contaminated all of my footage. But perhaps worst of all, my director's vision had not yet matured. I didn't know the angles. I would leap from spot to spot, frantically straining to find that perfect perspective, knocking over chairs and candles and Kempo trophies in my desperate ardor. Then, when I finally settled upon a spot, I'd film for approximately fifteen seconds, blink wildly, and make a sprint for the next location.

But none of this much mattered. Pitts complimented me profusely on each mediocre execution, exhorting me to add yet another chapter to his increasingly voluminous interracial library. Over the course of a few short weeks, I lifted myself out of my youthful poverty and entered solidly into a middle-class existence. The Burbank mall was visited; expensive Polo flip-flops were purchased. I wore them constantly in the LA autumn warmth, like a badge.

The speed of my transformation was startling. After a season of desperate, humiliating struggle, life was suddenly both easy and sweet. I felt more charming. Taller. For the first time in ages, I had enough money in my pocket to afford to buy a bag of weed. I cleaned my studio. I vacuumed the carpet, washed the windows, emptied the trash, scrubbed the bowl, changed the towels, and wiped out the microwave. All of a sudden, my place gleamed white, spacious, and exciting—a secret, bohemian laboratory. I spent long, happy evenings alone, listening to music and fooling around on the computer. One night, I even broke out the pen and ink, did a few modest little drawings. Most of them weren't very good, but that was beside the point. Finally, I was winning.

TEN

My new life was one of great leisure. I took long, pleasant walks around Echo Lake, attending to the ducks with bread crumbs; I participated in numerous classes at my yoga studio, where I held sway as a humble janitor. The woman who owned the place grew fond of the careful way I swabbed her floors. I saw no need to inform her of my double life. Instead I merely smiled beatifically and grew into a peaceful tree posture, my well-formed deltoids pumped up from diligently pushing my mop.

Yet my life felt imperfect. True, I could now afford foodstuffs that did not come canned for less than a dollar. But I was still alone and lonely. I saw vaginas up close and personal on a fairly regular basis, but those were not for me. They were greedily swallowed up whole by the twin thrusts of Bert and Darth, my Negroid swinger superstars from Oxnard and Long Beach.

I'd spat a good game at my parents about my artistic plans, but even I had to admit that the shenanigans I was pulling for Pitts were far from art. On my porch in Santa Cruz, I'd dreamed about giving the viewer something new, something totally unexpected, but in truth, the ill-conceived crap I was churning out was nothing surprising. In terms of my own edification, the only thing that I'd gleaned so far was that in this particular genre, it wasn't just the female participants who were objectified (on the basis of their looks), but also the males (on the basis of their race).

My muckraking intentions had been real. But since I'd arrived in LA, I'd somehow found myself kowtowing to the status quo. A bisexual woman had fucked me in the ass, true; but I could not rest on those laurels for long. The truth was, I'd gotten lazy. I'd let my lack of cash serve as a convenient excuse to malinger creatively. With growing alarm, I realized I had to get back to my ideals, and quickly, before some terrible *Invasion of the Body Snatchers*–type change had been completed in me, and I lost all innocence forever.

These women weren't *props*. They weren't even really "porn stars," except by label. They were regular people who, for some reason, had decided to get naked and raw. Only telling their complete individual backstory would humanize them. And only the honest explication of the *filmmaker's* desire could legitimate his gonzoid enterprise. It was time to make some groundbreaking sexual cinema. It really was. Plus I was incredibly horny.

One day at Pretty Girl, as we were quaffing a few warm Budweisers and suffering through a screening of the latest edition of *Party Pigs*, Gus turned to me and said:

"So, you fuckin' any of these girls?"

"Not really," I admitted, with a laugh.

"What the hell's the matter with you? These girls *do* like to fuck, you know."

"Well . . . I don't know how to talk to them," I confessed. "I'm too shy."

"Shy? Shy? What the hell's *shy* got to do with it? Why don't you just piggyback a scene or two?"

"Piggyback?"

"Oh, Christ," Gus said. "Rookies all around me. Listen, man. You find a girl that you like, okay? A semipretty one, who's not too far gone. Then you tape her for this thing that you keep shooting, the black thing, right?"

"Sure."

"But *then* you say"—he giggled, his voice rising squeakily like a teen's—"*How's about a little something for me, too? How about a little something on the side?*"

I frowned. "This kind of thing gets done?"

"All the time! I do it every time I go out. Nowadays, I don't even shoot unless I can get my balls licked."

"I thought you said . . ."

"I know what I said. But I was kidding. Look," Gus said, licking the suds from the rim of his beer can with a grayish tongue, "I get my balls licked. Minimum."

"You pay them?"

"*Sure*, I pay them!" Gus crowed. "I throw in an extra hundred, and they're happy to get it."

"And they usually say yes?" I asked, dubiously.

"They *always* say yes," Gus said. He stared at me. "That's their job, in a nutshell, right? They *say yes.*"

I made up my mind, then, to follow his directive, and when Clarence tossed me perhaps the best-looking girl at PGI, a twenty-year-old actress named Kate Frost, I was in business. Now, I *knew* Kate Frost. She was a name—not like Jenna Jameson or anything like that, but she had her own modest following. Kate had starred in a couple of Stagliano films, got flown to Rio with him. That *meant* something to me.

Nervously, I decided to call her. Kate Frost was very lively on the phone, the kind of person who was always hanging up on you about twenty times in a row because things were always *happening* to her while she was driving. But she had a good sense of humor and an open, honest manner that went along with her scattered nature, so, in truth, I didn't mind that much.

"So, it's eight hundred bucks," I repeated.

"Eight? Wow, Sam, for two guys? This is so bargain basement. I mean it really is. I just want you to know that you're getting a total steal here. My normal boy-girl rate for *one* guy is a thousand bucks."

"I know that. I know, Kate. Thank you."

"Oh, you don't need to *thank* me, baby. It's my pleasure."

"Maybe, if you're interested," I said, shifting into gear, "you can make a little more."

"How so?"

"Well, how would you feel about doing something on the side, with me? I'll give you a hundred bucks."

"A hundred *bucks*?" she squealed. "Come on! You must be kidding, my blowjob rate is four hundred."

"Four hundred? Wow. I don't know, Kate," I said, grinning. Haggling was good footage. I held my video camera a foot away from my face, capturing the audio. "I could go up to two. That's the best I can do."

She was silent for a moment. "Are you cute?"

"I think so."

"You'd better be," she said doubtfully. "Two hundred dollars isn't much money."

In the end, I emerged the victor, as we agreed not only to do the add-on scene, but to postpone it to the day following her session with Bert and Darth. Good—she'd be coming to my house clean. I could ravish her alone, with dignity.

Now I started getting excited. Browsing in a thrift store, I came across a Superman suit. It was a kid's costume, but made from a cheap plastic material that stretched easily. I managed to jam myself into it. Surveying myself in the store's dressing room mirror, I liked what I saw. The plastic pulled my balls high. Compacted them neatly.

Kate's evening in Long Beach went off without a hitch. Bert and Darth lashed into her with crazed devotion, of course, but they did that to everyone. Indulgently, I let them have their fun. Secure in the knowledge that I would get mine the following afternoon.

I slept fitfully that night, and when I woke, I immediately donned my costume, then set up the video camera to record myself chopping a crude aperture in the nylon fabric of the crotch, so I could get sucked off and be Superman at the same time. That taken care of, I moved on to hair and makeup. Blunt metal scissors made a chopping sound as they clopped their way through my tangled pubic garden. I had to be careful, so careful: any mishap would put me out of action permanently. I was in no position to give up an inch.

It was almost exactly twelve when Kate called me. "Sam? Hi, it's Kate. Look, sweetie, I'm so sorry, but it looks like I'm going to be a little bit late. I am caught up in some really awful traffic here in the Valley . . ."

Porn actresses were notoriously late, of course, and this one, obviously of a mercurial, fiery spirit, would be no different. "That's fine, Kate," I said. I would charm her into my web. "Just get here when you can."

"Oh, great," she sang. "It shouldn't be more than an hour or two."

"An . . . hour?" I repeated, my heart falling.

"Yeah. I'm up here on Sepulveda, and I just realized, Notorious is *so* close by. They owe me a check, so I'm just going to stop there for one sec."

"And then you'll come over?"

"Absolutely. I am so there. Look, Sam, don't worry. I *can't* be late for you. I have *school* later this afternoon. I go to massage school."

"Do you really?" I said, surprised.

"Yeah!" said Kate. "What, you think I wanna be in porn for the rest of my life?"

Half an hour later, she called again.

"Sam! Here's the deal! I need, like, an hour. I'm so sorry. I'm over here and I'm at Zane and they don't have my check!"

"I thought you said you were going to Notorious."

"I *did*! But then I remembered I did *Naughty Little Nymphos* for these guys like *months* ago! It's time to pay up, you know what I'm saying?"

"But do you have to get it today?"

"No! Not at all, baby! I just wanted to check with them and see if it was there while I was in the neighborhood. And now I'm gonna come see you right now, okay? Are you ready for me?"

"Of course," I sighed. "Thank you for calling me, Kate."

"Oh, no, thank *you*, baby. I'm gonna be over there so quick. I just have to stop by this *one* last company and see if they have my chromes. But it's right over here on DeSoto and it will take me like literally fifteen minutes. And then I'll be right over. Okay?"

An hour passed. Nothing. Waves of daytime foot traffic passed by my storefront window, people chattering in rapid Spanish, carefree and brusque. Through the thin ceiling of my building, an awful tuba-mariachi music began to wail. I tried yoga breaths to calm myself, invoke a world larger than my own. Not useful. I managed to pass a little time by smoking cigarettes joylessly and checking the charge on my already fully charged video camera. I took stock of my life, perched there on a wooden stool in the middle of my kitchen, naked save for a superhero costume, with a dickhole.

Finally, just when I was starting to lose my shit, she called.

"*Hey*. Guess what I just realized?"

"What?"

"I didn't bring a *toy*," said Kate.

"What?"

"I didn't bring a *toy*. You said you wanted me to start off masturbating, but I didn't bring a toy."

"No," I said sharply. "No. I didn't say that. I don't care about any of that stuff."

"Oh," said Kate. She sounded hurt. "Okay. I was just letting you know."

"Where are you, Kate? Are you still coming?"

"I just exited off of Alvarado right now. I'm not far from you. It's just, it was a bitch going through like, um, the 101 and I think it's the 110 and all them merge together. It's just a pain in the ass going there."

I was silent.

"All right, sweetie," said Kate. "I'll see you soon. I just wanted to like, tell you about that."

"Just . . . come, okay?"

"Of course," Kate said. "You know, you shouldn't worry so much. It gets you nowhere."

———

And then, without warning, she was at my door.

"Kate! You made it!" I said, letting her in.

"Yes." She put her bag down and gave me a big hug, bumping into the camera. "*Finally!* I wouldn't have been so late, but you live by some really shitty traffic areas."

"Yes," I breathed. "Totally." I had already forgiven her. Completely forgotten about it. Staring at her, I was captivated. I was salivating, dazed, high on her perfume. She looked that good.

"Well, where should I change?"

"In here," I said, motioning her toward my small, makeshift bedroom. I carried my camera after her, not wanting to miss a thing. "And I can watch, okay?"

"Okay!" she said brightly, moving past me, totally at ease, as if perverted things like this happened every day to her. She had this amazing *posture*. Her body was very rudely alive.

"Did you get your chromes back?" I asked.

"My whats?" She slid off her sweatpants, revealing an ass that was extravagant and glossy and full of light. Reaching into her zippered black gym bag with a dainty finger and thumb, she withdrew a tiny plaid skirt.

"Your chromes?"

"Oh," she said, laughing ruefully. "No! Those fuckers, I'm gonna *kill* them." She stripped off her shirt. Hands behind her back, she unbuckled her bra, unveiling gorgeous breasts. I gulped. Her stomach was exposed and muscular and firm and hypnotic, worthy of coveting.

Maybe I'm making slightly too big a deal of this. But Kate was the embodiment of my fantasies—the Hot Girl whom I had never been able to touch. In high school, I had listened to fables about wild nights in the North Carolina woods told by the strong boys of our school, they on the soccer team, they who were so naturally graceful, who at age sixteen had heavy, muscular chests, who could kick the ball equally forcefully with their opposite foot, thick socks pulled up perfectly over white-blue shin guards, them running swift and true despite a hangover from the night before when they got steaming drunk around a mystical campfire with the prettiest girls in school who drank beers that tasted so good and got swingingly tipsy and punched the boys accidentally in the left eye, laughing hysterically with their short skirts in the North Carolina night, blackening the boys' eyeballs, their retinas bloody and sweet. *I could have been there with you, too — in the woods! Look at me now! I'm not a bad guy to have at a party, huh?*

"You are cute," Kate said, startling me. "Give me that camera for a second."

"What?"

"Give me the camera," she repeated. I handed it to her. She turned it around on me, and all of a sudden I was vulnerable. "Tell me about yourself."

I ended up jabbering about the last time I was on film, when I'd felt the brunt of the strap-on. "It was, um . . . very exciting. And very, very *new*." I didn't want her to think that I did that kind of thing all the time.

"You should tell my friend Jim about that. He'd *love* to put you in a movie."

I frowned. "I don't really want to make a name for myself like that."

"You wouldn't," Kate said petulantly. "It'd just be like, another point on your résumé. Now, how are we going to set this up?"

Together, we arranged the camera on a tripod, dickering over proper height and distance. "You want to get your shot centered," Kate advised. "See all this open space you have here? You want to bring it in . . . here, move towards me . . . that should be fine."

Hanging my head, I backed away and let her make the executive decisions. It was mildly embarrassing, but she was probably better at this than I was. I tugged at my Superman costume, nervous. Go time.

Though I'd like to, I can't go into great detail about what we did that afternoon. It feels too private, too sacred, even though I paid her $200 in cash. I *can* say, though, that Kate Frost impaled herself onto me like a demented seal in heat for almost a full hour. I *can* reveal *that*. And I can also state that I totally embarrassed myself and lost all professional dignity and distance by lapping up at her comely and delicious vagina with the enthusiasm of a deranged Italian pig snuffling for truffles. If she was faking her ardor (yes, the question has crossed my mind), she did an excellent job at it, snowing me completely. We kissed with a passion that surprised me. I felt high, emboldened, risky, brave. I reveled in the proud swells of her perfect dancer's body, delighting in her skin's high, blinding sheen. My penis stretched, doubled in size, and emerged from the hastily cut hole in the crotch of my Superman suit like a long-dormant groundhog seeking the sun.

It was amazing: every configuration, every shot that we designed, seemed guided by a strange kind of destiny, a wild sort of luck. We changed camera angles with alarming regularity and brazen spontaneity, moving together as if by instinct, codirecting as one conjoined mind, and incredibly, every single shot worked. Our compositional integrity was never compromised. Even more remarkably, our passion never receded. I rustled her hair against my face in spasmodic agonies of blond-brown joy, smelling frankincense and rosewater. Her spine was slick, somehow hot to the touch. And she said crazy things to me, things that got my hopes up.

"I *love* you, you're just great!" With her hand on my cock: "I could *definitely* fuck this."

I blossomed, sprouted, grew ten feet tall, with mighty roots and strong limbs. Together we were Young and Beautiful, and I have it all on tape. The Luckiest Kid on Earth and the Best Porno Girl in the Whole World. Finally, I'd found her. The woman who held the key to ecstasy and sexual bliss. Vaporous gold clouds exploded around my head, striking me behind my eyes. As I climaxed deliriously, I slumped atop her, heavy, exhausted, and drenched with sweat.

"Sam," said Kate, laughing. "Come on. Get up. Don't die on me now."

I kissed her gently, apologetically, all over, worshipful, thankful. A totally aware being, in our resplendent universe.

ELEVEN

Kate showered quickly, in my disgusting shower, seemingly unbothered by its grossness.

"Would you mind telling me what time it is?" she called out.

"I gotcha, baby!" I yelled back, naked and stupidly happy. I gave a quick euphoric glance to my alarm clock. "It's three thirty-six!"

"*Three thirty-six?* Oh my God, baby, I have to *go!*"

Kate emerged from the shower and wiped her body dry hurriedly. She pushed her clothes back on.

"Will you dance for me before you go?" I said, pointing the video camera at her.

"No, sweetie!" She gave me a kiss on the nose. "I have to go *now!* I have an appointment. I *knew* this was going to make me late!"

"But you had fun, right?" I said, doubtful for the first time.

"Oh, it was *so* good. Now, where did I put my purse?"

And she hustled out onto Glendale Boulevard, toward her car.

—

I spent the next few days at home, replaying the incident in my mind and on tape, wondering if what transpired between me and Kate had been real. According to my TV screen, it had been, indeed: the informal, amateur attitude had somehow served up a mishmash of real, honest desire. It was by far the best pure porn I had ever made, and when I threw it up on eBay, unedited and unchanged (I even included my opening pube-trimming scene, as a nod to the ugliest kind of truth), buyers seemed to agree. Ninety-nine perverts ordered a copy in its first week on sale. I had to go out and buy another VCR to keep up with the transfers.

But it was our romantic connection that troubled me. I'd called her about ten times since the day of our shoot, but she never seemed to be answering her phone. I left a few casual messages, trying to sound unconcerned. Like that ever gets you anywhere.

I walked around tired and depressed for the next couple of days. It was as if something deep inside me had broken. Even Bert and Darth took notice.

"Sam," Bert said, clapping a fatherly hand on my shoulder, "you can't get all bent out of shape over these women."

"But Kate was *different*," I insisted. "I can't explain it. We had a connection."

"A connection? You got a taste of good pussy, is what happened. You'll get it again, my friend! Try to remember that."

"I'll try."

"Look, we called her, too," Darth confessed.

"Of course we did!" Bert exclaimed. "I've been callin' each and every one of these girls, after every shoot! Think I ever get a call back? *Ever?* Of course I don't! But you don't see it bothering me none."

I understood what Bert was saying, and I tried not to let it get me down. But damn: that beautiful smile. That wild spirit. I had been so sure that we were going to be partners in crime, spending our weeknights sniffing drugs off each other's bodies, projectile-vomiting together, not a care in the world. But it just wasn't happening. Porn girls just weren't that into me.

Meanwhile, Pitts kept sending me money. He seemed to have no shortage of it. Being an idiot, I always paid everyone in cash. I grew adept at walking around Long Beach with thick bundles of bills concealed inside my camera case. Sometimes, before a shoot, I'd drive into a McDonald's parking lot, lock the doors, and spread the wad all over the seat next to me. I was lucky I didn't get shot in the face.

The nights grew cooler, and I bought an expensive jacket with a built-in reversible hood. So what? I was still sad. I wanted to snuggle up next to someone beautiful, to press my face into her sweater and whisper at her from one inch away—to tongue her beautiful neck and lick her beautiful eyelids and pull her perfect hair, tease her, call her names. It wasn't fair.

But I made my first real friend that fall, a guy named Isaac. He was a painter in his last year of grad school at Art Center. Isaac made horror movies on the cheap, was completely obsessed with women, and could talk a blue streak about absolutely anything in the world. So we got on fine.

He was also getting sober, which fascinated me.

"I *hate* going to meetings. Hate it. You have never met a more self-absorbed group of people in your entire *life*."

"So, why do you keep on going?"

He smiled gently. "Because the shooting range isn't open at night."

Soon, he permitted me to watch his film. Very bloody. Friends murdered each other with baseball bats and plastic bags.

"That's *gross*, dude."

Isaac frowned. "Don't you have to have a strong stomach for the stuff you shoot?"

"It's different."

"How so?"

"My gig's cum. Don't go in for blood. It freaks me out."

Isaac, on the other hand, liked all kinds of films equally. Or so he said. Porno mattered, according to him, because it offered meaningful insights into human psychology.

"You did a very strange thing with that Dennis character. Utterly naked. I loved it."

The compliment made me blush.

"So, what's your next move?"

"Not sure," I admitted. "I haven't been able to think of anything very good."

"And you're too busy shooting for this guy in Seattle to do anything for yourself. I get it. Totally get it. Happens all the time. Look, I've been thinking, there's a couple of movies you need to see. You've heard of *Up Your Ass #18*, right?"

"Of course," I said, suddenly defensive. The idea that an outsider might have his own intellectualized take on pornography rankled me powerfully. "An Anabolic production."

"Exactly. So, you know the scene in that flick where Lexington Steele and Mr. Marcus are giving it to Alexandra Quinn? I was watching it for like the trillionth time yesterday when I had this realization: *Quinn's* the one who's controlling that room. The guys are playing to her, looking to her for approval. In effect, she's actually topping *them*—though she does it through what looks like submission."

"Well, sure, maybe," I muttered, upset that I hadn't come to that conclusion first.

"It's called power-bottoming," he said, matter-of-factly. "But you know what's *really* sort of interesting, which you might want to try? Fatty porn."

"Huh? Why?"

"Oh, man, are you *kidding*? Okay, I mean, at first, I was with you: I was totally baffled as to how anyone could find rolls of decaying flesh appealing. But then it came to me: people who dig this stuff are actually fascinated by *death*."

"*Death?*"

"Sure. It's all about guilt. A guy who perceives morbidly obese women as sexually attractive is compensating for his own mixed feelings about being alive and prosperous. Fatty porn is a *great* way for conflicted individuals to embrace failure and success at the same time."

I didn't necessarily follow everything Isaac said, but in my heart I could sense he was part genius, so I kept hanging out. In my own half-assed way, I began to try to untangle the black-on-white porn dynamic I was now being paid to reinforce. Clearly, an element of racism was central to the whole idea—*look, it's a chick who's so slutty, she'll even fuck a black guy!*—but the question was, who, exactly, found that concept so sexy that he was willing to pay to watch it? Was it an Alabama man, high on the cuckold pleasure of imagining his wife taken from him by a strong, dark buck? Or was it a frustrated, nerdy black man who spent his nights envisioning vengeful scenarios just like these?

I had grown up understanding Blackness to be a visual marker of "cool" and "tough," particularly when set up in opposition to a suburban kind of Caucasian lifestyle. But the problem here was that Bert and Darth didn't provide *quite* as much contrast as one might have hoped. They were being set up as "sex machines," I supposed, but one look at Bert's hungry eyes, damp with aging desire, pretty much took the air out of that balloon. I was in charge of a charade, all right, and it was plenty transparent enough to anyone who cared to detect it—though I'm not sure many did.

Hoping to take my mind off my romantic and professional failures, I decided to pay a visit to porno's version of the public library: the adult video store. My local branch was a sad, fucked-up smut shack named "Stan's of Hollywood," down on Third and Western. The energy at Stan's was foul beyond belief. It was profoundly weird and desperately lonely—but like all porn stores, Stan's constituted an edifice of epistemology: a tiny berth from which to behold, and perhaps decode, the byzantine history of smut.

And make no mistake, Stan's selection was impressive. There were so many tapes, in fact, so many staggering pyramids of cleaved genitals and crimson buttocks, that if you faltered, even for just a moment, vertigo and giddiness could take over, and you'd be dragged into an avalanche of bad decision making, leaving the store hundreds of dollars poorer. Over the years, I'd learned to be careful. Not all tapes can be trusted.

Entire *eras*, in fact, are suspect. I'll come right out and say it: I dislike most pornos from the 1970s. Film buffs can go on all day about the celluloid-laden "Golden Era," but the truth is, 99 percent of those movies are garbage, embarrassingly crude follow-ups to the more imaginative and better-shot exploitation films that preceded them. Even standout efforts like the Mitchell Brothers' *Behind the Green Door* and Radley Metzger's *The Opening of Misty Beethoven* feel like they've been written in a single afternoon by some half-smart fourteen-year-old boy. And not that it especially matters, but the wank factor on those films is so low that it's almost not worth mentioning.

Of course, the films that followed them were no more skillfully conceived; if anything, their scripts were even worse. What's exceptional about 1980s pornography, though, is the *music*. Everyone jokes about the "campy" wah-wah of 1970s porn tracks, but that funk-band-in-a-box sound isn't *campy*—it's unlistenable. The 1980s ushered in Video Sex, but it was also the Age of the Synthesizer; we shouldn't forget that. The fuckings of superstars Randy Spears, Tom Byron, and Peter North (and the women! those aggressively coked-up, highly aerobicized, poisonous-silicone-betitted women!) were set to the strangest of keyboard sounds. To me, the retarded computer-generated loopings actually *work*: complementing video-tape's bleary, vacant resolution to perfection, synth sound created a production value that is lo-fi at its very best. It provided an ambience that underscored the majestic *cheapness* of pornography—its poverty of connection and hope.

And then the 1990s happened. The '90s are a problem. When you watch a 1990s porno, you're getting an up-close-and-personal look at some of the scariest tit jobs ever created. Full-to-bursting, *Alien*-style false breasts, full of gristle and hard-packed meat, mark their hosts like a disfiguring tribal brand. And though it hardly seems possible, the men from that era are even scarier. Thong tans and long Fabio hair were the flavor of the day, creating a douchebag panache that, combined with blank, hungry eyes, quietly implied, "I'm so blitzed on stolen meds and Mexican steroids that all I want to do is get naked in front of a huge shoulder cam and do whatever the fuck I'm told." Performers in the '90s would do absolutely *anything*—as evidenced in Leisure Time Entertainment's *Kinky as They Cum #2*, wherein a succession of rat-haired degenerates strap mammoth prosthetic wieners to their groins to simulate a host of bizarre sex en-actments. But *Kinky* isn't the only flick where you witness this kind of deviant pantomime: a rash of terrifying penis-replicant movies were released in near-simultaneous succession in the spring of 1993 by several unrelated companies, and the occurrence was too peculiar to chalk up to mere chance, or even drug-induced collective dementia. By the later part of the decade, thankfully, nonsense of this kind was almost unheard of, and many actresses had begun to move back toward the "natural" look, but the damage had been done.

Now we had arrived in the New Millennium. And I was carrying the torch. It was an awesome responsibility. For the first time, I took a careful look at the hapless hordes of men who surrounded me, shuffling mutely among the aisles, whirling adrift in their angry, psychic energy. They deserved something better than this. They needed me.

And yet—what could I really do for them? Even at my best, I couldn't give them what they really wanted: a loving relationship. My heart fell, momentarily, for I was in that same boat, too. *Oh, Sex Shop Faithful: pathetic and weak, we might not be making eye contact, but in some strange, unspoken way, we are a team, and I think we all know it. Every one of us has admitted, just by walking through that door, just by agreeing to stay awhile, that we simply can't get with the program. That we have dreamed, more than once, of a world in which women existed only as props.*

Maybe we were scared of real women. Perhaps we were just frustrated. As we passed one another in the aisles, eyes fixed firmly on the racks, I could sense the ire and the silent arousal of the men around me. It sounds weird, but I felt reassured by the understanding that we were equally confused, equally burdened by the weight of conflicted emotions. We wanted to lavish whispered praises and gentle sensuality on sweet, graceful women—then we wanted to fuck them in half, call them whores, and make them disappear.

I wandered for a while. Eventually I came across a beaten copy of *Naughty Little Nymphos*. Kate's tape. It was a weak consolation, but it was something. I paid my $29.99 and got the hell out of there.

TWELVE

While I was growing up, my psychoanalyst dad had his office at home.

Originally a teacher by trade, my father fell in love with the couch during the mid-1970s. Gradually, he came to the decision that he wanted to dedicate his life to the practice of psychoanalysis, so he downsized expectations at his first job and went to night school for half a decade. He added the office on to our house in 1983. A full-time home practice began in 1985. My most vivid childhood memories include the continual stream of unfamiliar cars that rumbled up our gravel driveway every afternoon, punctuating my solo games of Wiffle ball, interrupting confidential conversations with my dog.

Back then, I'd wave and say hello, never feeling there was anything strange about the situation. Innocent and happy, I played child-host to a steady procession of men and women who were paying to engage in expensive psychotherapeutic wrangles with my dad in his soundproofed office.

But damn if, looking back, I don't feel a bit used. The sight of the doctor's little boy had undoubtedly served as a sort of trigger: a prompt, a key to unlocking some parent-child memory of their own. Unwittingly, I'd positioned myself as an emotional pawn, a jumping-off point for an hour of probing therapy. I'd been duped, and what's more, I'd never been properly compensated. So if I'd set out to torture my folks just a tad with my new profession, was I not merely taking a little of the back pay rightfully owed to me?

Of course, I couldn't much complain about the way they'd chosen to deal with the admittedly weird news that their only boy was making a living in the skin trade. Essentially, they'd settled on a "don't ask, don't tell" policy with me—live and let live—and I liked that just fine. So when they called me up to announce they were coming to visit me out west, I wasn't quite sure how to react.

"They're holding the American Psychoanalytic Association conference right there in Westwood," my dad said. "Isn't that an amazing coincidence?"

"That is *wonderful*, David."

"Don't be sarcastic, boy. And try to stop calling me David. It sounds odd to me. Your mother and I thought it would be an excellent opportunity to spend some time with you."

"Well, I'm sort of busy, but . . . I guess."

"All the way across the country and all you can say is, 'I guess'? Come on, cheer up! We'll take you out to dinner a few times. Are you eating?"

"They have food out here, David."

"You know, I just don't understand it. Why can't you call me 'Dad'? What in the *hell* is so *burdensome* about saying the word *Dad*?"

A few evenings before my father's conference was scheduled to begin, I greeted them in their hotel room in West LA. They looked good: my father tall and bearded and gangly and impulsive, you could see it in his eyes; my mother smaller and rounder and calmer and darker. Despite whatever I did to discourage them, my parents still seemed to like me very much. Their beaming faces shone when I came on through the door.

"How was your flight?" I mumbled, untangling myself gingerly from my father's warm embrace.

"Just fine," my dad said.

"We *like* Los Angeles," my mom chimed in.

"What do you mean?" I asked. "You've been here for about half an hour."

"It seems like an interesting place," my dad said.

"*Interesting?* That's like your favorite word," I said testily. It was. He used it to describe everything.

"So maybe it *is* my favorite word!" my dad said, his smile a bit tenser.

"We're just very glad to see you, Sam," my mom explained.

I sat down heavily on their hotel bed, resisting a loutish teenage urge to turn on the TV. "Well, I'm still alive, as you can see."

"Yes!" my mom exclaimed, laughing.

"Have you been enjoying yourself?" my dad asked.

"In what sense?"

"Have you been able to establish a group of friends? A type of community?" My dad was crazy about community.

"I guess so." Did Gus count as a friend? Did Bert the Lover?

"Do you miss Santa Cruz much?" my mom asked. "I wasn't crazy about that place," she added.

"What's wrong with Santa Cruz?" I asked, defensively.

"It was a bit slow." She grimaced. "Los Angeles is a real city. It has more resources for a person like you."

"Well, I'll drink to *that*." I flashed them a grin and lay back, testing their pillows. "We got some great resources out here, for a guy like me."

"That's very funny, Sam," said my dad. "Let me just ask you a question. How long do you intend to keep on doing this?"

"As long as it takes," I said, smiling.

"As long as it takes to *what*?" he said, crossing the room, hovering over me and folding his arms. "Would you mind explaining exactly what it is that you're trying to do?"

"It's complicated, Dad," I said, sitting up. "I *told* you that." How do you explain to your parents that you are completely revitalizing the face of modern urban pornography?

"Try me," he said in his most patient tone. "I guess what I'm trying to wrench out of you is this: what is the damn *point*?"

"David," my mom said. "Don't start. We just got here."

"Is this *art*?" my father demanded. "Is that what you're trying to tell me? That to you, this is *art*?"

"Yes!" I said vehemently. "Why is that so difficult for you to believe?"

"Because I cannot imagine for the *life* of me how porn can be art! *How* is it art? Tell me that!"

"I don't *know*," I said stubbornly. "It just is. That is," I amended, "if it were *done* right, it could be."

"Can we get something to eat, please?" my mom asked, tired. "You two have all weekend to go over this."

"Yes," I sighed. "Let's get something to eat."

"Fine," my father said, satisfied. He had made his point. "How about sushi? I bet Los Angeles has some very good sushi."

It really was difficult to explain to them why I wanted to be in porn. I mean, what was I going to say? *Well, Dad, I want to be famous and admired for my art even though I don't have enough talent to do that and also I deeply loathe the idea of a desk job and hey, by the way, I don't mind a cutie with incredible legs pushing her superb golden ass into my face until I can't breathe. Okay?* My parents didn't want to acknowledge my sexuality any more than I wished to acknowledge theirs. No one wants to see their son getting a blowjob on grainy videotape. It can cause short-circuiting in the brain.

And yet, in a way, this whole ordeal was good for us. I was a pretty private kid growing up—I hated to talk to anyone in my family about what I considered my personal life. I never brought a single girl home, never once spoke about any of my crushes, kisses, or teenage romances, not even to my older sister, with whom I was rather close. Now, in a geyser of retribution for all my years of silence, it was all boiling over in a very public way. To their credit, my folks were dealing with it better than I had imagined. Apart from a little squabbling, they never explicitly asked or ordered me to get out of the game. They clung hopefully to the flimsy lie that I was only filming porn, and not participating in it, but then, I encouraged them to that end. Frankly, I was scared to conflate my own family and my sexuality. There was this hip artist I'd met, Leigh Ledare, who'd made the beginnings of an art career by photographing his mother naked and giving blowjobs to guys. It seemed sort of dark, even to my standards.

But maybe Leigh's pictures were just a more truthful take on familial dynamics than I could stomach. Certainly, the family had its place in porno—it just wasn't usually referenced in quite so overt a manner. Now I could almost hear my poor parents wondering, *We must have done something wrong . . . what was it?*

I couldn't explain it myself. The Freudians might have gone for an early-childhood explanation: my foray into porn constituting a search for the emotionally distant mother's elusive breastfeeding nipple. But I had to say that my own relationship with my mother was a lot less tortured than by all rights it should have been. She was a sweet, funny, loving lady. A bit avoidant, maybe, and certainly not the type to dig into her own feelings with a trowel, like the old man was apt to. All in all, though, I felt quite fortunate to have such a solid and sensible parent around to counterbalance the more unpredictable (and sometimes more exciting) emotional wallops of my father. As far as I could tell, I did not want to photograph her naked.

The following morning, they picked me up in their rental car, and we headed down to San Diego, to the zoo.

"Nice place you've got there," my mom said, laughing.

"I like it," I said shortly.

"Good friends with the neighbors?" my father asked.

"They're my best friends in the whole world, Dad. Before I found them, I was lost."

"Don't be sarcastic. You know, a community serves a simple but very vital function."

"Sam, do you need any shoes, or anything like that?" my mom interrupted.

"I'm fine," I groaned. "I *am*, Mom. All my needs are taken care of."

"That pet shop looks rather eccentric," my father said, his eyes twinkling mischievously.

"You'd be surprised," I mumbled, grumpily. "They've got an iguana in there that would knock your socks off."

We rolled down the highway at cautious speeds, and in poor humor I watched the scenery bleed by. Being chauffeured by my parents, having them pay for my meals, infantilized me—it didn't feel too porno. And the prospect of going to the zoo filled me with equal parts boredom and sadness. I always left there with a renewed resentment for humanity.

On the other hand, zoos delighted my father.

"The San Diego Zoo is no *joke*, Sam! What do you think about flamingos?"

"I don't know, Dad. The last one I saw looked depressed. Maybe it was because he'd been taken captive and put in a cage with painted rocks?"

"He wasn't *depressed*," my father said, shaking his head at the drawings in his bird book lovingly. "What a wonderful animal."

"Birds are dumb, Dad. They have tiny little brains."

"You're very wrong. They're *clever*. They have an instinctual knowledge base that you or I could only dream of!" Excited, he riffled the pages of his book, in hot pursuit of the blue-throated macaws. My mother and I traded knowing looks, amused in spite of ourselves.

We made our way to the zoo, walked across the hot parking lot. At the ticket house, they paid for me, and I put up a weak fuss that embarrassed even me in its halfheartedness. Pushing his way through the turnstiles, my father immediately raced ahead with his loping, awkward strides, book in hand, leaving my mother and me in the dust.

"There's the reptile house," my mom said. "Want to take a look?"

"No. Thank you kindly, though."

She laughed, shaking her head good-naturedly. "Go easy on your father. He just cares about you."

"I *am* going easy on him. You should hear what I *want* to say."

"Oh, Sam, Sam. What are we going to do with you?"

"You could stop offering to buy me shoes," I said. "That would be a nice start."

"Hon," she said gently, "you have no idea what it's like to be a parent. You worry about your children. You can't help it."

"But I'm twenty-four years old!" I cried, exasperated. "I'm not a kid anymore!"

"Yes, I know, sweetheart. I'm sorry. I suppose we still feel some responsibility for you, for where you end up."

"Well, stop it," I said. "I want to take care of myself."

"We'll try, Sam," my mother said. "Or, I should say, I'll try." But, as if to amend her statement, she slipped her hand into mine, and we walked that way until we caught up with my dad, who was experiencing a zoophile's unpunctured joy, and wasn't afraid to show it. A long hour spent inspecting the best of Southern California's ornithological captives gave way to a hell-bent rush toward the Africa subdivision, where spindly giraffes and drowsy elephants gamboled. Elephants were my father's special animal, his favorite since he was a little boy.

We hiked to the far end of the zoo, chatting and kidding around. Finally we arrived upon a huge, dusty field, where two lonely elephants fanned each other with palm fronds. My dad gazed out at the big, wrinkled beasts with an adoring expression on his face.

"Aren't they beautiful?" he asked reverently.

"Yes, Dad," I said. "I guess so."

But they were beautiful. As unnatural as the whole situation was, even I had to admit that the elephants were beautiful. Long, eggshell-colored tusks protruded from the huge beasts' upper jaws. They rubbed them into the ground gracefully, using a kind of motion that seemed unstoppable, rhythmic and eternal.

We watched for several minutes without speaking. My father, still looking at the elephants, spoke first.

"I suppose we can't dissuade you from continuing down this path you're on."

"No," I said, "I suppose you can't."

"If you ever wanted to see someone . . ."

"You mean like a psychiatrist?" I laughed. He was always encouraging me to go see someone. "Come on."

"I'm merely *mentioning* we could help you pay for it."

"Thank you. That is very tactful."

"How is that inappropriate? Ellen? Help me out here, how was that inappropriate?"

"David, I think he'll tell us if he wants to see a psychiatrist," said my mom gently.

"I was only putting it out there," sulked my dad. "Boy."

I shook my head and laughed softly, watching the elephants.

"Sam?" asked my mom, somewhat hopefully. "Are you dating anyone special?"

"Not really, Mom. We'll see."

"Been to see the Dodgers yet?" my dad asked.

"No," I said. "That's on my list."

We stood there, looking out at the dusty earth, temporarily lost for words.

THIRTEEN

When my folks left, I decided to get down to Mexico. Only three months before, it would have been an impossible dream. Now I had money to burn. I rumbled down past Tijuana, elbow sticking out the window, garbage mountains in my rearview. I decided to keep driving.

Rosarito was the next town down, a calmer, beachier side of North Mexico. I found a room and walked out onto the sand, smelling roadkill and tacos. I sat down, stared up at the sky. I could hear the surf as it rose up and fell.

When I returned to Los Angeles, it was softer. Winter was coming. The hot desert sun that had blazed down upon me so rudely took a couple of afternoons off. I sensed mystical secrets in the air, but I was about a hundred years away from getting a handle on them.

Soon I fell into a porn-making rut. Reb's agency continued to comport itself as a second-rate operation should, disappointing its customers in all the ways that truly mattered. Sometimes both Reb and Clarence would disappear for days on end, to be replaced by Shawn Sawitz, Reb's obese son, who didn't like me. Those would be cold days. But then Reb would return, and with him Clarence, and before I knew it, I'd have a brand-new messed-up eighteen-year-old on my hands. Just like magic.

You'd think that the youngest chicks would be the most fun to shoot: full of piss and vinegar, sparkles still in their eyes, golden haunches glistening, without cellulite or sag. But in fact, the B-List Kiddies were some of my toughest cases. Starved for love and attention, they'd already figured out by the age of eighteen that selling ass was the quickest possible route to easy cash and low-rent fame. Most of them hooked, and they all wanted me to *admire* them. They radiated this weird, false courage that made me feel sick and broken inside.

One such working doll was "Honey." She was eighteen and a week, and already had about three scenes under her belt. Honey was bunking temporarily at Reb's house in North Hollywood. Reb had a standing policy of putting up actresses who had nowhere to go, but he wasn't sleazy about it, didn't demand sex from them to complete the transaction. He was pretty old, around sixty by my estimation, so maybe that temptation had passed. In any case, the only duty the Honeys of the world had to fulfill in exchange for room and board was to notch one scene a month for Reb's production company. In return, you got a clean bed and three squares a day. Just like jail.

It was a fine, balmy evening when I picked Honey up for her shoot. She was dressed in her costume already—miniskirt, chunky heels, rubber blouse. She narrated her story: crazy mom, no dad; passed around to a bevy of foster homes by the time she was six; running away from some, abandoned by others. She was a pudgy, pink little girl with mousy brown hair, a fat little stomach, and several bluish tattoos. She also wore horn-rimmed glasses—without them, she was nearly blind. Honey wasn't a wild girl. Her disposition ran to thoughtful and quiet. Under a different sun, she would have been a druggist, or a baker, or maybe the person you speak to when your airplane ticket gets fucked up.

"So, ya like porn so far?" I ventured.

"Heck, what's not to like?" she said, cheerily, gazing out the windows at a new world whizzing by. For some, porn is an easy cloak to slip over the shoulders.

Her shoot was full of the same nonsense as the others. I was getting to know these men well. Darth Callous worked best from behind. Dripping with sweat, dreadlocks bouncing, dark sunglasses adjusted by an index finger's push back to the bridge of his nose. Bert was slightly more creative—sometimes I'd find him suddenly standing up, knees slightly bent, thighs firm and strong and ham-like, eyes alive and burning with a child's delight.

I could hardly pretend my working life was satisfying. But the money provided a constant, soothing balm. And shooting camera for a living—never mind the context—satisfied my deep-seated need to feel like a working artist, further corroborating my fragile conviction that I was living a life altogether unique and unequaled by my peers. Guilty.

After the shoot, when I'd folded a bundle of cash into Honey's unbelieving hands, and we were driving back to her NoHo home, I asked jokingly, "So, those dicks big enough for you?"

"Oh, they were nothing," Honey remarked casually, laughing. "I used to get raped with a Clorox bottle on the regular."

"What are you talking about?" I whispered, feeling suddenly sad and sick all over.

"Sure," said Honey, still smiling. "These foster parents I had when I was thirteen? They used to do it every night."

"That's so fucked," I mumbled.

"Oh, boy, you think *that's* bad? They used to shove *scissors* inside me, too. *That* was a lot scarier."

We fell quiet for a while. Although, admittedly, not that long. Soon we changed the subject and spoke of other things. And on the way home, I got us Burger King, because it was too late to cook.

The months passed, and something about my life felt broken. I remember an AA meeting at a church in Echo Park, which Isaac convinced me to attend. Hot coffee and plenty of cigarettes. "I'm an . . . addict of marijuana," I confessed to the group, red-faced. Then I sat down, feeling like a total ass. They applauded anyway.

"These people are mindless," I whispered to Isaac.

"I know," he whispered back, smiling politely. "It's torture."

I remember New Year's Eve on the streets of Echo Park, nursing a tallboy with Tenzeno, leaning up against his storefront window. At the stroke of midnight, I watched someone throw up into a trash can. I remember January, when the days got shorter, and the wind had a bit of cut to it. One afternoon, a city employee came. I watched him try to plant a small tree in a squarish hole in the concrete sidewalk. He struggled for an hour, then gave up and threw the tree in a Dumpster.

February came. I remember thinking, *I must find a hobby.* Hoping for the best, I signed up for some improv classes. Such a bad idea. My ability to be funny on cue was, shall we say, exceedingly limited. I coasted for two weeks on old material, then ground to an agonizing halt. I quit. The Zing Bats would have to get by without me.

Bizarre cornflowers bloomed in cow dung in the fields, though, and I started getting fan letters from a porn addict who'd bought one of my early tapes. He lived in Oakland and went by the name of "Willie Timberlake."

Sam,

I'm a filmmaker with no productions in the can, I'm a musician with no albums made, I'm a movie scorer but I haven't written a complete score, I'm a writer who hasn't written a fucking book; and that's lazy. I'm all about lazy. I wish I smoked pot so I could use it as a fucking excuse. At this point I'm just a manic writer, harvesting my inner porn flower.

I am struggling to explode, fucking spit out product and be someone, but I feel like every time I jump to my feet I just as dramatically drop my ass in front of my computer and commit myself to an exhaustive three hour search for "+Israeli+porn +1970's." Am I the only one?

He was not the only one. I gathered the letter closer to my breast and read on, a small smile slowly spreading across my features.

Christ, my only achievement is a fucking BA in communications. Ouch! I still can't find a job where I can be something other than a chump drone. Ebb and flow back to bed. All this goes to say that it's great to see somebody being creative and it's pretty fucking inspiring. Keep working behind the scenes, and eventually it will catch on.

Can I tell you something embarrassing? I used to jack off with my friend Clint before I could even cum. We would do it for like an hour, both of us hiding under the same blanket, somehow not ashamed to be grabbing our cocks, but still too modest to be unexposed. We were just doing what seemed appropriate. It definitely felt mature.

Clint had this huge stoner dad who had every single Hustler since '76 stacked in his bedroom. I remember going into the bedroom and thinking to myself as I walked around huge columns of Larry Flynt's brew, "Your mom sleeps here too?" Jesus.

Not only did his dad have every Hustler ever made, he had tons of tapes, too. The VHS revolution of the early 80's hit him hard. Clint's dad also made tapes of him fucking Clint's mom. One time Clint's little sister, 5-year-old Tina, threw in a tape. "Look at this!"

On comes Clint's mom giving Jerry a sweet hummer. Clint's mom was trying to keep her eyes in the monitor to see what she looked like, so she was constantly looking off-screen. Tina died laughing. Clint was really embarrassed. For years, I fantasized about Clint's mom giving me a blowjob and taping it. For years.

Sam, there is a darkness!

March came. I endured several more AA meetings. My apartment grew dirty, and I decided to let it stay that way. Cleaning while sober was about one-tenth as fun. Feeling lost, I decided to try growing my hair out. Soon, it looked like I was ready for my Bar Mitzvah.

Bert and Darth started to bore me. Bert lived in Oxnard, where he held down a good job as an electrical engineer. And yet he would drive two and a half hours through bumper-to-bumper traffic to get to Long Beach, over and over again, just to "get the pussy." It depressed me. I met a boring twenty-eight-year-old who taught fifth grade in the Valley and started courting her. We talked on the phone every night. Boy, she could talk. She could talk with the best of them.

If I think about it real hard, I can remember the night we shot Divina, an eighteen-year-old Latina with baby fat still on her cute bones. She showed up to Darth Callous's on a Tuesday evening in a blue-black convertible pumping bass, with a stoned friend and a see-through plastic backpack. I escorted them up the stairs and into the bedroom, where Divina got half naked and squinted up at me with red eyes, hair in rollers, and I tried to explain to her that I needed *facial* cum shots—and that was okay, right? My guys come three or four times a night apiece, they are like genetic freaks that way, *and that was okay, right?* She stared up at me blankly, giggling every so often, hollow-eyed in a black bra with a tiny little stomach and braces.

Willie Timberlake's letters kept popping up in my mailbox. I devoured them gratefully, chuckling at their savage self-deprecation and naked hope.

> *You know,*
> *As a teenager I would always beat off straight onto the floor as a testament to supreme laziness and depression. I would bust a nut on the floor and lamely dab at it with a paper towel a few minutes after I goddamn felt like it.*
> *When I first started having sex, I couldn't wait to bust out some of the porno moves I had seen. St. Patty's day, 1998: I was twenty one. I got really, really fucking drunk and buttfucked this fat chick in the living room while my friend and his room-mates slept in their bedroom. And I didn't just quietly slip it in, either. I made her fucking squat on her knees and open that fucker up. I asked her, "In your mouth or in your face?" She responded mouth, so I ejaculated onto her face. Fade out, fuck the credits, and just show the goddamn copyright.*

I didn't feel cocky the next day. I didn't normally gloat over sexual conquests. I was always too busy moving on to the next mission.

Each morning, I woke up to the cheery LA sky. The weather started to feel vaguely mocking. After more than two months of laborious phone conversations, the schoolteacher finally consented to have sex with me, my first legitimate piece in quite some time. It was surprisingly bad. She kept getting on top of me. I did my damnedest, but it was no use: I just couldn't fuck uphill properly.

My job repeated itself over and over and over, like a single frame of video caught on an endless loop. Only the girls were different. I remember goths with stringy hairdos, at whom even Darth Callous wrinkled his nose in disgust. I remember wiggers who slow-danced with Bert in long gowns, while I ate french fries mournfully. The seventy-five-pound weakling from Redlands whose husband adored her and waited patiently in the car while her little bones made rent money. The registered nurse with Lee Press-On nails who exasperatedly separated her own thick buttocks to assist Bert in anal entry. The beautiful brown-haired girl who just giggled when they went to mount her, as if no one had ever tried that before.

I began fantasizing about leaving. In my head, I envisioned a horrible, fantastic event pulling me out of the industry by force. What would it be? A knife to the guts? A positive AIDS test? Somehow, I knew the bottom was going to fall out on me, and soon.

But nothing kept happening. One night, I picked up a buxom thirty-five-year-old blonde named Rikki Lixxx from a sad Woodland Hills apartment and drove us toward Long Beach. We rode in silence for a long time.

"I've got to get out of LA," Rikki said quietly, looking out the window. "I'm so over this town."

"Aren't we all."

She turned to look at me seriously. "I'm thinking about Brazil."

I gave Rikki the once-over. Her eyes looked very tired. Even her mouth looked tired. Her breasts were the precise size and toughness of bocci balls. "Brazil it is."

You know,

Timberlake wrote,

> *Sometimes I think that watching a porn chick get fucked is almost like a celebration of serious issues, getting off on their issues because we all know it's there, right? It's really obvious with the amateur try-out shit. They are being abused, exploited, and just about the same time your dick gets hard it dawns on them that they are getting a really raw deal and sometimes that is enough to push us over into our socks or napkins. Porn is like the mosquito bite of the male soul; it fucking stays swollen.*

April bled into May, and May into June. I maintained separate memberships at Video Hut, Videoactive, Jerry's, Stan's of Hollywood, and Mondo Video. I spent many, many thoughtful hours browsing under the fluorescent lights, comparing and contrasting their porn collections. I was becoming an authority. I was good for the industry.

One evening, I scheduled a shoot with a woman named Tess Nicole, a semiknown porn star who, like so many of Reb's actresses, had long since shot her wad. Now, after years of inactivity, she was staging some sort of "comeback." She was still beautiful, though.

Some women were simply destined to be beautiful for their entire lives, in spite of every peculiar destruction they chose to visit upon themselves.

"I had an . . . accident," Tess confessed softly.

She was applying her makeup in Darth's hot bathroom. I tended to hang out with the girls when they did their makeup. I considered it one of the perks of my position and didn't allow Bert or Darth to follow me.

"How's that?"

"I . . . hit my head."

"When?" I gazed at her small breasts and delicate rib cage. Sure, maybe it *was* a trying job. But I got to be around many delicate rib cages.

"Maybe a year ago. I'm not exactly sure." She looked up at me, in the mirror, and frowned. "I don't remember stuff very well lately."

"How has the work been?"

"*Pretty* good," she said hesitantly. She offered a small smile, like a little girl. "Only, it's weird. Sometimes, I think everyone is *related* to me."

I left Tess to finish her makeup.

"She good to go, Sam?" asked Bert.

"Oh yeah," I said quietly. "Red hot."

Tess called to me from the bathroom. "Hey, look, I'm feeling kind of *funny*."

"What do you mean?" I asked.

"It's just . . . well, listen, do you think these guys have any vodka?"

"What do you mean? To drink?"

"Yes," she said, firmly. "I think I need a drink."

I fixed her a shot of vodka. She knocked it back cleanly. "Again."

She had another. And then one more. I sensed our momentum fading.

"Tess, I don't want to rush you," I said, "but these guys have day jobs. We should probably get this thing rolling."

"All right," she relented. "Just a little *baby* one. And then I'll be fine."

I poured her a final drink, and she sipped deeply from it, and we both walked into the living room, where the boys awaited her with great anticipation and hunger.

Tess got down on her knees in front of the bed. She craned her head toward the men, who had already stripped to their boxers and stood towering over her like thick, damp trees. Her hair was blond and the strands were silky and fine. Her face was beauty itself, and her bright pupils were engorged with the blackest life.

"What should I *call* you guys?" Tess Nicole asked pleasantly, placing a demure hand behind each of their thighs.

"You can call me Bert," explained the elder, smiling proudly, running his hands through Tess's silky hair. "Bert the Lover."

"And I'm Darth."

"*Darth?*" Tess stared up at me for a second, and then burst out laughing. "You mean, like—*DUH, DUH-DE-DUH* . . . ?" She hummed the tune to *Star Wars*, then burst out in hysterics. "Luke!" she cried. "*I am your father!*"

Wordlessly, we watched her giggle. "I'm sorry," she gasped, finally, waving a hand weakly in the air. "It's just, since my accident . . . I think everyone's *related* to me."

Once under way, the scene progressed in fairly straightforward fashion. Tess, like a canny point guard in the twilight of her career, still had a few good moves left in her. Arching her behind, she looked back over her shoulder, touching her tongue to her teeth in a queenly, catlike gesture. Her nostrils flared elegantly; her lips quivered with passion. I was just starting to think she was one of the Reb's patented hidden treasures, when, upon Bert the Lover's third ejaculation—this one on the rim of her muscular vagina—Tess burst into wracking sobs.

"*Get the* fuck *away from me!*" she wailed. Her aristocratic face collapsed, her eyes twisting into pained slits and her chin protruding wildly.

Bert and Darth, scared, took a step back and reached for their shorts. Tess sobbed at a volume that hardly seemed prudent. We wrapped her in a towel and led her into the bedroom, where she fell onto Darth's bed and continued to howl hysterically, like a trauma-tized child.

"How thick are these walls, bro?" Bert said nervously.

"Not very," Darth answered. "Make her stop, Sam."

Tess didn't stop. She wept miserably, with the power of a natural disaster bent on destroying everything in its path. Her voice rose in volume and power; her sobs made the pavement shake. Then, quite suddenly, the storm broke, and she stopped. And Tess stood up, her eyes bugging wildly, and whispered, "I've got to get out of here."

"No!" I said, leaping toward her. "Tess! You're not dressed!"

"You stay away!" she screeched. "I need fucking *air*! Someone open this window or I'm gonna *die*!"

Darth looked at me questioningly.

"You better do it," I said. "Open the window and close the blinds."

Darth popped his window a crack, let the ocean breeze waft through. "See? That's *air*."

Tess pushed past him and bashed her head into the screen. She fell back hard onto her naked buttocks. "*Fuuuuuuuuck!*"

"Please, Tess! *Please* stop crying," I begged her. "Just sit down on the bed . . ."

Tess whirled to face me, her eyes puffy and red. "Get your hands off of me!" she hissed. "Get your *fucking hands off me,* or I'll call rape."

That shut me up quick. "Take your time, hon," I whispered, and backed into the living room, praying.

Eventually, the sobbing stopped. Tess walked out slowly to join us, still clad only in her towel. "I'm sorry," she said quietly. Her hair and eyes were ruined. She pointed at Bert. "I thought he was my brother."

"That's okay," Bert said. He attempted a weak laugh, but it came out terrible.

"Things just . . ." She sighed, seemingly lacking the strength to finish the thought. She looked beseechingly at me. "Things just haven't been the same since the accident."

A few hours later, we escorted Tess back to her Redondo Beach motel room, because she didn't feel all right to drive, and we understood that we had to get her home. Bert drove her car, and Darth and I followed behind. The 405 was black and peaceful. We got to her motel, and her room was on the second floor. We clopped up the steps, and inside, the bedclothes were distressed. The floor was littered with all kinds of porn clothing and powders and suitcases and agate crystals and blocky pyramids of half-charred green incense and purple astrology books. On the west wall, there was a framed painting of a seashell. In the corner on the floor, there was a black hair curler still plugged into the wall. Tess looked over at me as she drank a glass of motel water, and she shook her head at me while the liquid was still in her mouth.

She swallowed. "I feel a lot better." She looked around at all of us. "If you want . . . I think we can finish this."

FOURTEEN

A saner person would have quit right there. And I thought about it. But circumstances conspired to keep me in the game.

Once again, it was Pitts: in the form of a single tempting electronic missive, he took me one step deeper into the world of high-stakes pornography.

I've been thinking about this for a while, Sam, he wrote. *We gotta say good-bye to Long Beach. We need to ramp up our game if we're going to compete with the big boys. We need* production value. *I found a house in Malibu, a real peach: Oceanfront view, sprawling 18 acres—you never seen anything like this. Private. In the hills. Gated entrance. That sound okay to you?*

Puzzled, I said yeah, sure, it sounds great—and before I knew it, he'd promised me not only a bedroom in the house, but a healthy raise to boot.

We're gonna get real busy, Pitts warned me. *In fact, you may want to bring someone on board. Help carry the load. Who do you know who can shoot camera?*

I pondered that one for a while. I was set to give one of my friends the ride of a lifetime—but who? The question was, did I know anyone who really *got* porn? A regular person wasn't going to be able to hang for long. They'd do two weeks, see the bleeding insides of a person's body, and bolt.

But the answer came to me in a flash: the guy who'd been sending me letters. Willie Timberlake. Granted, I didn't know him from Adam, but the guy was my age, and his writing style had me interested. A healthy disregard for the laws of common decency notwithstanding, he was a damn good read—full of rage, torment, and confessional vigor. Bit by bit, I'd begun to look forward to his letters, to the experience of reading them and laughing at their crazy, manic hope. How could I not love someone who had the balls to confess this to a total stranger:

> *As I got older, I fucked a lot of crazy chicks, I mean true red-flag chicks (one girl told me as I slipped my cock into her big ass that I was a lot like her dad). Their pussies were always sopping wet, and I thought dealing with psychosis was okay as long as I was getting laid.*
>
> *At some point, I learned to disengage my penis from chicks that needed to be saved by daddy, and redirected my radar to women who had self-esteem. The weird part being I still like the fucked-up chicks, and the self-esteem chicks don't get it. My girlfriend couldn't possibly comprehend porn. To her, it is gross and foul. She saw an email that said, "amateur Japanese teenagers" and freaked. "This is what you like?" she cried. I'm a dirty old man at 24. I still don't know how to deal with her not understanding.*

You've asked me what porn I like. The porn I like makes me feel like shit, but it doesn't have to. Maybe it could still be "bad" but good at the same time. I'd love to see a woman finally say "You know, I DON'T like being called a bitch, but I DO love your huge cock spreading me wide open and it feels excellent!" I want to witness porn from the point of view of DWARVES, POORLY HUNG BLACK MEN, RUSSIAN MAILORDER BRIDES, ASIAN SCHOOLGIRLS, UP-TIGHT HOUSEWIVES, FEMALE COPS, AND BITCHY RESTARAUNT STAFF. The other side!

Feeling quite sure I had the right man for the job, I impulsively asked Timberlake to quit his job, move down from Oakland to Malibu to join me as brothers-in-porn, and to make a little money while doing it. Quite a little bit of money, actually.

"Is this *happening*, man?" he asked me, when I made the call. "Am I really being invited to Los Angeles?"

"*Malibu*," I corrected.

"Okay, to *Malibu*, to shoot porn?"

"You'll shoot so much porn, your head is gonna fall off," I promised. "Buddy, you'll shoot so much porn, you're going to *hate* porn."

"Couldn't happen," Timberlake bragged. "I love porn more than any man in America."

"You have a place to stay, too," I said, smiling. "Rent-free. A room in a *mansion*. I'm gonna live there, too. Beautiful, no?"

"But . . . why me? I mean, how the hell is this even possible?"

"I saw something in you. Baby, you were made for this business."

But in person, Timberlake wasn't quite like his acerbic letters—or perhaps, he was *too* much like them. Redheaded and skinny, Timberlake's cartoonish face appeared to have been thrown together with a random mix of ingredients: incongruously pretty eyes, closely shaven facial hair, and a big, beak-like nose. Jarringly, he often seemed not to know at all what he was talking about, yet was highly verbose nonetheless. It was my first lesson in the fact that we, as people, are often not quite the characters we appear to be on paper.

"Southern California is *chock-full* of schmucks," Timberlake declared. "Boy oh boy, I think I *knew* that in my bones before I came down. Still, seeing these assholes in person stings a lot worse than I thought." I squired him around Echo Park for a while, taking him to taco shops, trying to decide whether I'd made the right call. It was hard to tell. I remember getting stuck with him on the 101 freeway, turning to the radio for some relief, and immediately getting into a squabble over what year some Eddie Money song had come out. We started out laughing and bantering like brothers, but soon, when it became clear neither of us was going to budge, the conversation turned sour and snappish.

And it didn't take me long to realize that Timberlake was given to some pretty volatile mood swings. He'd appear crazily enthusiastic one second, then dark, depressed, and distrustful of me the next. "We've landed a really big fish here, man. I'm in the mood to make some money. *I WANT NICE SHIT! AND I WILL GET IT!*"

"Slow down there, partner," I said, frowning. "We'll get you some money."

"Slow down, my ass! I've worked so many hellish and shitty jobs in my young life, and already I've got a mountain of debt under me. Porn's my big chance to get over, man! I am staying down in LA, getting fucking *dirty*. We're gonna get so rich, we'll use twenties for shitpaper."

And then he'd laugh.

Timberlake may actually have been more self-aware and emotionally intelligent than much of his behavior implied. He analyzed himself continually. In more introspective moods, he could be as open and funny with his difficult past as any person I'd ever met. He had no problem, for example, letting me or anyone else in on the fact that he'd been conceived on a one-night stand and had never met his father, or that his mom was verbally abusive to him for his entire childhood.

"My mom *yelled* a lot," he explained to me. "She lost her temper a lot. Sometimes she was cruelly strict, and other times she didn't care if I existed. Some days she would fly into an uncontrollable slap-and-scratch rage. Other days she was euphoric and bursting with love. You know what's fucked? Now I'm the same way with my dog." He grinned. "Sometimes I'm nice, other times I'm an asshole."

Like me, Timberlake covered up a lot of his hurt feelings with humor; unlike me, he tended to push people away from him with alienating and annoying behavior before they could reject him on more concrete grounds. "Fuck your art fantasies, bro," he told me. "Fuck your parents. There is just me and there is money. I have already had myself a million different ways. Now I must have money."

A few days before work was scheduled to begin, Pitts flew down from Seattle, and we scheduled a Saturday Night Pornographers' Assembly at the Saddle Ranch, a tourist restaurant on the Sunset Strip. All the boys were there: me, Timberlake, Pitts, and even Pitts's little brother, who seemed to be serving as a kind of silent bodyguard. They made an interesting pair. Pitts looked like Mr. Clean, with a waxed bald head and piercing blue eyes and a great build, standing about five-foot-five at the most, while Pitts's little brother was built just like him and he *looked* exactly like him, except he was even shorter and had no shine in his eyes. It looked like he had been built out of leftovers.

We made our awkward introductions and got seated at a mediocre table. Timberlake, hyped for the future, barely noticed. He fairly vibrated in his seat, the glamour of West Hollywood seeping directly into his impoverished bloodstream like a hypodermic shot.

"*Oh-my*-GOODNESS that's a fine chica!" He jabbed at the air with his index finger, making no attempt to disguise the motion. We turned to observe a girl at a table directly across from us who was wearing an indigo cowboy hat and what looked like an Oilers jersey over a sports bra and tiny Abercrombie shorts. An Indigo Cowgirl was about par for the course at the Saddle Ranch, but she definitely was a looker, with almond eyes and Hooters-quality silken hair. She was maybe twenty.

"So let's get her a contract," Pitts suggested.

Timberlake exploded with a saucy snicker. "Let's get her a *contract!*" he repeated. In a good mood, Timberlake laughed as a matter of course (often at things that weren't funny, sometimes at things that were, but truthfully, he laughed at every third thing that was said, although nothing got said by Pitts's brother, who was staring down at the tablecloth with a kind of intensity that bordered on druggy fascination).

I was puzzled, trying to figure everyone out. Not only was this the first time I'd teamed up with Timberlake in anything resembling a professional situation, but it was the first occasion Pitts and I had ever met *in vivo*. We'd conversed so much over email that I had harbored a weird illusion that I "knew" him—but now I was realizing that, as in the case of Timberlake, I'd understood precious little about the real Pitts.

He was a compact piece of a man: but while Timberlake and I towered over him awkwardly, Pitts projected an impression of ultimate serenity and confidence, sitting there at the head of the table, studying his menu sedately. With his pumped-up biceps, shining head, and hard little jaw, the man was not quite handsome, and the blue in his eyes was too cold to be very appealing. But you simply couldn't stop *looking* at him. Diners from across the room continually flicked their eyes toward our table, watching him involuntarily for several moments before turning back to their own dinners.

In our society, charisma comes from many sources. Some are born with it; others accumulate it over time. Money, more than fame, remains the best modern-day shortcut—and Pitts had earned a great deal of money by understanding the growth potential in Internet pornography at a time when nearly everybody else in the business was still tied to DVDs. He was a visionary in a field full of guys who had stiff cocks for brains, and his business acumen had won him not only house and home, but had granted him a quiet power of personality that no stone could ever break.

He represented a side of the sex industry almost completely unseen by me: those who were driven by potency of character and cleverness, instead of pure, desperate salacity. Obviously, Pitts was at some level interested in sex; most men who choose to make porn their life's work are. It was my guess that he didn't mind the scum factor, either—the soul-crushing garbage one dealt with as a matter of course, on a daily basis, at every level of the sex industry. But by the unhurried, polished ease with which Pitts contemplated his menu and gazed about the room, taking in the city around him, it was plain to see he was, at bottom, a businessman.

"What will you gentlemen be having tonight?" our waitress asked.

"Steak," Pitts said, folding his menu, handing it back to the waitress. "Medium. Mashed potatoes."

"Steak," Timberlake said, tapping the table rhythmically, inspecting our waitress's pad to see if she wrote it down right. "Well done. Green beans."

"Steak," I said, looking into our waitress's eyes politely, while I used my peripheral vision to calculate her tit-to-waist ratio. "Rare. Salad."

Pitts's brother remained silent.

"How about you, sir?"

"Steak, I guess," he mumbled, staring at his hands.

"And how would you like that done?"

He glanced up at his brother, and Pitts nodded. "Medium," he mumbled out the side of his mouth.

The waitress wrote it down dutifully. "Any sides with that?"

Pitts's brother just shook his head glumly. After a long, weird moment, the waitress left.

"Okay, so let's get down to business," Pitts said. "First thing is, we clearly need to hire some new dudes."

"*Clearly*," Timberlake said.

"No more Bert and Darth," Pitts said, laughing.

"No *way*, man," agreed Timberlake. "Sam shot them into the *ground!*"

I frowned across the table at Timberlake. "I wasn't aware they were so objectionable."

"They were fine," Pitts explained. "They served a purpose. But now we need to take a step up in quality."

"Well, like I always say, Mr. Marcus and Lexington Steele, that's the best black wood in the business," ventured Timberlake.

I laughed. "Sorry, but how the fuck would *you* know?"

"Connoisseur," Timberlake explained to the table in general. "Seen a lot of black dick."

"No offense," I said, "but I *think* Lexington Steele's a bit out of our price range. He gets about one thousand dollars per scene."

"Hey, you want quality scenes, you gotta pay for it, right?" Timber said happily, tilting back in his chair until the front two legs left the ground. He looked back over his shoulder at the waitress's high legs as they strode confidently, like a racehorse's, across the floor of the Saddle Ranch.

"There's a fine *line*," I said, my eyes flashing. "Look, if we need new guys, I can get them for us. I know a guy, a black agent named DK. He can find good talent for us. And they won't cost a grand a scene." I smiled sharply at Pitts. "I got it taken care of."

"Great," Pitts said. "I like it." He excused himself and got up to use the bathroom.

"Hey, Samuel," said Timberlake, "we doing okay? I don't want to step on anyone's toes."

"Then *don't*," I said.

"I didn't mean to say anything."

"Let me handle the talking, okay, guy? I mean, you're the junior partner, are you not?"

"I am," Timberlake assured me. He patted my hand. "Don't get your panties all in a bunch. I'll let you deal with all further negotiations."

I was ready to snap something smart back, but Pitts came back and sat down at the table calmly, so I shut up. And as we waited for the food to arrive, I looked across the room and recognized a girl from Brown whom I had once kissed. For a moment, I thought about going up to her—we hadn't seen each other since graduation—but then realized she wouldn't want to see me. Even more, I wouldn't want to explain what I was doing with my life now, anyway.

But I couldn't help but look at her. Her name was Sandra, and she had been kind of compelling. She was one of those students who would make these long, rambling, tortured, yet somehow incisive comments in classes, which graduate students would fumble to answer in their excitement. But on a date, that kind of neurotic emotional rigor was poisonous. Sandra had been very pretty at school, and I saw that she still was. Her nose was hawkish and powerfully nostriled. From across the room, I watched and remembered her.

"Back to the plan," Pitts said. "We need better girls. You know what I mean? Younger. Cleaner. More *innocent*-looking. I want this stuff looking like a father's worst nightmare."

"Can *do!*" Timberlake exploded, laughing, before I could stop him. "So I'm watching this scene, the other night? *Tiny* blond girl, bobbed hair, braces, 'bout nineteen years old. And she's just *beggin'* for it! Beautiful! But the *best* part? Right at the *end*, she's all, *Cum on my braces!*"

"Keep your voice down," I begged him.

"Cum on my *braces*," he repeated, sniggering like a madman, fingering wormholes into a couple of pieces of bread in the basket, ruining them. "Can you *believe* it?"

"That's the kind of stuff I'm talking about," Pitts said, nodding his head. "We're renting a really great house here. Wait till you guys see it. It's very *refined*. I need us producing scenes that demonstrate a kind of *contrast*. See what I'm saying?"

"Luxurious surroundings," I said, "dotted with stark degradation."

"Filthy," said Pitts. "Kinda, well . . . evil."

"To chicks with braces!" Timberlake proposed, raising his glass. "And black dick!" A passing waitress glanced over at our table, frowning, unsure if she'd heard correctly.

We all raised our glasses and sipped from them happily.

"We should talk about money," I volunteered.

"All right," Pitts agreed.

"You mentioned a raise."

"I did," he said.

"Do you want to hear what I was thinking?"

"Yes, please," Pitts said, looking cautious for the first time that night.

"Well," I said, "I was getting around four hundred dollars for Bert and Darth. But since the stakes are higher now, I figure me and Will should get paid around five hundred for a regular shoot."

"I can live with that," Pitts said, smiling.

"Great," I said. "But there's more. If you want another guy in the scene, I think we should receive a small bonus. Say, six hundred for a three-on-one?"

"What's the rationale?"

"An extra guy is more work for us," I explained. "We have to book and organize each guy, take care of 'em, shoot 'em, and then get rid of 'em. I readily admit the job's not rocket science, but the truth is, it's no cakewalk, either."

"Well, okay," Pitts said cautiously. "Are you done?"

"Not *quite*," I grinned. "Same policy as we go up the ladder: four guys is seven hundred dollars, five guys is eight hundred."

"You want me to pay you guys *eight hundred dollars a shoot?*" Pitts said, incredulously.

"Only if there's five guys," I said simply. "You know, five guys represents an honest-to-God gangbang. That's what the big boys are doing, and it takes a hell of a lot of organizational prowess, not to mention top-notch camera skills. Which, luckily, we've got in spades."

Pitts was quiet for a moment. "So you guys want to get rich, huh?"

I shrugged, then I stared him solidly in the face. "Yeah," I said. "We want to make money."

There was a moment of awkwardness. Fleetingly, I wondered if I had gone too far. But then Pitts nodded. That's all he did: nod once. I couldn't decode from his expression how much anger versus respect was in there, but either way, it didn't matter. I was going to get what I'd asked for.

I bit down on my smile. Underneath the table, Timberlake kicked me in congratulation. From across the room, I watched Sandra wave her supple, thin little wrist, explaining something to her friends. I watched her, but not longingly. We didn't belong in the same world any longer. I was glowing, cold and excited.

Dusk the next evening, Timberlake and I arrived at the mansion for the first time—though the word *mansion*, as it turned out, was an overstatement, actually, and not quite right. In fact, the place was more of a Spanish-style villa, with a red roof constructed of thick Santa Barbara–style stone shingles that rested atop velvety white exterior walls that reflected Malibu Barbie sun all over the place, which was punctuated by a host of bizarre lanterns that led down to a rolling green, which led down to an Olympic-sized swimming pool, which was bounded on all sides by a brick patio, atop which sat a faction of inordinately ugly, stiff, white wooden deck chairs that waited there for you to perch upon them, gazing restlessly out at the world beyond you, high above the LA smog, insulated from its poor-person traffic.

Malibu is marketed as a place to escape, and many people receive it that way. But it is deathly lonely as well, and no one ever speaks of that part. Neighbors exist only behind the tint of their black BMWs. When they come knocking at your door, it is not to welcome you to the neighborhood.

A security gate closed us off from the world, anyway. In Pitts's master bedroom, a high-powered telescope had been installed; aside from that, we were isolated. It was an ideal place to make degenerate pornography—to videotape long, exquisite white legs being parted by black dick.

Timberlake and I took a hushed, barefoot tour of the grounds, shivering with enormous delight at the colossal lawn, the shrubs and the slips and the sprouts and the almost obscenely lush greenery. Manicured softwoods brushed against the fine hairs of our cheeks like a mother whispering good night, sweet dreams.

"There's *got* to be a fuckin' gardener living on the property here, man," said Timberlake.

He was right. Luiz was our caretaker's name. He was a sweet man with a poor command of the English language and a semi-retarded black Labrador that followed him around with a devotion bordering on beauty. There was a wife in the picture, too; Luiz let us know that if we saw fit, she'd be available to clean the place every week.

"No," I said, imagining the tableau. Your average conservative middle-aged Mexican woman would likely faint dead at the sight of three panting black giants towering over a little half-dead white girl. Even the after-trash, the grab-bag pile of crumpled panty hose, bloodied tampons, turkey neckbones, wrapped-up toilet paper, browning apple cores, and spent douches could easily send her into apoplexy. "We'll probably take care of it."

Timberlake and I parted a sliding-glass door and went inside the fifteen-room villa. The smell of furniture polish wafted up our nostrils and into our brains. A brand-new Canon XL-1 video camera lay quietly atop the glass living room table.

"*Nice!*" Timberlake exclaimed. "Opening day present?"

"It well may be," I said, staring at the huge camera. "Quite a thoughtful gesture."

"I guess I'll be shooting with this bad boy," Timberlake said.

"Suit yourself. But it's your funeral."

"How's that?"

"Too heavy," I said. "The XL's not a porn camera. It's got great picture quality, but you'll have to support it on your shoulder. It'll wobble when you try to get in close. It's gotta weigh ten pounds, easy. You should shoot with the smaller GL-1, like I do."

"Like I *said*," Timberlake repeated, defiantly, "I guess *I'll* be shooting with this bad boy."

He gave me the kind of look that says, friend, that's the story, and I shrugged at him and left him to go investigate the kitchen. It was endowed with a rich person's Sub-Zero refrigerator and a range-top gas stove with six burners and a honey dripper of balsamic vinegar and a green-tiled island plopped right in the middle of the floor for chopping up yellow peppers and making pots of delicious Chinese tea. There were plenty of cut-glass vases for placing flowers and stainless steel cutlery and mirrors and tea whistles and full-frontal air-conditioning. In the next room was a Samsonite washer and Sony dryer with all the Clorox bleach a man could want and a broom closet filled with mops with heavy-duty handgrips and a small transistor radio and buckets of detergent and brooms with black bristles and stipple-fingered yellow gloves and a bucket and a family-sized box of Whipple fabric softener with a picture of a cuddly teddy bear on it.

The living room contained sectional couches and an expensive green throw rug and digital cable television with hot exterior speakers and a remote control that glistened blackly. A chandelier of outstanding golden ugliness tinkled down from the rooftop and a magical staircase rose up from the middle of the room to the top floor, where Pitts would live and hold court. The Classy Bathroom was up there, too, where starlets would snap on their fishnets and apply their own makeup to their cheekbones, clogging their meth pores, creating the smoothest surface known to man: *peachy*, punctured by maroon lips, *peachy*, punctured by eyes blue, *peachy*, punctured by whorish jet-black lash-clogged mascara and clean hair until you got to the skull, where a filmy layer of dandruff and shame coated their heads and the rake of a fingernail would yield a quarter inch of greasy white flake. A stall shower loomed behind you, flanked by a tower of baby wipes and theater lights with exposed yellow bulbs encircling mirrors that were never streaked. A hair dryer fit directly into the wall.

Next to the bathroom was a guest bedroom whose walls, empatterned by circular brushstrokes, offered an attempt at faux-finishing. This same room boasted a thick, verdant shag rug that hungrily swallowed earrings and lipsticks and hastily gnawed candy bar crumbs. There were rumors about this house: notably, that a famous hardcore band had lived here a few months before us and recorded an album within its walls. I pictured them out on the lawn, weirdly unhappy, gazing into the turquoise pool, writing their grungy lyrics. This house was richly fuck-ugly, it rented for ten grand a month, its net worth was $10 million, and yet it was putrid, just obscenely sick, with strolling lawns and crunchy chemical-grass and birds overhead pooping into your hot tub. I breathed in the essence of the house and its walls and its monstrous oaken furnishings, and knew what I would do here.

Like those who had lived here before me: I smelled the money.

It was evening, and the chlorinated pool water was warm. It felt incredible on my face and my hair. Incandescent 250-watt underwater halogens illuminated my legs and chest, making them glow ghostly and white.

"I'm having an anxiety attack," Timberlake mumbled.

"What are you talking about, man? We're on easy street here."

"Pitts is going to fire me," he whispered.

"Pitts is not *firing* anyone," I said. "He's up in his room, tending to business, happy as a clam. What in hell is wrong with you?"

"I've had four jobs this year already," confessed Timberlake, treading water with a mildly agonized expression on his face. "And I was fired from every one."

"*Four* jobs?"

"Yeah. At first I was blaming the places where I worked — shitty pay, stupid hours, lack of perks, and horrendous bosses. But now, after job number four, I've got to lick the balls of reality. It's *me*."

I frowned. "You can do this, man. It's super easy."

"Anxiety attacks are strange," Timberlake continued, as if I'd said nothing. "I basically just watch myself having them. Part of me thinks it's funny, almost cute and endearing. Meanwhile, the other part of me is wigging out."

I floated on my back, weightless, regarding the spray of stars clustered overhead. You could live in Los Angeles for years without ever really seeing stars with any clarity. Streetlights always dimmed them out. But these Malibu stars were coming through with pristine clarity.

"Look," I said, coming out of my float. "You-will-do-fine. Okay? I'll make sure of it. I'll help you."

"I don't need help," Timberlake spat back. "I *understand* porn, okay?"

"Well, bro, you were just *saying* . . ."

"Sam," Timberlake said, "can I ask you something strange? Have you ever jacked off at *work*? I have. It was one of the most incredible rushes of my entire *life*."

"I don't want to hear about—"

"I could hear the woman in the office next to me moaning about how *delicious* her lunch was. Meanwhile, on the computer, I'm watching this fine Latina with the biggest bubble butt I've ever seen. Even through crappy digitization, I could still see ripples of pleasure coming up in waves off of her fat ass. My whole *groin* was hot. It rocked."

I shook my head, confused. "What does that have to do with your *anxiety* attack, dude?"

Timberlake stared back at me, laughing abruptly, as if I'd farted in the pool. "Nothing. Why?"

"You said you were . . ."

"The attacks always pass, given enough time. Employment, what a silly fucking debacle. I have three pairs of slacks suitable for work. Only one of them has cum stains on them."

I gazed at him, momentarily stunned. Timberlake peered back at me, curious.

"We still headed to see that black agent tomorrow?" he asked.

"Sure," I said, mildly confused. "But just a second ago, you were . . ."

"Just let me ramble, dude!" Timberlake exploded, radiating a gigantic smile, splashing in the water. "This is how I roll! Free association! I rented two Euro-porns last weekend. *Ter-ri-ble!* The women were unbelievable, but man, the French can turn the most beautifully naturally titted, fat-assed gaping anus fuck scene into depressing tedium."

Sighing, I climbed out of the pool. "I'm going to sleep, buddy."

"Hop to it," Timberlake said. "I'll swim here for a while longer. Beautiful in here."

That night, I traipsed around our enormous house quietly, deliberating where to shoot my very first scene. Each and every room seemed a superlative backdrop for whatever sleazy scenario I might dream up, from the immense, high-ceilinged den to the drafty, impersonal salon, to the elegant and stuffy dining room. Hell, even the *garage* looked good enough to fuck in, with Pitts's immaculate Mercedes-Benz holding court in there.

Observing the riches around me, I had to wonder, what in hell was I *doing* here? How was it possible that in such a short period of time, I'd come from filming a piss video in Periwinkle's low-rent living room in Santa Cruz to this Malibu villa-on-a-hill? It boggled the mind. But after some minutes, I concluded that I deserved everything I'd been granted. It is truly the privilege of youth to believe that worldly advantages have been bestowed upon you for a reason. Yes, I concluded, this was my destiny: to know porn in all its varied forms. To discern, in the most intimate terms, the opulence contained therein.

Even so, the house was a bit much. As a nod to humbler origins, I'd decided to take up residence in the pool house, a tiny but adorable carpeted luxury cabana, fifteen by fifteen feet in size. It had been designed to serve as a discreet, freestanding changing room for guests headed to the large, exposed-brick outdoor Jacuzzi tub positioned a scant twenty feet from my French front doors. Shyly, I hung my few clothes in its closet, vowing to buy more flamboyant and expensive gear as soon as my first paycheck came in. I placed my toothbrush on the edge of the sink; it looked shabby there, amid the polished shine of the basin.

I looked around for something to sit on—for now, my pool house lacked any furniture. Never mind. I would purchase a bed, eventually. If things turned out the way I hoped they would, mere household expenditures would prove little obstacle. Porn would provide me a bed to sleep in.

Bright and early the next morning, we headed to DK's Royal King Talent Agency. DK stood for Derrick King, but nobody called him

Derrick, and only his mother called him King. Forty years old and gifted with a white toothy smile and greasy, dense hair, DK was the only black agent in the game.

"I got some *terrific* guys for you," DK announced, spreading his hands wide. "This one brother? Bruce Vain? He looks like an *Adonis*."

"All right," I said, trying to sound agreeable.

"Vain's a gentleman lover," DK said. "Soft-spoken, but just top-notch." He winked, nodding all the time. DK emanated the sweet perfume of a fallen record executive: habitually short on luck, yet unable to wrest himself from the deluded conviction that he was just *inches* away from that next big score.

"That's terrific," I assured him.

"Now, Lucky Starr is a *big*-dick brother," DK began. "But *extraordinarily* sweet. Nonthreatening, if you follow me."

"Cut the bullshit, all right?" Timberlake interrupted. "We need some guys who can get *gangster*." His eyes roamed belligerently all over DK's office, taking in the box of Kleenex, the broken sticks of incense, and the couch-bed in the corner, which looked suspiciously well used.

"*Gangster?*" DK said, chuckling good-naturedly. "Sure, I follow. Ever heard of a fellow named Wesley Pipes? He'll fit that bill to a *tee*!"

"Never heard of him," Timberlake said, icily.

"You'll have to excuse my partner," I said. "See, he's not really familiar with all the players in the industry. Hell, neither am I. That's why we had to come to a stone pimp like you. We heard you were the best."

DK beamed at me and laughed. "You heard goddamn *right*, bro!"

I could feel Timberlake projecting distrust and disapproval beside me, but I couldn't help but beam back at our new friend.

Maybe DK *was* sleazy; maybe he was a bit disorganized, a little impulsive. Nonetheless, I liked him. So what if he was going to spend his commission on stonewashed jeans? Just talking to the guy, I could tell he was here to help.

"Oh," I said, "I almost forgot. How much are these guys going to want to get paid?"

"Liz?" DK called. "Hey, Liz, earth to Liz, sweetie? What's everybody been getting lately?"

White Liz, DK's major-league porn secretary, emerged from behind her computer for the first time. She was wearing headphones, but she slipped them off. "Say what?"

"I *said*," DK grumbled good-naturedly, "how much are the fellas getting over at Deep for a gangbang nowadays? How much are they paying over at Devil's Films?"

Liz shrugged, gave the matter a moment's thought, then answered, "Three hundred dollars is pretty standard for a gangbang."

"Three hundred could work for us," Timberlake said.

White Liz slipped her headphones back on her head and zipped back behind her computer. She was a catch by any porn agent's standards: not only was she twenty-two years old, with bright eyes, tight pants, curly red hipster hair, and blue-black tattoos running up and down her arms, more important, she seemed not to mind too terribly the freaky environment into which she'd stumbled by answering a classified ad in the back pages of the *LA Weekly*. While everyone was always trying to convince White Liz to get naked and get nasty on camera ("just like one *foot* fetish scene, baby"), she'd kept her wits about her, calmly relating to all parties that she had no interest in performing. She simply held on to her job for DK and fielded all the abusive phone calls meant for him, and also set up his clients with jobs.

"Fine. We'll need the names and numbers of five strong black male performers," Timberlake said. "With *huge* dicks."

"No problem," DK chuckled. "You guys are a trip."

I leaned back on the couch, trying to catch White Liz's eye. No dice.

"In exchange for your help," Timberlake said, "you'll receive five hundred dollars up front, no questions asked."

"You got it!" DK said. "*Deal*. And I look forward to working with you from this point out." He grinned happily, as well he should have: no one really paid for male actors in those days. It was a charity if you did. Agents received $75 to $100 for every actress they referred your way, but the men were a different matter. Male actors tended to fend for themselves, getting their own bookings, rarely remaining faithful to one agent the way that most of the girls did.

But we had deep pockets now. That was the difference. As DK rummaged around his office for paper, I scribbled out a check, which DK accepted most graciously. Carefully, he wrote down five porno names on a piece of paper. I looked the paper over and nodded, then passed it to Timberlake, my junior business associate, who looked it over and nodded. We turned to go.

On my way out, I couldn't resist eyeing White Liz one more time. She had a nice aura about her. There was dignity in that package. At the last possible moment, she finally looked up and stared right back into me. I gave her my best smile, but she just raised an eyebrow at me in a way that I couldn't decipher. DK looked up from his rummaging, noticing us, and immediately he emanated the most furious schoolboy lust toward Liz. There was no hint of malice there, no jealousy; he was just dying of horny. Liz just laughed at him, and laughed at me, then returned to her work, typing rapidly, headphones glued to her ears, a single Parliament Menthol on her desk, waiting to be smoked in the sun.

FIFTEEN

Descending upon the house like a black superhero here to save our asses, Lucky Starr warned me immediately, "I'm condom-only. I got a girlfriend, a fiancée. And she don't play that."

"But we can't *use* you if you're condom-only," I informed him, irritated. Fucking DK.

"Yeah, okay, but see, I am condom-only," Lucky said, backtracking quickly. "*But,* I'm gonna make an exception, just for you. Because I like you and everything. Plus, I really need the work."

I smiled and extended my hand. "So pleased to meet you."

Lucky Starr came as promised: he was black, and yet he wasn't *threateningly* black. In fact, he was basically harmless, and he actually made me feel like a black guy myself. It was a funny thing, and I doubt if I can explain it as well as it needs to be explained. I mean, Lucky Starr was honest-to-God black, grew-up-on-the-South-Side-of-Chicago black, ex-gang-member black. But his fiancée was white, like *British* white and fat white and funny white and loud white; just weird white. Lucky's best buddy was white, as well: slant-eyed Russian white, *Mongol* white, *chunky* white, and maybe carrying-a-gun white. *His* main problem was that he believed he could *rap*. And beatbox. Both he and Lucky did. Often, I was made to listen to the diseased fruits of their labor.

"This is one hell of a setup that you got here," Lucky said, strolling about the grounds. He removed a pipe from within the pockets of his short pants and tamped it full of purple kush.

"We like it," I said absently, gazing out into the distance at Catalina Island, hazy but visible in the noonday fog.

Lucky torched the bowl, then exhaled a thick plume that nearly enveloped his face in a white cloud. "You want this?"

"Nah, never touch the stuff," I demurred.

"Like hell you don't," Lucky said, smiling through the smoke, his eyelids lowered.

"Oh, I wouldn't mind a *small* hit," I confessed. "Just to taste."

The smoke hit the corners of my head from the inside out. I coughed a little, which brought out a little giggle. I glanced, embarrassed, at my new black friend, but he was giggling, too. Together, we took quick care of the rest of his bowl, and we became quite high, inebriated and dazzled, on top of a mountain in Malibu. Poolside, on white deck chairs, together in collective weed delirium, we were on the rise.

"Man, I swear, I would move *in* over here, if I was y'all."

"We already did," I confessed. "Me and Timberlake got rooms."

"Who's Timberlake?" Lucky asked.

"That crazy man coming toward us," I said, pointing to the redhead as he approached, holding his Canon XL-1 video camera and waving at us. "Say hi."

"You guys! Do something more entertaining," Timberlake ordered, waving at us from behind the camera's lenspiece. "Right now, what you're doing is terrible."

"You better enjoy playing with that camera now," I warned him, "because you're not going to be doing *any* kind of shooting once we get our scene started."

"Aw, bullshit," Timberlake said, disappointed. "I figured we'd take this first one together."

"Then you were sadly mistaken," I said. "I don't codirect. Besides, you don't need my help, remember? You can just sit back and watch how it's done. See how a pro *crafts* a scene."

"What, you *new* at this, bro?" Lucky said, laughing loudly. "Oh *shit*, this fool is here to get *schooled*?"

"I've been looking at porn since before you had a *penis*," Timberlake snapped.

"That don't make no sense," Lucky said, momentarily confused.

I smiled, happy and high. "Willie T, meet Lucky Starr," I said. "He's here to ramp up our production value."

Timberlake shook his hand grudgingly. "You're pretty gangster, I guess."

Lucky laughed pleasantly. "Good to meet you, too."

"Pop quiz, Starr," Timberlake said brusquely. "I've been thinking this over, can't get it off my mind. You do this every day, right? So you must come across some real pigs. Now, how can you *possibly* maintain your erection if you're doing a *truly* ugly girl?"

"First of all, all women are beautiful and lovely, whether inside or on the exterior," Lucky said.

"Yeah," Timberlake said.

"Second of all: Viagra."

"Are you *serious*?"

"'Course," he said, looking at me blankly. "What?"

"I just thought . . . no one ever admits to using Viagra."

"'Course I use it. I ain't secretive about my dick."

"No," I considered. "I guess not."

"Viagra's the *shit*. I mean, seriously, I *love* that shit. Dick all *hard* and shit."

"We get it, Lucky," Timberlake said. "Thanks."

"But you want to know what's truly the bomb? *Caverject*."

"What's that?" I said.

"Okay, don't quote me on this, now, 'cause I never tried it, understand? But from what I *hear*," Lucky said, "you *inject* that shit right in your dick. Right at the base."

"Ooooch," Timberlake hissed, guarding his crotch.

"It ain't *that* bad," Lucky said dismissively. "Be professional, son. See, with a *pill*, you gotta be *somewhat* turned on for it to take effect. Girl smells funky? You having a bad day? Well, then it just might not happen for you. With *this* stuff? Man, you just prick yourself and fifteen minutes later, someone could come up to you and tell you your *daughter* just got hit by a car. You'd stay wood, no problem."

Brian Pumper arrived shortly thereafter. He was a handsome son of a bitch with a perfect haircut, a solid boxer's body, and a giant light-skinned cock and balls. He was more than just a pretty face with Polo jean shorts and Nike ankle socks, though: at twenty years of age, Brian was one of the youngest working male porn studs in the business, and he already had earned a reputation as one of the best. Pumper didn't know how to drive a car, so he was escorted by DK's limo man, a geriatric Jew named Jerry. Jerry's limo had plenty of scratches on it, and it smelled like anal lubricant inside; nevertheless, a limo is a limo.

"Fellas," Pumper addressed Timberlake and me quietly, pulling us aside on that first day. "I get paid *four*."

"Seriously?"

"Definitely. I'm definitely serious." He looked toward Jerry for assurance. The old Jew nodded obediently.

"You really couldn't do three hundred?" I asked.

"No," he said, gazing down at the ground. "I get paid four."

Pumper. He had grown up alone and abandoned in West Babylon, New York, a precocious, lonely boy raised by his maternal grandparents. Now, suddenly granted the job of his dreams—of everybody's dreams—and more money than he knew what to do with (not to mention a source of unlimited, though degraded, "attention"), he had developed into a big-mouthed black narcissist sex addict with mild sociopathic tendencies. Well, fine. I could forgive all that.

Timberlake and I looked him up and down, and finally I said rather gruffly, "I'll have to clear it with my boss." We ran upstairs to Pitts, who peered down at Pumper's figure on the lawn from his post in the master bedroom and immediately caved. "The kid's got a great body," Pitts said. "Pay him his rate."

All we needed now was a woman. And shortly thereafter, she arrived. Our lady's name was *Tasia*. Tasia was new to the industry and four foot eleven if she was an inch. She sported braids and a bubble butt and an aerobic upkeep that, combined with high cheekbones and an exceptionally pretty freckle face, belied the fact that she was here to guzzle cock and let cum drip off her face and onto the carpet.

As soon as Tasia arrived at the house (escorted by a driver of her own, a young man who emanated a leech-like quality that suggested he was angling to become her manager), Timberlake and I buzzed heavily around our actress like two drunken fruit flies. "Mostly I've done lots of dancing," she told us. "Lots. Also, I was at the LA Exotic Erotic Ball, and I met Max Hardcore there. He *loved* me!" She had never performed in a full scene, though—much less one for Max, who had a rather gruesome reputation—and certainly, she had never taken on two fellows at the same time. "But I'm giving this a shot," she said, sensibly.

Before very long, Pumper and Lucky joined our swarm, dislodging her manager with a swift twist of their broad shoulders. "This her?" Pumper asked me, in his deep baritone, caressing Tasia's curvaceous tush while she giggled.

"Yup," I laughed. "Tasia, meet Brian Pumper and Lucky Starr. Soon, you'll be having sex with them."

"Oh *my*," Pumper murmured, doing his best Isaac Hayes. He refused to address Tasia directly, even though he was nose-nuzzling her breasts. "She is *ripe*, fellas."

"Guys, guys," Tasia giggled. "How about giving me some *air*?"

"Yo, you heard the lady," Pumper announced, waving off the rest of us, but moving not one inch himself. "This delicate flower must be allowed to *breathe*."

"Upstairs?" I suggested gently, herding our group to the wooden steps, where we swung around the spiral of the staircase up into the mammoth guest room. There, Lucky and Brian sat down on our vast guest bed and stared at each other guardedly. *Who would get to lick the pussy first? Who would sloppily swing his cock into the other's thigh?*

I clapped my hands meaninglessly a few times, then nodded at Timberlake, who took Tasia by the elbow and steered her into the bathroom, as she giggled. I watched her face to see if she was duly impressed by the finery and rich, peachy towels, then passed her a seven-page model's release to sign and initial. As she worked her way through the document, I warmed up the GL-1 (which weighed only two pounds, 12.8 ounces, and was a true porn camera if you asked me, which no one ever did, with an external Sony unidirectional microphone attached to the shoe atop the apparatus, though that didn't come with the model and, in fact, I had had to buy it in downtown Santa Cruz when all of this was just beginning—I had *seniority*, see?), and I glanced at Timberlake to see if he was checking this all out, studying the master, but he wasn't even looking at me. His attention was focused on Tasia and her tight tan breasts and her almond eyes and svelte forearms. Her sensational tiny body. Feminine essence fogged his windshield, engulfing him.

Tasia giggled at both of us, we who were so obviously whiffing her perfume. Nerdish lust and tiny boners sprouted from us; we were stuttering and stammering, begging for a piece of the pie. Ah, Timberlake. Already I could sense that he and I were so clearly a pair, awkward in the best tradition, brothers in dorkhood. It was just obvious. But instead of feeling comforted by our allegiance, I resented him for it. I regretted the association with his weakness: with his obvious, corny remarks, the flip of his wrist. I was going to be *rich* now, in a mansion; I wanted to be around *men*, like Lucky Starr. Suck up some of their strength and their powerful black energy.

"All done, guys," Tasia said with a smile. She handed me the model release. She posed shyly in front of the brown oaken door of the guest room, a black tube top cupping her little tits, black shoes on her feet, heavy and weird. Behind me, Timberlake observed silently, maybe sullenly. Lucky Starr and Brian Pumper shuffled their feet restlessly, wanting in. I said no. I pointed my camera at her, recording her, savoring Tasia all for myself. Her face was gorgeous. She had no imperfections on her remarkable little body. No drug scarring on her cheeks. No little zitlings rouging her buttocks.

There was nothing complicated or even interesting about what happened next, which was the blowjobs. The blowjob scene was always my favorite part of the shoot, not just because they were pointless from a reproductive point of view and thus reassuringly perverse, but also because the girls' faces would occasionally mangle and distort from the effort of wrapping around the large cocks; sometimes they would choke, and saliva would drool out of their gobs, and their throats would close up, their eyes watering, and it pleased me in this horrible way I was scared to describe to anyone. I just got *off* on it, got off on the fact that sometimes they looked like monsters, vaguely inhuman, and although I had only just met Tasia, a little part of me longed to see her upside down and humiliated and lonely and slammed to the ground . . . not *all* of me wanted it, just a flicker of me wanted it.

"This is one beautiful woman," Pumper announced to the world around him. "I would like to make love with her."

"Brian," I whispered. "Talk less."

"All right," he said, looking hurt. Tasia was holding on to the shaft of his penis with one hand, trying to get her fingers all the way around it and failing to do so. "Look, all I'm saying is, this bitch is one delicate flower who really *gets* me."

Pumper flipped Tasia upside down and began to plow her in impossible circus positions. I filmed, my forehead frowning in pure concentration, one hand outstretched to the side, to aid my balance. I tensed, ready to pounce, prepared to record every moment of available footage. Downstairs, the doors creaked open: a pair of intruders slipped off their shoes stealthily and tiptoed in, slinking up the regal staircase to join us. DK and White Liz, our neighbors in porn. Limousine Jerry followed their lead. White Liz yawned. Jerry, startled at the sight of Tasia's tiny anus, coughed up a gob of phlegm in the background.

I shot them all a look that said: *Quiet on the set.*

Tasia, mind-blowingly flexible, curled into yoga backbends and Möbius strips, hand meeting ankle meeting head. Lucky saw that aerobic madness and raised it, tilting Tasia's chassis on an impossible bias, hopping up on one leg to impale her good. I hefted my video camera to one shoulder, shifted my weight, zooming in and out *slo-o-o-w-ly*, the way I had learned from the masters. *No one make a sound.* Pumper edged into the fray and simply stole Tasia for himself. He hoisted her tiny buttocks into the air and carried her over to an eighteenth-century cherrywood fuck-bench with a hand-rubbed finish, antique brass hardware, and snag-free drawer bottoms. He seated her on his lap, and there she rested like a Chihuahua. We all watched Pumper pump, and he pumped, and he humped, caressing his giant foal of a penis, triumphant, not sweating at all, Olympian, beaming, emanating light from the proud, shining beacon of his smile. He cupped his massive mulberry-colored balls in his palm, confirming their heft. Tasia seesawed back and forth, concentrating, still wearing her odd, giant shoes.

By the time it was over, by the time we'd smothered the wet fireworks, commemorating yet another ritualistic frenzy, however scripted, the Malibu day was fading into night. DK clapped Pumper on the shoulder, rubbing his well-formed deltoid with a strong hand. "My man! You rocked it, once again." Pumper glowed in the fatherly approval. Lucky kissed Tasia on the check, collected his check, and dipped out. The sound of beatboxing followed him fading into the night. Tasia sipped coyly from a bottled water. Sidling up to me, she said, not shyly at all, "I want to do a scene with *you.*" She flashed her eyes at me, gave me a long hug. With her eyes, White Liz shot daggers at Tasia. They all made the exodus to their cars. As she left, White Liz turned to me, looking at me hard, as if to dare me to look away. I grinned at her and shrugged my shoulders. I couldn't control someone like Tasia. If a Tasia or any other porn girl wanted to climb on my vines . . . well, there it was. Pumper jumped into the backseat of the limo, saluting me like a soldier, and DK laughed and dug it, and I waved as they all drove away.

That night, I showed Timberlake how to write a check out to himself.

SIXTEEN

The following morning, Pitts wished us farewell and Godspeed.

"Got to head back to Seattle for a little while," he said. "Take care of business up there. But don't worry. I'll be available by phone if you need me."

"But . . . who's gonna handle the house?" I asked, surprised.

"You guys," Pitts said, laughing. "I can trust you not to burn the place down, right?"

"Right," Timberlake agreed. "You can trust us."

Will's inaugural shoot was that afternoon. His girl's name was Veronica Light and she didn't have a manager or a driver, so it was up to us to drive into West Hollywood and pick her dumb ass up at Reb's PGI. Even though I had only been up in the mountains for about two days, the hard, yellow light and bad smell of the real LA now disturbed me. After enjoying a steamy stall shower and only wiping your ass with baby wipes, you really got used to being a rich guy and comparing yourself to Tom Selleck in the fogless mirror. The smoggy, transsexual, hard LA light really bothered me now.

"So, you like this town so far?"

"Love it," Timberlake said, dryly.

"What about porn?" I asked him. "Got any questions?"

"Sam." He looked at me. "Come on, man. This is the easiest job known to man. I'm gonna knock it out of the park."

I sighed. "I'm there for you. Just so you know. I got your back."

Veronica was eighteen years old and sitting on a stoop out in front of Reb's. She had bottle-blond hair with deep, dark roots. Her hair was as short as a boy's; you looked at her and just imagined she had cut it herself with a pair of scissors standing naked in front of a mirror one afternoon when she was bored and drunk and possessed by Satan. Reb's Pretty Girl had the ability to give us just the craziest talent in the land, C- and D-listers who would do four or six scenes and absolutely fade the fuck away or commit themselves to mental asylums. To exist for a good long time in the adult industry, one must be thick-skinned and lucky; also, it helps to be pretty. Veronica Light was chubby, bordering on ugly. Some companies actually preferred the ugly girls, Extreme Associates for example. It fit their degrading aesthetic. They hated women and wanted to represent them in the absolute worst light possible, so it helped if they hired really ugly young girls with pleasant pancake tits who would eat hamburger meat out of a garbage can. But there weren't enough companies like Extreme out there to support the Veronicas, Butters, Charitys, and Candyliciouses of the world. So they would do their four scenes and then disappear, and then the next one would arrive.

As Timberlake snaked through traffic like a demented Italian race-car driver, simply *daring* the complicated LA gridlock to stymie him, I stroked Veronica's shoulders from the backseat. Sleazy, I know, but I couldn't help it—she was glassy-eyed and her affect was weird, but all in all, she had something to her. She sort of reminded me of a dippy aunt or a matron on the Hebrew School bus, and something about that made my dick stand up on end. She seemed receptive to my rubbing, and looked back and let her hand come back into the backseat. We held hands for about ten minutes, her sweaty little palm in mine. She wore jean shorts and I looked at her thighs. They were illuminated by a patch of sunlight that came through Timber's windshield and only disappeared for a few seconds at a time as the car would slip beneath an overpass.

"I'm exactly twenty-five-and-a-half-years old," Timberlake announced to the car. "I start my porn career today."

"I'm eighteen and a half," Veronica Light said, bouncily. "I started my porn career two weeks ago."

"My mother *called* me on my birthday, you guys," Timberlake said.

"That was nice of her," I commented, still stroking Veronica's little hand, wondering if I could put it on my penis. Or if that would be too much.

"I did not enjoy her call. She called me at twelve-oh-five A.M. She has never called me past eight P.M. in the seven years since I left home. She seemed to be manic, and I found her emotional disposition and the very fact that she was calling me to be invasive. Her call made me angry. I was not super friendly. In fact, I was cold. She tried to get my fourth stepdad, a man whom I've only met once and spoken to once, to sing 'Happy Birthday' to me. He refused. I said thanks anyway. She told me I was ruining something perfect and fun, and hung up on me."

"Your mom probably missed you," Veronica decided.

"She doesn't know how to do it right," Timberlake said. "Hey, am I headed in the right direction?"

"You're good," I assured him. "Ride the Ten to the Pacific Coast Highway. Super easy."

"I want to jack off," Timberlake said. "I must be honest and say that the type of women in porn that I find most arousing have similar body types to my mom."

"He does this from time to time," I explained to Veronica. "He rambles."

"I *like* it," Veronica said, taking her hand back and caressing her own breast. She seemed to be checking it for lumps.

"I've let my mom back into my life several times," Timberlake said, steering the car carelessly with one hand. "Each instance has been disastrous and ended with damage done to facets of my personal life that my mother never had access to in the first place."

"My oh my," Veronica Light whispered, clutching her tit.

"I remember when my mom forced me to go to her psychiatrist. He diagnosed me as bipolar in five minutes. I guess he thought he was psychic, I don't know. He opened up his top desk drawer and it was filled to the brim with Zoloft samples, and he tossed a bottle to me from across the room. 'Give it a go.'"

We rode along, watching furniture stores and vintage shops stream by us. Soon we found the on-ramp to Highway 10 and merged into an army of vehicles. Wheels were turning in Veronica's head. Finally she spoke. "I don't think your mom is *mad* at you," she said to Timberlake, shyly. "I think she wants to say . . . 'I'm sorry.'"

Timberlake frowned grimly, pushing his maroon Subaru to its limit as it choked and sputtered. "*Dude!* That bitch was seriously unstable! To this *day* she's nutty. Her Social Security benefits are about to run out so she's thinking about going back to vocational school for the fourth time. She's been a medical transcriptionist, accounts payable, data entry, and now I think she makes *dolls* in her spare time.

The kicker is, every time she goes back to community college for a shiny new career, she gets the highest grades in the class. She fucking *excels*! My mom isn't dumb, she's just really fucked up!"

Veronica Light patted Timberlake's neck sympathetically.

We twisted along the Pacific Coast Highway, taking in the Santa Monica coastline and the brownish desert hills. On the right, we passed restaurants advertising grilled trout and malty brews. We spiraled up the mountain, a winding ten-minute drive. When we reached the house, Timberlake punched in the security code, and the gate swung open. On our way to the front door, the immaculate house loomed over us, huge and impassive. Veronica's eyes widened appreciatively. "This is *weird*," she gasped. To her, everything was a revelation.

Neither of our actors was there yet, so I donned a brown Brazilian bathing suit and asked Veronica if she would like to stretch out in the sun with me. She said yes, although she had no bathing suit, so she just laid out in her bra and panties and in no time, she took those off, too. Some flab hung over her hips, but lying back on a white deck chair, gravity did its job, and all the flab settled back into the pit of her guts. Her tits moved off the center of her chest, hanging off the sides of her ribs like pale saddlebags. I squinted up at the sun, then gazed back down at my skin. I wasn't quite as tan as I would have liked, but I was working on it, which is more than I could say for Timberlake, who was fretting over his XL-1, reading the instruction manual nervously, paying no attention to either of us. I had a bag of stone-ground tortilla chips with me and a yellow pack of American Spirits, and I offered both to Veronica Light, but she begged off.

"You feeling nervous?" I asked.

"Nope," she said, smiling. "It's not a big deal to me."

"Do you want, like, a massage?" I said hopefully.

She shrugged.

Then I asked if I could kiss her. She grinned: "You really like me, huh?"

I nodded. Maybe I did, maybe I didn't. She seemed pliable, though; more, she was there. We made out for a little bit, but there was no pulse. After a while, I just stopped kissing her. Veronica Light smiled peacefully and put her concentration back into her own head. Instantly, it was like her nose was buried in some invisible book.

Timberlake's actors arrived soon/ thereafter. They were a pair of veterans named Darren James and Julian St. Jox. I knew St. Jox by name, because I had watched his high-top fade and big ass star in about a hundred '90s pornos. He was the face of the black '90s, along with Sean Michaels. He was about thirty-nine and had a great laugh and a nice belly on him. I liked the veterans—it was like having Wes Unseld and Elgin Baylor in your living room fucking a girl. Darren James was about thirty-five or so, a grown man with a perfect Marines body. He had about 1 percent body fat. Darren wasn't as fun as St. Jox, wasn't cool like him, but he was a Derek Fisher–like consummate professional, who could always be counted on to drain his free throws and maybe even sink a clutch three-pointer from the corner in the late stages of the game.

Timberlake got Veronica into the upstairs bathroom.

"But I don't have my makeup with me," Veronica said.

"Well, then take this," he told her kindly, folding a Summer's Eve douche into her young, troll-like palm.

Hurriedly, he photocopied Light's IDs on the big HP scanner/copier that Pitts had bestowed upon us, and then, before we could stop her, she was in her underwear, waiting expectantly for him to turn on the camera in the guest room. The lights were blazing up directly at the ceiling. St. Jox and James hovered nearby, curious.

Timberlake was ready to go, but his feet weren't set. When he perched that heavy gray XL-1 on his shoulder, the machine wobbled, and he had a devil of a time finding the on/off button, and when the tiny wheels were set in motion, the DV tape whirring and stirring, Veronica Light was like *Do I go now*, and Timberlake was nodding furiously behind his giant '80s shoulder cam, and she began frigging herself thoughtlessly, her thumb raking against the wrinkly skin of her clitoris, as she whispered, *"This is how I do it at home."* Timberlake struggled to one knee to get a different take on her masturbation, then thought better of it—"Sweetie? I need you to bend over?"—then rose to his feet, grunting, the mouthpiece of the camera rapping awkwardly against his thigh, vibrations visible to all of us.

Julian St. Jox made contact with Veronica Light—a respectful, sportsmanlike sort of greeting—as he grabbed her breasts and hocks, testing them for firmness. Neither spoke. Neither smiled. St. Jox led her to the bed, where with little ado, he claimed his prize. And Veronica Light began screaming, just screaming, not like your normal moans and groans—more like electric animal madness:

WHOOOOOOOOOOOOOOO*hoooooooo!*

WHOOOOie-HOOOO!

Jox, unperturbed, pinned her body to the cold, chafing mattress and pounded into her, getting his. WHOOOOOOOOOOOOOOO-HOOOOOO, and then Darren took over, and all of a sudden, as suddenly as she had begun, Veronica Light stopped screaming. In a lifeless sort of parody of porn passion, she said, completely deadeyed Dick, her eyes like two black, cast-iron skillets: "Give me some of that chocolate dick."

"Give me that chocolate."

"Give me that chocolate . . . dick." Dead as could be.

Then later, back to St. Jox, and again, the howling:

WHOOOOOOOOOOOOOOOeehoooooooo!

I watched it, confused and slightly scared. Timberlake and I made eye contact and shared a tiny laugh for a second. Were we frightened or amused? I couldn't tell, exactly. The windows were closed, our vast compound deserted and locked, no one to hear us.

SEVENTEEN

It was evening and hot with summer. Timberlake and I reclined at a picnic table on the back deck of the Reel Inn, our new favorite casual Pacific Coast Highway red-checked-tablecloth restaurant getaway, to which a man may retire after a long day of shooting hard-driving black porn. Having been porno millionaires for nearly an entire fortnight, we deserved a break.

"Terri is not *happy*," Timberlake sighed, fork in hand, spearing his free-range white trout.

"What's the problem?" Terri was his girlfriend, who was still up in Oakland, waiting for him.

"Oh, she's convinced I'm gonna sleep with one of these girls," Timberlake continued, staring at the space in front of him. "Paranoia." He sighed again dramatically, then dipped his forkful of fish into a ceramic ramekin of sudsy tartar sauce, contemplating it, cat-like and depressed.

"Think she's got anything there?"

"I love her, dude," Timberlake said. "I think about her at night and I sympathize with what she's going through. Oftentimes, I can't believe that I'm putting her through this ordeal."

I nodded, sipping from a plastic cup of water with lemon wedges. Around us, conversations buzzed. A couple who sat at the table to my left looked like they might be here on a date. The guy was in his early thirties, wore a fitted red baseball cap, and carried a couple extra pounds on his belly and man-tits.

"Look, T," I said, as gently as I could. "You're here now. You're checking porn out. Trying it on for size. If you hate it, you could always quit."

"What makes you think that I *hate* it?" Timberlake snapped, whipping his gaze from his fish to me. "It's fucking *hilarious*. Only an idiot would hate this job. I love this job. I'm not quitting. Not for anything."

"Okay, Jesus . . . you were talking about Terri, and I just thought . . . Don't bite my head off."

"I'm not biting anyone's *head* off," Timberlake said. "I'm *talking* about things. You're great to talk to." Timberlake picked up a piece of steamed broccoli with his bare hand and looked underneath it suspiciously, as if checking for a fungus. But then suddenly, his mood shifted and he was jovial. "Ohmy*god*: Aurora Snow!"

"I know," I grinned, pleased the storm had changed direction. "Incredible, right?"

"Splen-dacious, my good man!" Timberlake announced. He unleashed his crazy, loud laugh. "*Splen-dacious!*" Some of the people on the patio turned around to look at him. "She looked like a runway model. I was gonna come all over myself when she stepped through the door. Now listen," he said, his voice lowering slightly, "what *I* don't get is why *you* always get the hot girls and I always seem to shoot the dogs?"

"Just my good luck, I guess." I shrugged, looking past him, inside, to the girl working the cash register. She was about twenty years old, maybe ten pounds overweight, but it sat right, brown hair streaked with blond, looking busy and sweating lightly with effort and kitchen heat. Behind her, dishes got washed loudly, and I watched her heavy tits go up and down against her tight, dirty T-shirt.

"Good luck my wide *ass*. You're tilting the tables in your favor. Admit that, at least."

"I know this business," I admitted. "I know the girls. I know which ones I want. But hey, man—you'll get it. We've only been going for a couple of weeks. You'll get the handle."

"Why do you always say I'm gonna get it, I'll catch the handle . . ." Timberlake whined. "*Boy*, you act like this job's rocket science . . ."

"Excuse me," I interrupted him, "I think my fish is ready." I scooted out from behind the pine picnic table to retrieve my tilapia, my topsiders slapping the wood of the deck, triumphantly sockless in new shoes, the pads of my toes gripping the new leather.

Two straight weeks in the Malibu sun had browned my skin. Wandering around the compound one evening, I had discovered a fitness room, set off from the main house, carpeted and equipped with its own Soloflex machine. Several times already I had visited the fitness room, working out as the spirit moved me, pumping iron, practicing a variety of yogic poses, as well as using the elliptical and the stationary bike. Or reverting back to the good ol' basics upon which you can never improve: pull-ups, push-ups, and crunches. My hair was growing, too, past the awkward stage, curling in ringlets around my head. I rubbed myself down with good shampoos, no longer content to just take a bar of soap to my head like I used to. Somehow, even my *eyes* looked good. They had never looked right to me before. Now, for the first time in my life, I felt people watching my eyes as I talked.

"Look," I said, rejoining Timberlake at the picnic table, my plate balanced in my hand. "Just tell her, baby, my penis is *way* too small for these porn girls. Tell her they laugh when you pull it out."

"That might be true," Timberlake considered. "Ten of my dicks would fit inside one of Pumper's." He stared at me gravely.

"We're dealing with monster dicks here," I agreed, cutting into the breaded fish.

"*Cartoon* dicks," Timber laughed. He and I never tired of talking about penises. We never tired about talking about enormous boobs, either. There were downsides to shooting porn with a friend: namely, you never talked about anything but porn.

"What do you have lined up for tomorrow?"

"I'm not shooting," said Timberlake. "I'd like to, though. What about you, you shooting?"

"Nope. DK hasn't called me back yet."

"These agents are all the same," Timber said. "World Modeling is holding out on me."

"How about Reb's?" I suggested.

"Reb's is just skanks," he said disdainfully. He sniffed at his fish.

"Reb's has the ugly girls down pat," I agreed.

"Sure," said Timberlake.

"Veronica Light came from Reb's," I pointed out.

"Ohmy*god*," Timber hollered. The guy wearing the red baseball cap turned, annoyed. Timberlake didn't see him. "She *digs* your *schvantz*, dude!" He giggled. "You gotta get on that."

"What are you talking about?" I frowned.

"Veronica. I gave her a ride home, and the whole way back, I forgot to tell you, she kept on talking about how *hot* you were."

"Come on, you must be kidding me. She totally ignored me."

"Not at all," Timberlake said. "Man, I can't believe I didn't tell you about that night." He slapped his hand against his forehead. "She wants your putz. In her mouth. It's true. For the life of me, I can't figure out why, but goddamn, there it is. By the way, she didn't even remember where she *lived*. We were in the car together for about three hours. I almost gave up. She was loopy. Eventually we had dinner together at some diner in the Valley. Nightmare."

"Sounds romantic."

"Give me some credit," Timberlake said.

I sighed. "So where did she live?"

"Huh?"

"Where'd you *drop her off?*" I said testily.

"Jeez, you know? I can't remember," said Timberlake. "Everything looks the same out here." He grinned at me and picked up the broccoli in his hand once again and sniffed at it carefully. He chuckled, then threw it over his left shoulder.

"Now look, *goddammit*, you guys!" yelled the guy with the red baseball cap.

Timber whirled to face him. "What?" he said, a huge smile on his face. He was laughing, loud and hearty. "Are you making a broccoli *arrest*, pardner?"

"No, I'm just . . ." Red cap looked at his date, who was watching him and watching us dispassionately, like we were TV. She wasn't so bad. But her hair was mousy, and she was holding herself a bit too tightly, like something might unwind if she let it go. Maybe her large intestine. Maybe she was waiting for the date to end so she could go home and take a nice smelly shit that would snake its way around the toilet bowl.

"You're just . . . *what?*" Timber grinned. He was a master at getting under someone's skin. When threatened, he was rapid and relentless and viciously annoying. Timberlake would take a punch to the face happily, if it meant that would piss off the guy who threw it.

"We're very sorry, sir," I interjected. I put my hand on Timberlake's. "My boyfriend's having his period."

"Yeah!" Timberlake exclaimed. "Right! My *boyfriend* and I are just having an argument about who gets to be on top tonight." Both of us gazed longingly at each other, then started laughing uncontrollably.

Red baseball cap stared a hole in us, but he didn't get up. He just exhaled deeply and shook his head. Likewise, his girl said nothing. Her eyes said nothing. Her arms were squeezing around her middle, holding everything in.

A couple of nights later, White Liz called me. She certainly had an interesting flirting style: half insults and half compliments, alternating the whole time, so you were constantly off balance. Neat little trick. At first I was too intimidated to keep up, but luckily, I managed to marshal together what little balls I had and invited her over to hang out on a Friday night. *Maybe we'll try out the Jacuzzi*, I said in a Pumper-like tone. She laughed but then agreed, and I was glad. Suddenly I had a date to look forward to, with a normal girl.

On Friday, Timberlake asked, "How do I look, dude?"

"What the hell are you talking about?" I said. "Why do you care how *you* look?"

"*Liiiiizzzz*, man! I gotta look good for little Lizzie! She's a hottie!"

"She's coming over here for me, douche," I reminded him.

"It's Friday night. She's open game."

"Open *game*? You are fuckin' crazy, kid. *She-called-for-me.*"

"Relax, relax. I am merely trying to look *good*," Timberlake said, grinning. "Got my hair cut today—what do you think?" He reached up on a high shelf for a glass tumbler, exposing the wobbly line carved in his reddish neck hair.

"Looks like you went to SuperCuts."

"I went to SuperCuts," he announced. "It was the only place I could find! I think they did a great job, though!"

"You fucking tool," I said.

"*Hey*," Timber began, with an outraged look on his wide face, but just then the doorbell rang. "*I'll* get that."

I buried my head in my hands and let him bring White Liz into the house.

"Hi, guys!" She smiled at us. "Where should I put this?" She held a twelve-pack of Tecate.

"I'll take that, darlin'," Timberlake said suavely, winking at me, removing two cans from the box, then stopping, as if remembering something important. "Beer, Samuel?"

"Yes," I said thinly. "Hi, Liz. Thanks for coming over."

She smiled. "Thanks for having me. You look cute."

"*You* look cute." She did. White Liz had curly red hair and tiny tits and a tiny ass and summer-ripe skin and all her tattoos were complemented by a sharp way of dressing that wasn't afraid to use Lycra to show off every little inch of her tight twenty-two-year-old body. Her face was her best feature, though: pixieish and lightly freckled in a childish way, yet the eyes were bright, intelligent, and even wry.

"What about me? Don't *I* look cute?" Timberlake preened.

"What's with him?" Liz asked, frowning.

"I think he's chaperoning."

"I am not," said Timberlake. "However, it is Friday night, and seeing as my girlfriend is in Oakland, and I have no other plans, I will be preparing my evening meal in the same dining space as you two. That is, if you don't mind. After all, you don't own this place."

"You can join us, dude," White Liz said. "More the merrier."

"See, Samuel?" Timber said, pleased. "More the merrier."

I'd planned on making pasta, and Timber said he would prepare *a rice pilaf*, but in the end, we all decided to just order a pizza. As we ate, we sat around the table and talked shop. White Liz regaled us with DK stories.

"You guys, he's *disgusting*. I seriously can't deal with it."

"What does he do?"

"Well, first of all, he *loves* it when he gets a new girl in there. It's like his birthday. First he brags for a while about how much money he's going to make her, and who his connections are. He *always* mentions the Ice-T video."

"Ice-T?"

"Yep. Ice-T produced a porno this spring; you guys didn't know about that?"

"Nope," I admitted.

"Yeah, well, DK got him all his girls. So within the first ten minutes of meeting any new girl, he tells her how he *supplied* all the *talent* for the porno that his *good friend Ice-T produced!*" The last few words were in a deep baritone, which I assumed was White Liz's impersonation of a buffoonish DK.

"Then he takes the girls on a 'tour' of the grounds," she continued, disdainful. "Sometimes I have to come with him, to legitimize his whole act. He's always got his hand on the small of the girl's back, and he's like dying to put it on her ass, but he's too scared. Then at a certain point, he asks me to 'go get his video camera' and he mentions that he'd like to 'take some test shots.' It's all so fucking predictable, it would be hilarious—that is, if I hadn't seen it like a million times by this point."

"He's a decent man," I said to Timberlake.

"*Decent?*" Liz snorted. "He's a fucking moron. He hits on me almost as much as he does on his girls! If he could figure out a way to get me naked, I swear he would declare it a national holiday or something."

"He hits on you?"

"He's in *love* with me!"

"Insatiable appetite," I commented to Timberlake. "Not his fault."

"Why are you defending him? He's *repugnant*. And he's not the only one! Brian! Brian is a creep-in-training!"

"*Pumper!*" we squealed, delighted.

"He's a sick kid," Liz said, looking nauseated indeed. "I think he's obsessed with me. I'm not trying to toot my own horn here, believe me, I'm not. I really think it's a problem. You know he can't drive, right? Well, yesterday, he told DK that he needs *me* to start driving him to his scenes. I was like, what the fuck? I'm a secretary, not a driver! Brian said he'll *pay* DK if I'll do it."

"He'd like to spend more time with you," I observed.

"He brought me flowers the other day," Liz said, seriously. "Lilies."

"You represent an older sister figure to him."

"Bullshit. He *wants* me. He told me as much. And if he romanticizes me, it's because I don't perform. In his mind, I'm, like, *cleaner*."

Timberlake folded his arms. "Perhaps you *are* cleaner," he pointed out.

"Perhaps," Liz said, a bit grimly. "And on *that* note," she said to me, her eyes narrowing, "did you have fun with that slut?"

"I don't know what you're talking about."

"The midget."

"Tasia?"

"Is *that* what her name is?" White Liz said, sipping her beer.

"Whatsamatter?" I grinned. "Jealous?"

"Just interested."

"She never called me," I admitted.

"Sam waits for girls to call *him*," Timberlake said, laughing. "The *ego* on this kid!" He rapped me on the arm playfully. "You don't mind that I said you have a big ego, right? I mean, it's kinda true. Eh, Liz? No?"

"He's okay," Liz said, grinning at me.

She held my gaze in her serious Liz way, but then she smiled, and so did I. From across the table, she grabbed my arm and pulled on it. "Let's try out that Jacuzzi."

"Hot," Timberlake reminded us. "I need that water *hot*."

The three of us donned swimsuits and charged yelping into churning, burbling wonderful waters. White Liz had switched to rum and Coke and we laughed, and I sipped from her tumbler, my face flushed from the heat and sweet drink, the water jets humming. Timberlake, awash with the pleasure of the night, glided tirelessly from one side of the large brick hot tub to the other, back and forth, his arms swanlike, enveloped in his own narrative. Meanwhile, Liz and I inched toward each other in the tub. The crickets were out, and the summer lawn was freshly cut, and we in the warm waters were surrounded on all sides by nasturtiums and vines you could reach up and touch. Above us in the summer night sky: a sprinkling of stars. The house was dark and thickly windowed, a rock star's mansion we'd stumbled into, with gates that closed noiselessly behind us. I inched closer to the beautiful red-haired twenty-two-year-old who was looking into my eyes more and more fetchingly, and thought, *Dear God, please will you bless Pornography, for her endless bounty? Amen and pass the bread.*

Timber slowed, catching his breath, and examined us, who were by now touching. He grinned. "Am I mistaken, or is there a certain *chemistry* developing here between the two of you?"

"*Right*," I said sternly. "Good night."

"Good night, sweet prince," Timberlake said. "Liz, I'll call you." Cloddishly, he launched himself from the tub, rivulets of chlorinated foam coursing into his eyes. Yelping, he sprinted toward the house, toward the stack of thick white towels, which he would use and then toss on the floor for someone else to pick up.

"How did you meet him, again?" White Liz asked.

"He came with the place. We're in discussions to slit his throat and feed him to the coyotes."

"Can I help?" Liz whispered, floating in the water toward me. My pulse quickened as she placed her face about an inch and a half away from my lips. Liz laid her hands on my face, her palms fragrant and wrinkled. In her gaze, I felt weightless in the water, and she wrapped her tiny perfect legs around me and rubbed up against me with her swimsuited cunt, her tongue on my neck. She was radiating confidence and lust. No hurt, no helplessness; no self-hatred or sickness.

"Let's go inside," she suggested, smiling, and we stood up in the water. Wet and dripping, holding hands, we walked into my pool house bedroom, which still lacked any sort of bed. I rummaged up a towel, and she stood and dried her body in front of me as I watched, admiring her: beautiful and breathless, her rib cage, her eye makeup running. She threw me the towel, and I tousled the fabric across my body, across my head.

She came to me then: one full head shorter, three years younger, a secretary of the porn industry, a child of the dance clubs, just wondering at me, sizing me up, smiling, taunting, being cute, maybe a little drunk, so what, she was skinny and tiny and we dropped down to the floor where I kissed her perfectly shaved and unscented pussy. I licked at her, the scratchy carpet playing against my knees, forgetting who I was, my ass sticking in the air, my fingers straying to her neckbone and shoulder, and I didn't want to crush her on the carpet and burn her back, so I grabbed her to me and her buttocks sat on my thighs and her back *arching*, her body *arching*, and White Liz nipped at my neck like a perfect little baby spider with strong thighs gripped around my waist and my cock grew and bulged and I put my hand on her porcelain throat, and I gripped the roots of her hair, and shook her head gently. I pushed down on her head, until her body fell and her back pressed the floor and I licked at her mouth. My fingers explored her lips and then her white teeth and then I was pushing my fingers into her mouth, *gentle*, and her nails raked into my back, scratching grooves, I rasped *Liz*, but it was way too late, because then we really *were* fucking, the way you do it the first time, when you are anonymous, don't know who you are, don't much care, and I crushed her body into the carpet, her hips and ass so tiny, her tailbone absorbing the brunt of the blow, her hugging me and moving under me and she looked at me so intensely, her freckles glowing, peering into my eyes with so much focus, such a sharpened spotlight, that I felt huge yet somehow vulnerable, and she said *fuck me* with a voice so urgent that I had to swallow twice.

That night, we slept on the floor together, huddled under a big orange comforter, our bodies forming one simple tangle.

It didn't take long before Liz and I were operating as girlfriend and boyfriend. We occupied a similar sort of space, living on the fringes of the industry—she as a fully clothed secretary, I as a director who didn't fuck. Both of us made our living amid the smut pile, but felt more comfortable pretending that we weren't exactly a part of the dirty excess, that we were somewhat removed from it. And to some extent, it was true: to real porn players, we weren't really part of the game; yet among our normal friends, we had secrets to hide. It left both of us feeling kind of alone. So it was hard to fight the feeling that our union, if not predestined, was at the very least something that should be explored.

"My résumé is pretty bad," I explained.

"I don't care."

"I have several black marks against me. I have committed sins on videotape and sold them on the Internet."

"I said, I don't care," repeated Liz. "What I want to know is, are you done? Are you over porn girls?"

"Sure," I said automatically. I paused. "What do you mean?"

"Can you be *faithful*," Liz said.

"Wow. Of course I can. Wow. How can you even ask that?"

"Sam. Come on. There's a new girl over at your house every day of the week."

"I know, Liz. You send most of them to me."

She smiled. "Oh, yeah. I'm like your supplier."

"You're my pimp."

"Whatever," Liz said, smiling. "Look. I like you. I just don't want to be worrying all the time that you're trying to get blown by some crazy whore."

"Liz," I said, giving her my best sincere look. "I'm tired of these girls. I really am. I used to be fascinated, I admit, but it was a phase. I'm looking for someone real."

"I don't know," White Liz said. She shook her head sadly, as if lamenting what she was getting herself into. But then she kissed me. She rolled on top of me and put her tiny muskrat body on mine and we laughed and pressed our faces together and kissed.

Everything is so *easy* when you are in a new relationship. Every single minor good thing about the other person is amplified by the newness of the situation. White Liz had a car, a ten-year-old tan Jaguar with a lockable glove compartment and a powerful motor and leather seats. She looked good driving in it. Nothing special, necessarily; but I decided I was in *love* with that car. How I adored riding around in the passenger seat, responsible for nothing, and listening to her good stereo system. We sped through Hollywood late at night and watched stoplights change from red to green. She was a fast driver; not only that, she dressed well. Not only that, she was a good email writer. In the beginning, the little things awe you, and it's very beautiful.

"Let's get Thai food," White Liz said.

"Terrific. I could go for some Thai food."

"What's your favorite?"

"I don't know—pad Thai? Is that too unoriginal?"

"Pad Thai is for beginners, certainly," Liz said. "Do you know *larb*?"

"No. But it sounds disgusting. What's larb?"

"Sam!" said Liz. "You *have* to try larb! It's the crown jewel of Thai food. Tell you what, I'll order some, and we can share it."

"Sure. I'm game," I said. I liked looking at her face as she drove through traffic, with my hand on her tiny, skinny, muscular thigh; furrowing her cute little brow with concentration, looking for the best parking spot. She was my girl now, and she was beautiful.

"I'm dating someone," I announced to Isaac.

"Incredible," he said. "Does she deep-throat?"

"She's not in the business," I said. "I mean, she is, but she doesn't get naked on film."

"That doesn't answer my question," he said.

"I refuse to talk about it," I said, proudly. "I respect her."

"God, you really *have* gone off the deep end," he said. "Well, when can I meet her?"

"You should come up to the house this weekend. Hell, bring some friends. Let's have a little party. Let's have some normal people up at that place, you know? I want to show you guys where I live.

It's very ugly, but sort of . . . impressive. Bring a bathing suit. Tell everyone!"

Isaac brought eight or so people to Malibu that Friday night, all art-school friends of his. Liz and I greeted everyone at the door, and Timberlake offered them drinks.

"None for me," Isaac said.

"What, you on the *wagon*?" Timberlake laughed.

"I am," Isaac said calmly. "Who's this asshole?" he asked me, hooking his thumb toward the 'Lake.

"He's nothing," I said, apologetically. "I'm afraid you'll have to deal with him."

"Yep, you'll have to *deal* with me," Timberlake crowed. "Cuz I am a porn-making machine, and I am going nowhere."

"I'm very sorry," I said, taking Isaac by the elbow, the better to escort him around the grand house.

The sun going down, we gathered around the circular glass table, the very same table where my porn actors congregated on a daily basis as they waited for their fuck scenes to begin, and we drank our drinks and listened to summer sounds. Some of Isaac's friends, charmed by the house and the grounds, wandered around on the lawn, doing cartwheels. "Whee, man, where the hell *are* we?" The contrast between the hipster east-side gallery life that they knew and a fortressed garden in Malibu was so pleasing for all, it was hard to exaggerate.

"You should come with me for just a second," Liz said to me, gracefully excusing herself from the table with a polite nod. I followed her and her tiny behind, which was clad in tight black pants that had some polyspandex in them, to a first-floor guest room that was crammed full with ugly knickknacks and a rocking chair. She swept a path clear on the ugly, brownish Early American desk, slapping a pair of doilies to the ground, and hopped up on the table.

"I want to make out with you."

"You what?" I asked, coming closer to her.

"I want you to kiss me." She stared at me for a second. "That okay?"

I put my head near hers, smelling her hair, and touched her silky clothes and skin, and we pressed into each other, our skins trembling with electricity and the happiness of something new. Then we moved to the bed, that thick and expensive pillow-top mattress. Not long after, we headed back out to the party, where the conversations were suddenly more provocative, and marked by a good deal more participation by us.

Hours passed, bugs chirped on the grounds, Liz was charming the girls, and I was smoking Isaac's cigarettes and having a deep and dirty talk with his best friend Harry, who was half Italian and half mean, but also a painter and a mathematician in his spare time. Harry had a lot of chips on his shoulder, and there was something pent-up and rageful about him, yet there was something excellent about him, too, you could tell, and you could tell the thing he was mad about was that he hadn't quite discovered how to let the world know how good he was.

"You guys have a great place here," he said, looking off into the impressive vista, at the purple mountains, folding his arms.

"Thanks," I said, sipping a beer. "You know . . . I really like that girl in there," I confided to him.

"Liz? Oh, yeah. You got *lucky*."

"Thanks, man. I think I did."

"She's good-looking."

"Very."

"I would pound her," Harry admitted.

"Sure," I said.

"I would actually do okay in porn," Harry said. "I have a super-big dick."

I said nothing for a second.

"I guess we should be getting back."

"Sure," Harry said, patting me on the shoulder. "Sure, sure. Nice place you got here, man. Best of luck with it."

We all listened to music and gabbed, congregating around the table until it was two o'clock in the morning and Timberlake was depressed and yawning. I brought out an excellent experimental ambient album that I thought would invigorate everyone's spirits, but instead everyone hated it and laughed at it. Eventually Isaac got the troops together, including his buddy Jams, who was wearing heavy-framed glasses and kept on talking about his painting style and the gloves he had to buy tomorrow to paint with and Jams's girlfriend, who *knitted* her paintings, and they got into their cars and readied themselves to drive on down the mountain. Liz and I retired to the guest room, sort of drunk, dead tired, and collapsed into the bed, keeping our clothes on.

"What should we do tomorrow?" I whispered.

"Eat breakfast," she whispered.

"What do you want to eat for breakfast?" I said gently, kissing the top of her head.

She snuggled into my chest. "Biscuits."

"I want hamburgers."

She said nothing, only cuddled more into me.

"Millie's," I mumbled to myself. "We'll go to Millie's, of course."

We curled around each other, into a sweet warm cocoon, apart from the rest of the world.

Three hours later, the sun was out, and it hit us in the face and we had to get up, and Liz brushed her teeth with my toothbrush and tried to smooth her wrinkled clothes. We drove an hour into Silver Lake and ate at Millie's, where I got a chicken-fried steak and a coffee. I remember the hot sauce that they brought to our table. It was the green kind, and it was delicious.

"Let's go over and see my place," I suggested.

We drove over to Echo Park and she saw the roach den, pushed the wire door open. I hadn't been home in weeks, but everything was still there, everything in its spot. My computer, my jar of change.

"I *so* need a shower," White Liz groaned.

"This, er, facility may not meet your expectations," I explained.

"I don't fucking care." She trudged over to the tiny stall shower I called my own, a far cry from Malibu. The beige paint that clung to the shower walls was rumpled and bulging with water stains. The nozzle was dingy, spewing one singular rope of water at you. "Are you just gonna stand there and watch me?" Liz asked.

"No. Of course not," I said quickly. "I'll give you some privacy. Let me get you a towel."

She showered, trying to wash the hangover off her, scrubbing her underarms with an old bar of soap. I waited for her in the anteroom and handed her a gray towel with little strings fraying off it.

"I'm so *tired*," White Liz groaned, collapsing in my arms.

"Come here," I said gently. "I know what you need."

She plopped down on my futon, *whoomp*. "What."

"Massage." I palmed her tiny muscular back, karate-chopped her little buttocks and thighs and the bottom of her calves and soothed her cute little feet, wrung out her traps with my strong hands. I pushed the erectors off her spine, *to the side to the side*, avoiding excess friction over the kidneys, kneading her thighs, stretching her quads, using my index fingers as pointer probes to dig around in the swelling curves of her delts, even paying attention to her cervical spine and occipital ridge. It was terribly hot in my little apartment, and soon both of us were beaded with sweat, sweat under my eyes and in my ears and on the backs of my wrists, but I kept at her, caught up in the moment and in the momentum of the work. Only when my energy was finally and entirely spent did I collapse beside her.

"That was crazy."

"Sorry," I whispered.

"For what?" Liz murmured. "I meant, it was good."

"No. It's too hot in here. I'm sorry my place is such a shithole."

"But I love it here," she whispered, unexpectedly. "Really."

Slowly, she turned her head to look at me. Her face was kind of mashed by the pillow and partially hidden, but I saw that she was smiling.

Despite being in a new relationship, and despite the fact that I was spending the majority of my waking professional hours watching other people getting nailed right in front of me while I filmed them for hours on end, masturbating was still something that I liked to do. Indulging in my own fantasy life, with the doors locked, in front of my own television, still retained its own attraction.

My porn tastes had evolved somewhat since the early, heady days of the Santa Cruz flea market. Like any connoisseur, I'd become less interested in your run-of-the-mill crapola. These days, I found that to get high, I needed something that pushed the envelope.

Though I'm ashamed to admit it, and even more loath to describe the contents therein, a videotape called *Slap Happy* was my porn of choice that summer. Due to my fascination with said tape (I watched it at least once every day for a while, which is absolutely remarkable for pornographic materials, which so frequently never receive even a single repeat viewing), a summation in these pages seems rather necessary to explain my burgeoning sexual preferences, and by extension, what happened next in my life. So here goes, and I'm going to choke through the guilt.

Slap Happy, 120 minutes in length and shot on videotape in the great tradition of gonzo, consisting of ten or so extraordinarily hardcore blowjob scenes ranging anywhere from six to fifteen minutes apiece, was a pornographic "movie" created in the year 2000 by a Canadian actor/director named Brandon Iron for the production company Extreme Associates. As described earlier, Extreme, owned by Rob Black, had made a name for itself from the moment of its inception in the late 1990s as the most disrespectful and wholly misanthropic video team in the United States of America. Their lines (among them *Cock Smokers*, *Creampie Milkshakes*, *House of Whores*, *Fuck Pigs*, *Euro Cuntz*, *Anal Blitzkrieg*, *Ghetto Bitches*, *Oral Hygiene*, *Spare Parts*, *Asshole O-Mio*, *Cum Catchers*, and, simply, *Go Fuck Yourself*) garnered huge fan support from mean old men who wanked at home alone; this was no "couples" audience. Dudes who were never going to have sex again loved Extreme's movies. Thick with hate, chalky with self-loathing, people got destroyed in Extreme's movies, and the directors laughed. *Slap Happy* only raised the bar.

The long and short of it (why put this off? sigh) was that Brandon's chosen girls, many of whom were young and anonymous looking—they were not "names"—would start off giving Brandon a blowjob, but within ten or so seconds, their hair was getting pulled and I mean *pulled*; it was like he was trying to yank off their wigs. And their faces were getting slapped, we're talking hard: *crack!* Then Brandon's monstrous penis was jamming around in their throats like a mop handle. In several of the scenes, his penis functioned like a plunger in the depths of the actresses' throats, and they would vomit a brown mixture all over his legs, and he would have to stop the tape. When enough footage had been filmed and enough mouth had been fucked as roughly as a pussy, he would take a moment and produce a washable marker from his backpack and pen one word across their foreheads, in red or blue. Sometimes it was SLUT; sometimes it was WHORE. Another option was CUNT. It depended. Then he would take his huge, thick dick in his hand—it was so big that he couldn't even put his whole hand around it—and he would wrench the foreskin up and down until he reached a climax, the video camera whirring on a tripod in a hotel room, and he'd masturbate onto their faces, usually aiming for their noses, and then he would use his giant dick, which was often still hard, to push his ejaculate into their mouths and, generally, the girl would swallow it.

I felt like a deviant watching *Slap Happy*, that much was for sure. But goddamn if it wasn't fascinating. First, I was shocked that this was even *legal*. Iron filmed short interviews with all the girls beforehand, asking them to nod and agree that they were "into rough sex," but it was so transparent they were doing it for the money and the attention, it was sad to see them lie. I mean, certainly it was possible that a handful of them were "kinky" like they said, and "adventurous," but for the most part, these girls were only eighteen years old, and some of them were obvious little drug fiends, the kind that Extreme specialized in finding and turning upside down until gummy juices ran out of them. Some were runaways with infected eyebrow piercings and boyfriends waiting in the car for them to get the money, some were midlevel strippers at some terrible club where the patrons threw soiled dollar bills at them, and some were just plain unlucky, and fortune had conspired to put them into the shittiest porno movie of all time. Iron astonished me in how open and unashamed he was with his rage. He wanted to slap someone—so he did it! (Was it that easy?) I was shocked at myself, at how my cock stood up on end and wanted to be alone with this tape while being touched.

I mean, I'm no beast. I still thought of myself as a happy-go-lucky, awkward kinda guy. That's why it sort of surprised me: that I liked to see their faces distort, wrap around a huge cock, and then choke—the sound of it—the gurgling, the tears in their eyes. It was like they were getting hurt and humiliated, drooling thick spittle, and sometimes there was a look in their eyes: hate. Or with other girls, it was even worse than that—there was this kind of sad *docility*. Sometimes I'd look at a girl, and I'd be naked and masturbating, and in the peace of my bedroom, I'd consider the video screen, and I'd think, suddenly, *She never had a chance. She just thinks she's a shit-hole.* She got dealt a bad hand, and now *Slap Happy* is getting made at her expense, and there are guys in basements all over Cleveland and Cincinnati and Auburn and Bakersfield slipping away from their wives after dinner with a quick *gonna work on my lathe for a little while, hon,* locking the door behind them, watching her slip deeper into a sad oblivion. Big, flat hand across her fucking face, whacked in the head with a left and then a right, jizzed on and throat-choked, falling over with WHORE scrawled in blue clown lipstick all over her dumbass rosy cheeks.

EIGHTEEN

It was evening and the house smelled like cheap lube. Timberlake and I sat around the postapocalyptic kitchen, spent from the day's porno labors, too exhausted to move.

"I've been receiving some negative emails from Pitts," Timberlake confided. "Hurtful stuff."

"Why the hell is Pitts emailing you?" I asked.

"According to him, I keep on shooting *dogs*. He says I need to get my act together and find some better-looking girls." Timberlake shook his head, miserably. "Pitts sure can write a mean email."

I put my arm around him. "You can sleep with me tonight, if you think it'll help."

"You *ass*hole. You unsympathetic prick. Listen, I was an asshole as a teenager. I admit it," said Timberlake. "But I grew out of it. You never did."

"I got straight A's back then," I said proudly. "My dad paid me to study for the SATs. Did I ever tell you that?"

"You were a nerd," Timberlake explained. "I had a couple of friends like you, a couple of goody two-shoes brainiacs. I had to work at *Little Caesars* for spending money. Boy, you were lucky. You got *coddled*."

"Fuck you," I said, laughing. "You have no idea of the dark night that is my soul."

"Dark night of your *soul*?" Timberlake said. "Dark this, kiddo: for a whole *year* of my life, I was forced to take lithium and Depakote. My mother and her abusive shrink stripped away every ounce of control I had in my life. Dude, I had long grunge hair when I was in high school! The Depakote made my *hair* fall out!"

"You must have looked very odd," I murmured.

"I looked *awesome!*" Timber roared. "You couldn't even *tell* the hair was falling out unless you got up close and looked. And see, that was actually the problem. My mom convinced the doctor that I was lying, so I could stop taking the meds. The quack wouldn't take me off the Depakote unless I brought them a Baggie full of hair. So chunks of my hair are falling out, and they expect me to walk around school putting it into a *bag*."

I opened up a kitchen cabinet and stared deep into it: nothing but a box of wheat crackers. I closed the cabinet, leaving a lube stain on the wood.

"Fortunately," Timberlake continued, "two weeks later, my mom hit the jackpot with a high-manic cycle and euphorically de-cided to move towns and let me stop taking meds altogether. Cool, huh?"

I said nothing, hearing the sound of the front door opening. Its smooth, oaken heft brushed against the floor. Keys jingled into a ceramic dish. A suitcase dropped against the ground. And Pitts stood there in front of us, back from Seattle.

"Good trip?" I offered.

"Let's go out to a titty bar," Pitts said, with an exhausted sigh. "I'm in the mood for it."

Timberlake cowered behind me, scared to death that he'd shot one ugly-girl scene too many. But Pitts was sincere: he just wanted to see some swinging tits. Pitts was like that. He was always sending you scary emails, but when you saw him in real life, he was never mad at all.

"Um, sensational," Timberlake managed weakly. But behind Pitts's back, he beamed, and went to go fetch his hat. It seemed Timber had nine lives. Outside, the crickets chirped.

We journeyed into the West Valley, chugging along in the Volvo. As I drove, I watched Pitts from the corner of my eye. He was tired from his journey, quiet and a bit preoccupied, but he held the power in the car, nonetheless. You simply couldn't stop sensing him. I mean, his tractor beam? You wouldn't believe. Hell, by the time we made it out to Bob's Classy Lady, pride of Van Nuys, he almost had *me* in his lap . . . Timberlake, too. We were telling all our best stories, *Man you should have seen Celine Maxima! They make 'em differently in Holland, I guess!* And boy, *Calli Cox can take one, she's a midwestern housewife-whore, best in breed!* He had us boasting and bragging and competing for his attention like he was someone's cool older brother.

Pitts was odd and impenetrable. That was his beauty. Like a lot of eccentric rich people who had focused their lives on one singular goal, he didn't seem overly concerned with making friends, but strangely, with Pitts, that didn't come off as narcissistic. More, it was patently obvious that he just wasn't *interested*. And because of who he was, and how he carried himself, you never considered resenting him for it. Instead it just added to his charisma.

We parked in the mostly deserted lot, loped our way to the front, showed IDs, and paid the cover. "Need a drink?" I asked the boys.

"Sure," said Pitts. He passed me a twenty. "Lemon Drop."

As I waited for the bartender to get our drinks (*Lemon Drop?*), I watched Timberlake and Pitts take up seats at a table underneath the strippers, laughing. Timberlake pulled out his wallet and put it on the table. Right then, I could tell he was going to squander every dime in there. Not to impress Pitts, or to show his gratefulness for keeping him on board, or anything like that. He was just a guy who loved to shit away everything good he had, including money.

"Here you go," the bartender said.

Clutching the drinks between my outstretched fingers, I tiptoed over the bumpy, cigarette-burned strip-bar carpet. As I walked, I gazed up at a dancing girl, transfixed by her tits. It was astounding: I could shoot every day for a month, the most graphic stuff you'd ever heard of, and still I never tired of seeing naked women. I wondered if there was something wrong with me.

"Thank you, Sam," Pitts said, as I placed our drinks on the table.

"Cheers, buddy," said Timberlake. He sipped at his beer.

Two girls named Golden and DanceHer writhed sexily up on the stage to a shitty song with lots of guitars in it. They wore pasties and bathing suit bottoms: you couldn't get fully nude in places where they served alcohol. Pitts sipped at his Lemon Drop, fished in his pocket for dollar bills, and dropped a handful onstage carelessly. The girls cased him from the corners of their eyes, their interest piqued.

"Strippers are interesting people," Pitts reflected.

"I don't understand them," I confessed. "They won't let me inside their heads."

"I've gotten to know some Seattle girls quite well," said Pitts. "We've partied, and they're fairly solid human beings. Strippers like me for my money, but that's understandable, as I like them for their looks. It's a totally workable, equitable transaction."

"I dislike their names," I offered. "DanceHer is not a good name."

"Well, first thing you have to realize is that they're not like you or me, Sam," Pitts said. "They don't have degrees, and whatnot. You shouldn't come to a strip club and expect to find yourself up onstage."

"Take DanceHer as she is," suggested Timberlake, dropping his own slew of dollar bills up onstage magnanimously. "You'll be happier."

Both of the girls approached the edge of the stage, leaned on the railing, and crouched athletically, bopping their asses together in a crude sexual pantomime and staring hungrily at Pitts, who didn't acknowledge either of them.

"I can't remember when I first realized that sex with a stripper was probably the dirtiest sex I was going to be able to find without actually going to a hooker," Pitts said, "but it was a big moment. Yes, *essentially* it was paid for, but it wasn't quite prostitution, either, and that felt important. I'd stumbled across that rare, fine line, a special no-man's-land where things were smutty and exciting, without being truly disgusting."

"Porn girls are in that category, too," I pointed out. "They're not really whores, except sometimes they are."

"Right," Pitts said, nodding. "I'm very curious to see what makes them tick."

"What makes them *tick*!" repeated Timberlake, hooting. He slurped at his beer. He was the kind of guy who got tipsy from a swallow. It all went straight to his head. "I know where *this* is headed!"

"I may attempt to meet a few of our starlets," Pitts admitted. "Curiosity." He pulled out a wad of bills and thumbed through them, finding a twenty. "Watch this. These women have excellent eyesight. They know when a twenty hits the stage."

Timberlake and I laughed. "They sense the big bills."

"Yes," Pitts said, shaking his head good-naturedly. "And the big spenders. Of course, I'd prefer to be admired for my looks, or my bravery, but in the absence of any of that, I'll take affection any way I can get it." He smiled a bit sheepishly, then blinked his eyes quickly, as if remembering something. "Oh, hey, good news. Rag Man's thinking of joining us for a while."

Timberlake's jaw dropped. "You're *kidding*."

Rag Man was a legend. He was our editor. None of us had ever met him, but we'd heard the stories. He lived in a musty basement in Pittsburgh with his wife and spent all his waking hours watching porn scenes with a jeweler's eye for imperfection. He ate porn and shat out boob jobs. His labial knowledge dwarfed that of an average aficionado. He laughed cruelly at what we had accomplished thus far.

"Not at all. Is that a problem?"

"No . . . it's just . . ." Timberlake's voice trailed off miserably. "Why?"

"He wants to shoot a second camera during both of your scenes. That way, we'll have more angles to use during edits."

"But that's crazy," I said. "I get all the angles we need."

"Maybe Rag Man has a different opinion," Pitts said, reasonably.

"You gotta understand," I said firmly. "We sort of have a *system* going. I like to create an intimate atmosphere for my actors."

"Yeah," cried Timber, unhappily. "Another body could tip the scales in ways we can't predict!"

"Take it easy, you two," Pitts said, calmly. "Take it easy. Rag Man's never been out to California before. He's worked as my editor for a lot of years—he deserves something nice. He wants to be *around* porn. See it up close. Don't you understand that?"

I sighed. I did. "Of course."

"So it's all right with you?"

"Yeah," sighed Timberlake. "But tell him not to yell at me, okay?"

"Nobody's yelling at anyone," Pitts said. He sipped at his Lemon Drop and dropped another handful of bills onstage, quietly. The girls kept right on dancing. "People say things they don't mean, sometimes."

Though my parents and I weren't exactly on the same page when it came to porno, I nevertheless felt the urge to apprise them of my newfound success. I knew I wouldn't be able to turn them around on the whole issue, but with so much money coming in, I figured maybe we could find some common ground.

"Daddy?"

"Son of mine. So nice to hear your voice. How are you?"

"Great, Dad, but how are *you*? How's the head-shrinking business?"

"Fine, just fine. I've found something that keeps me out of trouble. Not to mention my job assists me in staying up-to-date with the world around me. Did you know, for instance, that more and more people are using coffee shops as places to find life partners?"

"Is one of your clients a coffee shop owner?"

"I can't tell you that, of course. You see, my boy, there's a little thing called a *confidentiality agreement* that I enter into. You may have heard about it?"

"Barista?"

"It would be inappropriate for me to say."

"Hey, come off it, you can tell me. Do you have some *coffee* addict coming to lay on your couch every Wednesday and Friday? That sounds weird."

"Enough. I assume you're just being fractious."

"Yes, David, I am just being *fractious*. Just totally fractious. You have me figured out."

He sighed. "So. To what do I owe the pleasure of your call?"

"Nothin' much," I said nonchalantly. "Just that I'll be sending you a check in the mail quite soon."

"Is my birthday coming up so soon?" He laughed.

"No, Dad," I scolded him. "Don't you remember that grand that I borrowed from you way back?"

"Yes, of course," my dad said, his voice darkening. "For your . . . movies."

"Exactly!" I said. "Well, I can finally afford to get it back to you! Isn't that cool?"

"Very much so," my dad said, guardedly. "Now, if you ever need any money, like, say, if you ever decided to go back to school, or something of that order, I want you to know you can always depend on me and your mother—"

"You're missing the whole point!" I said. "I'm calling to tell you I don't *need* to borrow money from you anymore! I thought you'd be happy."

"I *am* happy," said my father. "Maybe." He paused. "What are you doing for your money these days, if I may ask?"

"Same old, same old. You know." I paused, then picked up the word and tossed it at him, like a tiny little bomb. "Porno."

"Ugh," he sighed. "I can't quite reconcile myself to the knowledge that this is what you want to do with your life."

"I want to be an artist, Dad, and—"

"Yes, yes," he said irritably, "we went through this whole line of reasoning once before. Yet for some strange reason, I *still* haven't been able to see what *porn*'s got to do with *art*."

"That's because you don't have my vision," I said smugly. "No one does."

"Then *tell* me. For the love of God, tell me. What special things are you doing out there in California, that makes videos of people having sex become *art*?"

"I just . . . I mean . . ." He had me there. "Well, right *now* I'm concentrating on making money. And believe me, I'm making it."

"Perhaps your artistic goals have been proven slightly unrealistic?" said my father.

"Money's where I'm at right now!" I bellowed. "But I'm still on my mission. You just wait, I'm going to put something together really soon."

"All right. Calm yourself. Don't *yell* at me. I'm still your father."

"I'll speak how I darn well please," I grumbled. "I've got a mind to send you a tape of my recent work, so you can screen it for your *clients*."

"Don't," my dad said, calmly. "And I'm saying please."

"Well, then why don't you just *trust* me? I mean, Dad, *seriously*! You wouldn't *believe* the place that I'm living in. We have a *huge* pool, and a giant refrigerator, and the *view*? It's spectacular."

"California's always been one of the more beautiful states," my father said, patiently.

"Man, I don't believe this! You should be proud of me! Hell, Dad, I made almost two *grand* this week! It's the easiest money in the world!"

"How long do you need to do this?" he asked. "How long?"

I sighed, long and deep. I held the phone at arm's length and looked at it. But then I brought it back. "Look. I really have no fucking clue, Dad. Maybe for a while. Maybe not."

"And then what? Got any plans? Teaching nursery school, perhaps?"

I laughed, in spite of myself. "I may have placed myself out of that job."

"Perhaps."

"Can you just have faith in me, Dad? Can you trust the person I *am*?"

"I *do* trust you. I love you. But sometimes I really wonder."

"About *what*?"

"If you're doing as well as you say you are."

"Gee, thanks for the consult," I said.

"Free of charge. Family rate."

"Okay, deep pockets. I guess I won't be sending you that check, then?"

"No, no," he said, calmly. "By all means. Send the check."

One night, as we were chilling at her apartment, drinking wine, lounging on her couch, I confessed something important to Liz.

"Sometimes I get sick of it."

"Sick of what?" asked Liz.

"This whole thing." I motioned at the air. "You know. The whole 'gangbang' thing."

"*Really*," Liz said. Boy, if there were a sarcasm scale, she would have been right off it.

"Yes," I said carefully. "It's goddamn stupid."

"Thank you, Sam, for this late-breaking news." She grinned, reaching for the channel changer. "What else have you got?"

Liz lived in an apartment complex on a hot and treeless street in North Hollywood, across the street from a junior high school, within walking distance of two liquor stores. Her bedroom overlooked the

170 freeway. The constant hum of traffic was never far from us. As if that weren't enough, an army of cheap plastic fans spun endlessly in every room, creating a miasma of white noise; it was enough to drive you bats. Also, Liz had a Chinese roommate named Lisa, who was very pretty and totally immature and loved pooing with the door open. I wanted to kill Lisa.

Their bathroom was like *the* horrible place to take a shit in the United States. Their towels were maroon, the wallpaper was bumpy, the door was painted yellow, and on all exposed surfaces, scissored and Scotch-taped pictures of the little monsters from the rock band Incubus stared back at you. As a team, Liz and Lisa adored them, wanted to embrace them, and be embraced. A sickly light emanated from one long fluorescent bulb that was paneled behind a thick plastic covering, and their toilet paper was matted and wet. It smelled like they had a tray of cat litter hidden in there. But there was no cat.

"I think porn is offensive," I continued. "To women."

"You are one sensitive guy, sweetie," Liz said, patting my hand. "I'm *impressed*."

Liz's bedroom was a touch better, although, in reality, it was a terrible place that gave me vertigo. The walls felt like they were made out of pasteboard and you could jump right through them and they would fold like props in a skit. Green fluorescent stars on the ceiling bothered me when I went to sleep, and there were black silken sheets on her bed, which spoke of a goth sensibility I couldn't relate to. And Lisa, I *seriously* disliked. She and Liz had their own secret language and goth giggling fits that left me out in the cold. I couldn't relax there.

"There," Liz said. "Now that we've got *that* covered, should we make some food?"

"But seriously," I pressed. "Don't you *think* about it sometimes? Isn't it, like, *gross* to you?"

Liz shrugged. "People are people." She got up from the couch and opened a kitchen cupboard, from which she removed a large stockpot. She turned on the kitchen faucet and began to fill it with water.

Perhaps I was being a tad ungrateful. Liz was well liked by my contemporaries; not only did all the porn guys love her, but so did many of the porn actresses. Daisy Dukes—small, thin, Latina, and owner of arguably the worst name in the biz—really looked up to White Liz. In fact, she adored her like a big sister. Liz was three years older, but she dug Daisy in the same way. They would go shopping together and buy underwear and talk about boys. Their relationship was important. I knew Liz was taking care of her. I could tell she cared about her. I had seen Daisy Dukes strangling on dick, but whom hadn't I seen strangling on dick, by this point? My *job* was making people strangle on dick.

"But . . . what about the girls?" I persisted.

"What *about* them?"

"I just think . . ." I drew in a long, slow breath. "I think some of them were molested when they were younger."

"Holy cow, Sam," said Liz. "This is some day of epiphany for you. When did you come to *that* groundbreaking conclusion?"

I eyed her sharply. "Don't make fun of me, okay? I just didn't . . . well, before recently, I didn't really *believe* that."

"Well, congratulations," Liz said, laughing. She lit a burner on her white stove and hoisted the pot onto it. "You've tapped into, like, the biggest stereotype ever! Girl gets pawed, girl grows up, girl gets pawed again."

"So what are you saying?" I asked, watching her fearfully. "You think it's true? Or, no. You think it's stupid. It's not true."

"God, you *are* trying to figure this out, huh?" She tilted her head at me. "You're kind of cute when you're *earnest*. You know?"

"Did Daisy?" I asked, my voice quaking. "Did she get . . . molested?"

"Her real name is Leslie," Liz said. "And since you're interested, no. She didn't."

"So why is she in porn?" I asked doubtfully.

"Why are *you*?" Liz asked, waggling her eyebrows at me.

"Not the same thing," I parried. "I'm not in front of the camera."

"That's not what *I* heard," Liz said, laughing. She mimed getting fucked from behind. "*Slide Bi Me*, anyone?"

"Who told you about that?" I cried, infuriated. "Timberlake? That little *fucker!*"

Liz collapsed into a fit of giggles, hugging her arms to her chest. "Nothing to be ashamed of, sweetie, *nothing at all . . .*"

"I'm glad I could be such a source of hilarity for you," I said dryly, waiting for her laughter to subside. "Are you done yet?"

"Yes," Liz said weakly. "Yes. Very done." She wiped tears off her very pretty perfect face.

"Then I'll answer your question."

"Go, baby."

"I'm in this game to make money."

"So's Leslie."

"I'm in it for the attention."

"Ooh," said Liz. "Good honesty! Points. So's Leslie."

I opened her refrigerator. "What are we making?"

"Pasta," Liz said. "Unless you want to get takeout?"

"I'm too lazy," I admitted.

"Good," said Liz. "Me, too. Pasta is good for you, anyway. It has amino acids."

"No, it doesn't," I said seriously. "So look. Maybe Leslie *wasn't* molested. But I've been getting this feeling from some of the girls that I shoot that they *were*."

"Maybe they were," Liz said, shrugging and pushing past me to grab a couple of water glasses, which she filled from the tap. "I have a couple of friends who *aren't* in the porn industry who had bad stuff happen to them. And those are just the ones who've come clean. Abuse isn't as infrequent as we'd like it to be, unfortunately."

I accepted a water from her and stared at it, frowning. "Or it's like, *collectively*, these porn girls have been fucked with. You know what I mean? In the collective unconscious?"

"Now you're talking over my head," Liz said. "Missed that."

"Women have been getting fucked over by men, degraded, for hundreds and hundreds of years!" I declared. "Reduced to a combination of ass, tits, and legs."

"You're a feminist!" Liz said. "This is really cute. A pornofeminist. Okay, I'm listening, very sorry to interrupt, but do you want spaghetti sauce? 'Cause we might have to go out and buy some."

"Yes. I do want it. Let's buy some." I took Liz by the shoulders. "Listen. I just get this sense that I'm tapping into something ugly. I'm *mining* something here, something secret and sad. And there's something *wrong* about it."

"Okay," agreed Liz. "I hear you."

"I have to stop doing it, don't I?" I asked fearfully, waiting for her reaction.

"Not if you don't want to," Liz said dryly.

"I . . . I don't?"

"Sam. Come on. Do you think that's going to make a *difference* or something? Maybe some of the girls you shoot have issues, and sure, of course they do. Porn's a strange diet for anyone to choose willingly. But are you going to change their past by quitting? Are you going to *heal* them by running away?"

"It doesn't change the fact that I make my *living* off of this totally gross set of actions," I mumbled.

"Well, true," Liz said. "Your life's pretty gross. On a cellular level."

"I'm going to hell," I decided.

"Well, I'm more detached from the action than you are, but I'm implicated, too," Liz said. "And I don't feel great about it. But what are we supposed to do? Quit? Have you ever thought about what you would do for *money*?"

I was silent for a moment, thinking about the new Kenwood stereo I had my eye on for the Volvo. Its parametric three-band equalizer and in-dash unit-integrated amplifier were only half a five-man gangbang away. "It'd be more difficult to get by," I admitted.

"You running away to satisfy your guilt isn't going to stop Leslie from staring up at the ceiling when she has sex. Is it?"

"Aha!" I said, pouncing. "I thought you said she *wasn't* molested."

"Well," said Liz, crossing her arms guardedly, sipping from her water, "she wasn't. But I'm not saying she doesn't think about leaving, too."

"I guess it's complicated," I said glumly.

"Look," Liz said. "I'm not going to do this for the rest of my life. And, despite your current level of involvement, I doubt that you will, either. So listen, sweetie, why don't you try to relax a little bit? Just pretend it's all funny. That seems to work for everyone else."

She gave me a small smile. Not one of her best, actually. But all things considered, it would have to do.

"Now," she said. "How about we talk about something else?"

Timberlake was a pretty crazy fucker. I really couldn't hate him, though, much as I tried. He was hyper and manic-depressive, yes, and I probably should have realized that before I brought him on

board, but he did all the weird little amazing things right, like teach
the girls yoga before their scenes. Instituting prescene Sun Saluta-
tions was a genius move on his part. He had Aimee Tyler reaching
up to the sky and bending her stringy little arms, her sexy squashed
thighs trembling before God in our secluded little compound.

Timber had other splendid ideas, too, like dressing up a girl as a
Klanswoman for her shoot. He actually *was* talented at porn, when
it came to the psychological side of things. He was excellent at creating scenarios, making up—off the top of his head—that Autumn
Haze was a teacher for new immigrants; that Friday was trying out
for an all-male baseball team. He inspired me to start using my
brain once in a while, if only to better impress Pitts. Without even
a word, the pace was starting to pick up. We felt Pitts's odd centrifu-
gal force when he watched our scenes, standing by, arms crossed,
evaluating them. He never watched more than a few minutes at a
time, the mark of a truly classy man (you had porn going down right
before your eyes, but you *chose* not to watch it). Likewise, he never
spoke to the male performers more than was absolutely necessary.
Regardless, they all immediately realized who he was and what
that meant to them, and they kissed his ass just enormously. God,
they *lined* up to kiss his ass. The mountains of purple marijuana
offered up to Pitts was legendary. Of course, he begged off all gifts.
Wouldn't have been appropriate. Like I said, the man was business-
minded.

After a day or two of frowning observation, Pitts called a roundtable, the agenda of which was essentially a mandate to start including more male performers per scene—immediately. "Guys, I
know it'll be a little harder for you to organize, but it's worth it. The
subscribers *love* it. What can I say? They're into nasty. You know? A
girl who will do a two-on-one is nasty. But a girl who'll do a *three*-on-
one? Much nastier." We shrugged. We didn't care. Timberlake and

I got paid an extra hundred bucks if we threw in another guy, so we were more or less thrilled about the new challenge.

Slowly, the house started getting more and more packed. We were basically the new employment agency in town for black male performers, and word was getting around. The organizational part of my brain, the same brain that liked to pretend I was the coach of a pro sports team, dug it a lot. I met so many damned Porno All-Stars up there. Weed was one of them, a light-skinned half-black, half-Cherokee from Compton, a reformed drunk who was just incredibly, incredibly gentle, puffing his Newports, talking about going to pick up his daughter after the shoots, and only being able to come when the girl rubbed his left nipple clockwise. Though he was somewhat of a handful, due to the nipple complication, I nevertheless loved Weed. Then there was John E. Depth, a New York porn performer with dreadlocks and a wide-nostriled face with a deep chocolate complexion and a quiet demeanor and a legitimately huge '80s porn dick that he could pick up with both hands and that would only get hard after about a half an hour of prodding. John E. Depth was six foot three and had no fat on his entire body. His butt was just thick, corded muscle.

We shot everybody, just everybody. Billy Banks was a grinning man with a bald bubble head who reminded me of an unctuous preacher, sermon in hand. Billy liked to clap me on the back good-naturedly, even though we'd just met, and say things like "We *family*!" We were most certainly not family. Billy rolled with a guy named Ned, a production assistant whose penis was basically terrible (which is to say, it was not in league with the Krylon spray-paint cans we had at our disposal) and who was kind of fat to boot, not to mention being far too light-skinned.

("Keep the light-skinned guys to a minimum," urged Pitts. "One per scene, max. Subscribers want to see dark skin.")

Thus Ned got booted after two scenes. I fired him myself. I saw the hate in his eyes. But Billy's other pal, Tony Eveready, hung on. He fit right into our game plan. Tony was thuggish, small, and compact, with cornrows and a southern accent. He'd been a player in the porn game forever, performing since the early '90s, taking breaks only when incarcerated. He'd brought a gun to the set until we told him not to; and then, after leaving it at home for one day, he decided to bring it again. "I felt naked without that shit," Tone said. "So now I'm wearing it, and what the fuck you gonna say about it?"

("Tony is a good example of the kind of guy we need," Pitts said. "He's ghetto. We need to push that.")

Eveready was a "pretty pimp." Cuddly and teddy-bearish one moment, violent and frightening the next. He loved firearms with a good heft to them, skunky strippers, short money, fast cars, fist-fighting, and drinking liquor directly from pint bottles wrapped in paper bags. He was an intelligent man, quite comfortable in prison, though according to him, everywhere was one.

Wesley Pipes was "ghetto," too: a real-life gangster from South Central LA who'd served ten years for trafficking and conspiracy, so gifted in the art of talking shit that he'd been able to build an entire *career* out of it. His awesomely sincere and impeccably expressed horniness for white women tickled all of our fancies. The singular desperation of his movements, speaking of ten long years of enforced celibacy, informed every one of his scenes. If you let him, Pipes would use up the entire hour all by himself, just *windmilling* from every conceivable direction, sneering, mumbling nonsense— *kick that leg up, can I kick that leg up? You might can win, baby, you might can win, but slow it down. Grind it on there real hard. Grind it on there real hard. Oh, shit. This white pussy got me. I ain't going to be able to take this one! Girl, you got this mothafucka at the tip!* Wesley was so amusing to listen to that he quickly became a favorite of ours. Timberlake and I hired him as much as we possibly could.

Sledge Hammer was another favorite son, a power lifter with a dick as big as a submarine sandwich (bread included), zitty New Orleans skin, and a wonderful dorkish laugh. He was a beta male if you ever saw one, unpopular with the girls, a mama's boy who collected *Dark Knight* action figures, yet he could lift a Hyundai with his left hand, and his penis was giant and inhuman, and always hard like a saber. "Hey Sam, *huh huh*"—he would grunt—"can you tell me when you're getting ready to shoot? I gotta, um, go wash off my dick." We all suspected he was injecting that Caverject shit, but what did we care? I wouldn't have wanted to touch it, much less let it pierce me, but a perma-schlong made our scenes far easier to shoot. A limp dick was all of our undoing. Timberlake, in particular, went absolutely crazy when he encountered one. He took it personally.

"Billy!" he cried in frustration one afternoon, when he was shooting a wobbly-Timberlake-special, out on the grass in front of the house with Austin O'Reilly, a blonde with big bazooms who was supposedly going to law school when she wasn't fucking black guys on camera for us. "What's going *on*, man?"

"Hold it, hold it, hold it—just give me a second," croaked Billy, grinning and blushing and sweating, his black skin glowing from the effort, the terrific strain of it. "I'm *about* to get my edge."

"You *are*? Well goddammit, you coulda fooled me!" Timberlake played the French auteur well, slapping his head with his flat palm, waltzing around with that huge XL-1 camera teetering crazily in the wind and bumping dangerously against his thigh. "We only have *so much time*, Billy, before the *sun* moves! And *then* how are our shots gonna match? Tell me *that*, man!"

Timberlake made to advance toward Austin, who, naked with her belly button pierced, her high heels on, her skin tan and flawless, her stomach flat, her lips poutingly pink and her buttocks glistening and sugary, looked *perfect*, just wonderfully *porno*—and Timberlake swiped at her cunt savagely with his thumb and forefinger. She gasped. Paying no attention, Timberlake held up his dampened fingers, sniffing at them maniacally.

"She's losing her *juices*, dude! She's dryin' up at record speed! Come on! Come on!"

"Hold it," said Billy, whacking furiously, his penis slowly gaining strength and thickness. "I . . . hold it . . . yo, *I got that shit, man*! I'm *ready TO GO!*"

"*Action!*" roared Timberlake. "Go, go, go! I need two straight minutes of doggy! Sledge, you're in the mouth! Weed, behind her! Attaboy . . . now, flip her! Let's see some *riding* action. Christ, *move*, okay? Okay, honey? Are you hearing me?"

Pitts and I watched him work, bemused, admiring his manic energy.

"Sledge, on the ground! You're my anchor! *Billy!* How's that wang workin'?"

"Like a *champ*! It's hard as *steel*, bro!"

"It better be!"

We stood next to one another in the weak afternoon light, watching man after man insert his penis into a honey of a woman, watched her do her sex cries and her laugh, the whole thing. Austin looked somehow happy up there.

"*Weed!* Stand to the *side!* This is important—I can't be focusing on your big hairy ass right now! For the love of Jake, *cammmaon!*"

And even when Timberlake suggested the DP, the double penetration, the famous porn move with the degree of difficulty of a 9.8, the one that entailed one member going into her anus and the other into her vagina, filled up and stuffed, Austin O'Reilly kept on smiling, taking it good-naturedly, like a champ.

"Billy, I need you in that pussy, and *pronto*! Move out the way, *move*! I gotta . . . I gotta . . . lemme wedge this camera . . . hold it . . . let me get my shot . . . you fuckers . . . all right . . . and steady now . . . *Fuck! Please! Oh my, that's a beautiful sight*, bootylicious sight—great wankin' day!"

I leaned against my car in the driveway, smiling, with my arms folded, watching this curious gaggle of humanity press up against one another. I watched them struggling and fucking and falling to the ground, apologizing and getting up to brush grass and dirt from their elbows and knees, then rising to the test again. I longed for a good strong drink. Something with ice cubes in it. Or maybe just a friend to talk to, someone who might understand. The Malibu sun was sliding down the hardscrabble hillside; the light was dying.

NINETEEN

White Liz hated being on top. She was so tiny and small. Her vaginal canal so shallow.

White Liz would whisper when we had sex, biting my ear, not the lobe but the hard cartilage. She was so *beautiful,* and her eyes were so pretty, though often there wasn't always a lot of eye contact going on—mostly they were closed, her forehead wrinkled with concentration. Eye contact or even talking a little bit during the act might have been good for us; though on the other hand, I would also have found it a little scary. Liz was *easy* to fuck, that's the main point: I was stronger and bigger than she was, and taking her wrists and pinning them to the bed was easy, and she would struggle to try to free her arms, and I wouldn't let her, not even for a little bit, my body pressing her down, her knobby little knees, her small and exposed breasts. We were connected, linked by an unspoken bond, but sexually, something between us was bestial: captive and tormentor, a means to some menacing end. Afterward, we'd shower together, kiss, touch fingertips. But in the moment, no, we weren't friends.

One night, soon after we'd made love, I was gently touching her body. I saw a dark spot on her thigh.

"Liz," I said. "What have you got here?"

"What's that, honey?" she said softly. She could fall asleep so fast after we had sex. I envied her for how quickly she fell into unconsciousness, how deeply she slept. It wasn't always easy for me to sleep in the same bed with her, or with anyone.

"It looks like a . . . bruise or something."

"You probably hurt me, you *animal*." She punched at me lightly, but missed. She was close to sleep.

"No, seriously. Baby. Wake up. You've got this thing on your thigh. Look at it."

"Ugh," said Liz. She sat up in bed. "Let me see." Below the ridge of her ilium, on her outer thigh, there was indeed a dark, swollen mark, approximately half an inch in circumference. "What the hell *is* that?"

"I don't know," I said, scared. "But it's not a bruise."

"Christ," Liz said. "It's a . . . spider bite."

The next morning, a cheery fat man who looked like a black-haired Santa Claus appeared in our kitchen.

"Pleased *ta* meet *ya!*" he bellowed, intercepting me in the kitchen. He stuck out a fleshy hand for me to shake. "Name's Rag Man! And you must be . . ."

"No," I grunted, my mouth all cotton, "you muss be mistaken." And I pushed past him to drain my piss-filled boner.

Some minutes later, we met more cordially over coffee. Rag Man was fifty or so, like the legends had it, and he was from Pittsburgh, where the beer ran freely and Yinzers reigned supreme. He sported a comb-over hairdo, mom jeans, and comfortable shoes. A flabby belly hung over the waist of his jeans, and his feet turned all the way out. You could see the rounded insides of his heels as he waddled quickly from room to room, checking out each view from each separate large picture window, with increasing wonder.

"Fuck, I can't *believe* this shittin' house! Sam, you guys have hit the *mother lode* up here! Sweet balls and mother of *fuck*! I guess all we need *now* are about two hot chicks apiece and about *twelve black guys* for a full-on gangbang! *Ha ha ha!*"

Note the dedication. Even in fantasy, Rag Man could never allow himself the pleasure of a hot chick draining *his* balls. It had to be the balls of *some black dude*.

"Can't wait to get my feet wet," he confessed. "I'm gonna be shootin' second camera, right behind you. That cool with you, dude?"

"Of course," I said. Of course it wasn't, but what the hell was I going to do?

"This is the culmination of a lifetime of hard work for me," he said, suddenly confessional in the midmorning light. I retracted from his old-man breath; he came closer. "Lemme be honest with ya for a second. Never in my wildest dreams did I think I'd have the opportunity to check this kinda shit out in the flesh."

"Mm," I said, noncommittally.

"To put it plainly, I'm honored to be in your guyses company." He stuck out his hand again. "Thank you, man. Thanks for including me."

I groaned. This was even more awful than I had imagined. Now I couldn't even hate the goddamn guy. He was too nice.

Rag Man moved his belongings into the orange-carpeted guest room on the first floor, the one that the talent had been using to take pregame shits and showers. "I freaking *love* this freakin' *Jew guy!*" crowed Rag Man, pointing to the small television screen in his room, where Larry David was running around nebbishy in his first season on HBO. "What a freakin' *dickhead!*" He stuffed raisins and produce into his face, delicious "California stuff," as he laughed loudly at hours of television: *Sopranos, Daily Show, Adult Swim.* "My wife don't let me watch this shit at home!" He smoked enormous bowls of powerful marijuana, but only at night. "Keepin' my head fresh for the work ahead!" His long black socks dotted the hamper with old-man disease. I missed my sweet, solitary mansion, the firm fantasy boobs of my women.

Timberlake felt his freedom particularly infringed. "That guy's *killing* my concentration," Timber said to me, as we jetted out from the compound at night. "*Murdering* it."

"You had no concentration in the first place," I said. "Did you?"

"You're wrong about that, you're wrong. I'm coming along. Aren't I? I can shoot a good scene."

"No, you never could," I said, as honestly as I knew how. "Look, why worry? What's the worst Pitts can do? Fire you?"

"I can't lose my job, Sam. I want . . ." He gazed into my face, wondering whether to trust me. "I want a new car."

And there it was. Timberlake's dream. The fucking moron couldn't live with his Subaru, and the way it wheezed when it went up a hill. He was slipping down to the Beverly Hills Acura dealership three days a week to wank off on the aluminum showroom floor. Wasting long afternoons there, conducting an extended flirtation with the lowly salespersons, talking *cars*, the way the rest of us talked about a woman's legs, thighs, and silky maroon lips. And one day, he threw down all the money he'd earned thus far—$4,750.60—and signed up for an indentured servitude that would cost him eighteen grand more. Timber's nearly new Acura was fast and gold and smelled like the absence of responsibility. It had a moonroof and perforated leather seats and triple-tread tires and reverse steering ignition with a five-disc CD changer and a digital odometer, plus a thrown-in radar detector that suction-cupped to the inside of the windshield or to your anus, as preferred.

"Why, man, *why?*" I groaned.

"You scared to see me looking good?" Timber crowed. He wore sunglasses. (Why was it that when a guy went out and got a new car, he immediately had to spring for $80 sunglasses?)

"You will never look good, not even if you lopped off Celine Maxima's head and glued it to your neck," I explained. "I'm upset because I'm *worried* about you. You're in debt, man!"

"This job's . . ."

"This job's supposed to get us *out* of debt, fuckwad!! Not the other way around!"

"It's just eighteen thou," Timberlake said grandly. "I'll pull that down in a couple of months. And meanwhile, I got the car of my dreams. Truly, I don't know what you're whimpering about."

Yes, it was true, I didn't understand cars much. A diesel Volvo older than most of our female talent was just fine for me. Rag Man must have felt similarly, rolling around town as he was in his rented Kia. "I ain't gotta impress no one up here," he told me. "It's not like my lady is up here, keepin' tabs on me."

"Oh yeah, we heard you were married," I said.

"Fucking-A-*right!*" he bellowed. "I love her, a lot."

"Wonderful sentiment," I said. "Beautifully expressed."

Rag Man nodded. "Fact is, we haven't been separated since we were married, thirty freakin' years ago, so this is a little weird for both of us."

"Does she mind you being around porn?" I said.

"What's to mind? She *loves* it! She's freaky, Sam," Rag Man confessed.

"Oh, I bet she is," I said hurriedly. "So, hey, about that Larry *David*? Let's see what's on—"

"I ain't come in her pussy in twenty years," said Rag Man, his tone hushed.

I didn't ask. But he would tell me anyway.

"*In her mouth.*" He grinned, triumphant. "Every damn time."

"Kudos," I said, weakly.

"*Nasty*," Rag Man corrected, smacking his lips.

Meanwhile, Pitts had started banging about one porn chick per week as the rest of us stared on, envious. Autumn Haze was one of his "dates." God, she had a pretty face. It was the face of a bubble-bath operator. Autumn stayed with us for an entire week, moving her suitcase, her thousand-toothed hairbrush, her spongy shoes and silky breasts into the master bedroom, constituting an odd sort of common-law wife/sex slave for Pitts. Despite the frequency with which he exchanged women, Pitts was not what you'd call a pig. Pitts honestly got *into* his ladies; he got *into* Autumn, found her fascinating. As did I. Autumn was a Northern California woman with a hazy far-off look in her eyes that spoke of stories she wouldn't mind telling but was honestly a wee, wee bit too drunk to remember. She could have been twenty-two years old or, equally plausibly, twenty-nine. Her body had felt the effects of gravity, but that face? Preserved in honeydew. She was as pretty as Jenna Jameson, maybe prettier; an A-lister who'd lost her way and had to hang out with us. But if Autumn knew she was slumming, she didn't give much of a damn. A borderline personality's spotlight of fame followed her around every corner, tracked her to the bathroom, and watched her write in her journal. She was voraciously sexual: when I shot her, she demanded not only that I get *four* fellows for her, but that she'd be able to select the guys in her scene. I was impressed. No other girl had wanted to pick before. Maybe no one had felt empowered to. Perhaps no one cared.

"Autumn's gonna rock this one out," Rag Man murmured to me. "Ain't she?"

"Yep," I responded shortly.

"Little scoutin' report for you. She does best in positions where her legs can extend to their full height," Rag Man recommended. "She looks tall and elegant. Dudes like that refined shit. Especially when it's combined with her slobberin' and whatnot."

"Thank you for the advice."

"No problem," Rag Man said. "She's a total whore, so this is gonna be easy. Oh! You're gonna notice that her left boob hangs a little bit. She might have a little one at home, is my guess. So if you can delay her takin' off her bra until about midway through the scene, it might make the scene a little hotter." He watched my face. "'Course, I don't want to tell *you* what to do."

I shook my head, impressed in spite of myself. "You know a hell of a lot about porn, don't you?"

He grinned happily. "You don't miss a trick, do ya, boy? We elders do have wisdom to impart, even beery fuckers like me."

"You love this crap," I accused him, smiling. We began to get the living room ready for the scene. I moved our green sectional sofa closer to the wall, and Rag Man strode forward to lend a hand.

"Hell yes, I do," said Rag Man. He grunted, nudging the sofa until it was perfectly aligned with the wall. "I was going to *movie theaters* way back when, man. Whackin' off next to other dudes, or just not whackin' off at all." He shuddered, remembering. "It was brutal."

"Then VCRs came out?" I said, hiding a box of baby wipes behind the couch, within easy reach for the talent.

"Yup. I got one of the first models, an '81 JVC top-loader. Cost me damn near five hundred dollars, but it was worth it. VCRs were way better. I saw a lot. I *learned* a lot." Rag Man nodded. "But when PCs came, I mean, the whole *thing* changed. Think about the way we're showing our movies, man—we haven't mastered a tape yet. It's all on the friggin' *Internet*! Just a few years ago, nobody was doin' this."

"Nobody was watching porno on the Internet?" I said. "Not even the geeks?"

"No bandwidth to do it on," Rag Man said. "Until the mid-nineties, the best you were gonna do was get some pictures off a bulletin board system. And that'd take you about half an hour per pic."

"Dark ages." I frowned, wondering where to position our lights so they'd illuminate the scene but wouldn't get in my way as I tried to shoot the action from all angles. I wasn't much for lighting.

"Indeed," said Rag Man. "Here, try this." He toggled a cord, re-positioned a flood, and the living room came ablaze in the glow of hot, vivid porn lighting. "I was part of that BBS crowd, believe me I was. See, I was rentin' videos, takin' em home, snaggin' vid-caps and postin 'em. People freakin' loved it. I wasn't chargin' any money for my service, of course," he said proudly. "Doin' it all as part of the love of the game."

"Then what happened?"

"Around '97, '98, computers finally got faster. More people were using the Internet, not just kids goin' to college. I started playin' around with video clips, and I hooked up my VCR to my computer with an RCA cable, started digitizing tapes. We still didn't have the capacity for more than ten-second segments, but still, people just went balls crazy. They was talkin' about me, posting comments. I was gettin' famous, man."

"But you weren't making any money."

"How could I?" Rag Man said. "It wasn't my content. This was all stuff I was renting from the fuckin' store, man. I was cuttin' movies up and postin' em on the Web, just because I loved the stuff."

"Well, I don't get it," I said. "If there was such obvious demand to see the movies on a PC, why didn't the owners of porn companies do exactly what you were doing, and charge for it?"

"If it ain't broke, don't fix it," Rag Man explained, simply. "That's how most people think, Sam. Remember, it's not like these guys were goin' broke. Everybody was still selling lots of DVDs, videotapes, too. Hell, they were making so much fucking money, it took an outsider to see the new business model."

"Which is where you came in."

"Naw," said Rag Man, his eyes glowing. "I was just a fat guy at home. I'd have kept on doing it for free and for fun until I died. I ain't no businessman. But *Pitts* came in and he saw it from a different angle. You know what he was doing five years ago? That guy wasn't no damn pornographer! He was cleanin' fuckin' carpets! Haw haw! But he's a *thinker*. He listened to the ground, picked up what was hot."

"Interracial?"

"You ain't no dummy. He sees the black thing, takes a guess that there's a big-time market for it. He thinks of a way of makin' money off the computer from it. It took some balls. He basically thunk up that monthly membership idea."

I shook my head, considering. It was all coming into place. "And he decided to bring in the guy at the head of the technological revolution to be his webmaster."

"He basically drafted me," said Rag Man proudly.

I couldn't help but laugh. I tamped it down, as much as was possible.

"He's got an eye for talent, that Pitts does," said Rag Man, smiling. "Oh, I been watchin' you, man! Don't think I haven't. You lucked into a great situation, and I think you got some real potential. Hell, I wish I'd been in your shoes, when I was your age. But everybody ain't lucky like you."

He took a good look around at the living room, surveying the scene we'd created, plumped up a few pillows on the couch, and smiled, satisfied.

Turned out Liz was laid up in bed. She couldn't even get up to go to work.

"I can't drive. It's like there's a *hole* in my leg," she explained to me over the phone. "It's fucking *disgusting*."

"All that from one little spider?"

"Your house has like, *brown recluses*, or something," Liz said. "Seriously, I'm stranded on my couch. The doctor said I was supposed to move as little as possible."

"Well, I'm sorry, Liz," I said. "Does he have you on antibiotics?"

"Of course," she said. She sounded pissed. "Well? Can you come and see me?"

"Sure," I said slowly, watching Lucky Starr lazing around the kitchen, waiting for Timberlake's three-on-one to start. Our eyes met and he raised an eyebrow. "Today might be a little hectic, though. I have a late shoot. And then I have the early slot tomorrow morning. Look, how about tomorrow evening? Would that be okay?"

"Whenever," she huffed. "If you can fit me in."

"Hey, don't be like that."

"Like what?" Liz said, and she hung up the phone.

"Christ, mannnn . . . ," I said, shaking my head.

"What's the problem, big man?" Lucky asked, coming over to slap a supportive palm on my back.

"You know. Ladies." I rolled my eyes. I pushed past him to open up the refrigerator, give it a good stare. Nothing in there that I was too excited about.

"Ladies ain't no problem," said Lucky. "It's when you *don't* have 'em, that they become a problem."

"Boy, you *are* a philosopher, huh?" I said, picking up a tortilla wrap and putting it right back down.

"I dabble," Lucky said. "I meditate and shit."

I wandered outside and tramped down the hill, sighing. What good were Malibu porno grounds, after all, if you didn't wander around them aimlessly once in a while? You had to put your time in, observing the foliage and the little bugs and slugs and things. Our gardener, Luiz, kneeled over a bush, trimming it. I waved to him, but he only coughed wildly into the bush and pretended not to see me. Boy, Luiz was shy. I felt horrible for a moment: here was this full-grown Mexican man in his late thirties, and for some reason he was *scared* of me. I wanted to draw him to my chest, tell him that I was *sorry* that we were shooting porn here, that I knew it offended him and frightened him and he didn't find it funny at all. I wanted to tell him, if he was a religious guy, then I honestly *apologized* for pushing broken flesh into his face over and over again and making him flee the area with his weed whacker whenever we decided we wanted to stage a double-anal outside in the buggy sun. I wanted to embrace him, tell him, *Sí, amigo,* I know your wife probably feels a bit uncomfortable here, *confused* that she must be confined to the house during weekday hours. But I only waltzed by him, staring woodenly at my arms, and didn't say a damn thing, of course.

These doubleheader days were a bit intolerable. When Timberlake would have a shoot and I would have a shoot, we'd utilize between us eight actors, which meant eight large and sometimes volatile egos to attend to—not to mention sixteen forms of ID, 4 sixty-minute Sony mini-DV videotapes, 10 Xeroxed seven-page stacks of model releases, 3 douches, 2 bottles of lube, 4 snug-fitting high-heeled shoes with giant soles, 7 to 8 automobiles featuring 28 to 32 absurdly expensive spinners, a black Panasonic stereo blaring hip-hop so loud it could make your eardrums bleed, crumpled half-drunk water bottle after crumpled half-drunk water bottle, 6 blunts, 10 Vanilla Cokes, 2 green dildos, and 1 blue strand of greased anal beads that would have to be thrown away immediately; ruined towels with blush and eyeliner wiped on them, costume changes up the ass, harried phone calls to AIM Healthcare to see whose test was out of date, scumbag managers, and people's older brothers watching with wide-open eyes. It made you want to wring your own neck, when you did it over and over and over again. Porn wasn't the problem. The people weren't really the problem, either. It was the schedule. It was the pace.

I called Liz again. "Can I come see you?" I asked her.

"What?"

"I changed my mind. I'm sorry. I want to look at your spider bite and watch how disgusting it is. I wanna take prom pictures with it."

"You're stupid," she laughed. "Yes. Come over as soon as you can."

"I will be over as soon as porno allows me, my dear."

I opened the refrigerator door again, looking for the surprise that never came. Nothing. In the distance, Timberlake was washing his Acura, slopping the doors down with a mop and a bucket and a brand-new purple sponge. He was whistling, happier than a pig in shit.

Rag Man had offered a couple of general suggestions to me. (He disliked Timberlake straightaway and tried not to talk to him when he could avoid it. Timberlake felt the same way.) The main one being that I try a bit harder to make the scenes *nastier*. That was his word: *nasty*. And Pitts was right there with him, too: nasty. They loved to say it. Whisper it at night. Rub it into each other's hair.

"Nasty sells, fellas."

"Nasty is as nasty does."

"Nasty's what we do. It's the quantity that we supply."

"Hey what's nastier than a whore gulpin' down about *twelve black guys*? I don't know, but if *you* know, then by all means, *tell me!*"

In a way, it was kind of nice to have someone telling me to be *more* amoral. That afternoon, I had arranged to shoot a five-man *blowbang* . . . quaint. My infantry consisted of Billy Banks, Brian Pumper, John E. Depth, Tony Eveready, and Domeniko, a high-yella fella gifted with an elephant's schlong that looked nearly supernatural, jutting out as it did from his narrow, malnourished body. Niko was a former hip-hop artist and, to me, was rather glamorous, as glamorous as anyone who carried around a fifth of tequila in his sweatpants could be, anyway. His main point of pride was that he'd once opened for R&B sensation Babyface on some long-forgotten tour. (Maybe it was bullshit? I couldn't tell.) In any case, he liked me, and I liked him, too. We gave each other Dap. And of course, there was Juliana. Seven years later, and I can still see her leaning over backward in a couch-chair, one of those square cushions with no arms on any side, to take what was coming to her. The skinny, twenty-two-year-old mother of one was blond, constitutionally cheery, Sacramento-born, naturally titted, and represented by Spiegler. Her little body balanced on top of the chair, and her legs hung off it, and her neck hung off it, so she was upside down. They waited in line to use her mouth. I ordered the guys, *spread your legs wide!* and *take your underwear off from around your thighs* so I could scurry in with my expensive camera and huddle there, underneath their cock and balls. Brian Pumper fucked her upside-down white-girl mouth, and drool puddled back up into her nose and eyes. Rag Man hung back behind me, shooting second camera, calling my name, and getting more and more fired up as the scene went on.

You knew *you could do this!*

and

That's a nasty little scenario, I cun'a done better myself!

Tony Eveready was not opposed to being a malevolent sadist, either, and so after he felt Juliana had taken enough gulletizing, he dragged her by the hair out the bay window and hurled her stringy body onto the lawn and dragged her slowly down the set of brick steps, one brick step, two brick step, three brick step four, down to the pool, and he shoved her head into the green waters. Chlorinated sheets of pond water enveloped her blond head. She sputtered, choking, and Tone dunked her once again, his hand never leaving the back of her head where he'd clamped a death grip onto her hair and Billy Banks laughed his forced, sycophantic laugh—*heh heh heh, that's a white girl for you.* I huffed with a pro's impatience and shouldered past all of them to get a great shot that would lure subscribers to spend another month's membership, and in the back of us all, separated out from this fart cloud of humanity, stood John E. Depth, looking stunned. His eyes were open wide and his mouth hung out. His monster cock was deflating in the hazy light of day.

"What in the *hell* are you people doing . . . ," he began, but then the sound of—

"N-*n-n-n-nnnasty!*" Rag Man trilled and then the fat man danced, turning from one out-turned instep to the other, snapping off a roll of photos, a deranged dervish, bobbling his TrX one-chip Canon Digital from one hand to the other, and from around his neck seizing his small and economical 530 pixel digital still Olympus ZR-90, popping flashbulbs in Juliana's soaked, ruined, and crying face.

Stick that big ole dick up in her grill, dog . . . came the chorus.

Lemme drop that dick all up in her head, dog . . . sang Domeniko.

I'm going to Rodney King *her!* Brian Pumper promised.

Yeah, Tony Eveready exulted, *beat that dick on her head like a baton.*

Billy Banks and Domeniko and Pumper formed a ring around her, and I was inside the ring with Juliana. She fell to her knees inside a roiling circumference of flesh and I fell to my knees right there with her. Inside it was black and blue and all we felt was hot breath and dick heat. She sucked and through her soul I felt the absence of pain. Juliana was choking and laughing and searing in the sun, and Billy Banks, town crier, felt his penis wilting again so to assert his masculinity and poor personhood he took Juliana by the forehead, his hand covering her nose and eyes, and he pushed the back of her head, hitting me—*Ow Billy! Ya Doofus!*—and we all laughed and he blushed, and I elbowed Pumper out of the way rising to my feet and his penis smacked against John E. Depth's thigh as he watched us all, unmoving and unrelieved, with a hollow pained look on his face. The clouds were parting and separating, pointing and laughing.

"That's one hell of a frightening wound," I said.

"Way to put it nicely, Sam," Lisa said. "You really have a way with words."

"And you really have a way with being an ungraceful host," I said. "I'm here to entertain my girlfriend. So, if you'll just leave us to our evening . . ."

"I *live* here, cuntwad," Lisa said, shooting me the bird and slamming the door to her room.

"Technically, you wouldn't call a man cuntwad," I explained

worriedly to Liz, who was lying across me with her legs spread out over my thighs and looking very cute indeed in just her undies and a tiny white T-shirt.

"I know, honey," said Liz sweetly. "Would you please get me a glass of milk? Or a beer?"

"Of course, darling. Which one do you want?"

"Just depends on which one we have," said Liz. "Since I haven't been able to drive, the fridge is kind of bare."

"Lisa should get off her fat ass and go to the store for you," I said.

"I'm broke!" came a muffled voice from the other room. *"You know that, Liz!"*

"Do you not have *three dollars* for a *gallon of milk?*" I said loudly. "Boy, what a *letdown!*"

"You weren't even going to come *over* till tomorrow night, asshole!" screamed Lisa. She pulled open the door furiously, her face tangled in rage. "Liz, you *know* I would have gone to the store for you if you needed it!"

"Go shave your chin, Lisa. Listen to what Satan's telling you to do," I said soothingly. "Liz is spoken for tonight."

"Fuckhole," hissed Lisa, slamming her door violently shut once again. All that slamming was going to blow this pasteboard house down. It really would.

"You don't really refer to a man as a fuckhole, either, of course," I said, looking at my girl for understanding and support.

"Sweetie? That beer? Or milk? Or whatever?"

"Right!" I said, leaping to my feet, running over to the fridge. The door was so light and so badly built with such crap metal, it took almost no energy to open it, and I pulled it too hard and its ridge smacked against the wall. "Sorry about that." I scanned around the fridge door for its contents. "No beer." I looked some more. "No milk, either. Pickles, if you want one." I took out a pickle and bit into it.

"Kill me," groaned Liz.

"No need to get bent out of shape. Because you know what *is* in here? A *month-old Diet Sprite.*"

"*Kill me,*" repeated Liz. I joined her on the couch, resumed stroking her white little shins.

"Am I not *so* good to you?"

Liz nodded in assent, but it looked like her mind was elsewhere.

"Pay some attention to me!" I whined. "Listen. Douche Boy got a new car."

"So what? I decided I hate him."

"I know. He bought an Acura. Can you believe that?"

"Yes, I can," said Liz, finally. "He's a fucking idiot. I can believe anything about him."

"He says he wants to go out on a date with us. His girlfriend Terri is coming down to see him, and Timberlake says, double-date time."

"What kind of girl would date *that* asshole?"

"I'm not sure. Someone with deep-seated issues?"

"Who *doesn't* have deep-seated issues, Sam?" said Liz. She looked at me. Watching me.

"Well, I'm completely normal, if that's what you're trying to say. I'm the normalest person in the porn industry, in fact."

"*I'm* the most normal person in the porn industry," said Liz, a tiny hint of a smile on her face.

"Then I'm the *second*-normalest. Can we agree to that?"

"*Yeah,*" said Liz, in a goofy tone. "Look, honey, I am *so* tired. I'm not sure what it is, but I think I better go to bed."

"Let's *both* go to bed," I said, waggling my eyebrows sexily.

"Yeah, but none of that," warned Liz.

"Aw, well what the hell . . . I came all the way over here," I began.

"I'm dying of a fucking *spider bite*, Sam!" cried Liz, outraged.

"You're hardly *dying* . . ."

"You see what I said?" came the voice from Lisa's room. *"Didn't I tell you he was only after one thing? He's unworthy of you, Liz!"*

"You should come out to the house tomorrow, Lisa!" I yelled, seething. "I have several large black friends I'd like you to meet."

"Racist!"

"Yes!" I crowed. "I am! I am *so fuckin' racist that all I do is make movies of black guys fucking white women! I am so fuckin' racist!*"

"Guys!" screamed Liz. "Guys! Both of you, stop! I'm like, succumbing to a *spider bite* here, and no one seems to *care!*"

I smooched my girl on the center of her forehead. Her apartment was brutally hot, and it sure smelled like cat litter in there, so I decided to take the hint and go on home, snaking a Parliament Menthol for the celestial heavenly breeze-from-the-side-of-the-window ride back on home to Malibu.

There was a nice little masturbation waiting for me when I got there, so no need to think about much else: how I was going to make anything better, including porn, including my life.

Slap Happy 3: *Valentine's Day. Michelle Raven has a lipstick valentine on her face. Brandon Iron invades her throat and she collapses to her haunches, looking vaguely shat upon. There is no part of her face that is not covered in maroon lipstick. An anonymous cameraman pans rudely down her body, kind of as an afterthought. She is naked on a tight-weave rug, in someone's commercial office space in the middle of the day. Muffled sounds of working chatter outside the door provide a counterpoint to Michelle Raven's goggling eyes. They are surprised*

and deer-like, hungry for their own kind of succor encircled in
ghostly glowing maroon war paint. The gagging that hiccups
forth from Raven's gullet further animalizes her. She is a walk-
ing throat, a tall savage who has checked her personhood at
the door, tranced out, a sacrifice to the suburban gods, and I
am frightened by how I find this not amusing, nor exciting, but
instead, somehow satisfying.

And then it was just me and my wonderful solitude, the moon,
the Jacuzzi, berries on the bushes, me in my green jockey underwear, walking on the grass, bugs on my hairy toes, two sweet tokes
on a leftover half-inch blunt that tasted of ashtray, a light frothy little
buzz, eminently manageable, clomping down poolside, my naked
behind pressing on the brick of the pool, clasping hands around
shins, shivering in the cold California 2 A.M. air, stoned and wonderful, starry, silvery, regarding my dripping underarms, the physicality
of life, and myself a record of its impermanence.

TWENTY

*L*ike that? Me eatin' on that pussy? Like that? Want yo ass licked? Want that little white ass licked?

That's proper. Oh, that's proper. That's a white girl for you, though. Always gonna be leading the pack in the nastiness. That's right, show 'em. Show 'em you nasty. You look at me, goddammit. That's right. Get that dick. Let go of it?

Shake that mothafucka? Shake it back and forth?

Yeah, that's right. That's my white girl, boy, oh, love my white girl! She just a li'l thang, huh? Dap that up, nigga? Ain't she jus' a li'l, tight-ass, pretty thang?

Don't fight it, let me get it. Don't fight it, let me get it. Nigga, stop playin' with me. You got to take it. Up and down. Up and down. That's right . . . I got this white pussy twisted. Don't you run from me. Don't cheat me. More. More. Strong dick. Strong dick.

Don't you run from me. You give me this little white pussy. There

you go. Oh, don't that shit look sweet on there? Do your thing, baby.
There you go. Tight pussy. Tight pussy . . . Li'l skinny deep *white*
pussy. Skinny deep *white p—(tape cut)*

Liz was back up on her feet within the week. A gauzy bandage
clothed her upper right thigh, and I couldn't touch her in that sensitive area, but for the most part we were back in business.

"Must not have been a brown recluse, after all."

"I don't care," said Liz. "I don't like your house anymore. There's
something wrong up there."

"Silly," I murmured. "Come here, okay? I want to help you feel
all better."

"God, no. You'd think I was just there for you to bang," Liz responded, swatting me away.

It wasn't long before she was back at work, where some of her re-
sponsibilities included sending us new flesh. Generally, Liz gave me
all the good girls. But this time she called Timberlake, and hipped
him to Ashley Moore.

I couldn't help but be disappointed at the snub. A new girl was
always an event, and a pretty one all the more so. No matter how
many women came over to our house, no matter how stupid, repeti-
tive, or depressing the sex often became, a new actress coming up
into the joint was always an occasion. We were pornographers. We
simply had nothing better to do than examine pictures of "the girl"
beforehand, analyzing her look, her history, her cultural heritage. It
was like Internet dating, but with the guarantee of a more satisfying
payoff.

We'd wait around the kitchen table, bullshitting, an hour before
she was supposed to show up, listening for the strains of her car in
the driveway, keeping the cordless phone nearby in case she got

lost. It was the responsibility of whoever was manning the shoot to go out and meet her when she showed, bring her and her porno suitcase, full of shoes and toys and butters, inside. You couldn't step over another guy's actress; it was horrible manners and anyway he'd elbow you out of the way, send you downstairs to eat doughnuts with Rag Man while he carefully guided the actress up the stairs to the bathroom, where he could watch her undress, get first glance at her naked, supervise her costume changes, maybe steal a caress. It was the privilege of our post. And fuck the other guy.

We simply had *rules*. And we respected them. The day Belladonna arrived on set, I literally snarled whenever Timberlake came within ten yards of her. If Rag Man had tried to butt into our conversation with some insight about her performance with Rocco Siffredi in *Italiano Fuck Racers* I would have clawed off his arm at the elbow. It was my right.

And thus, I couldn't help but be slightly bummed when Ashley Moore arrived and I got a glimpse at her. She was all leg, like about 90 percent shapely leg, and the other 10 percent was a huge smile on a cute but not intimidatingly beautiful face. A mop of brown-blond hair fell over her head like she was an emo kid and didn't have time to style it because she was just too busy skateboarding.

I desperately wanted to draw nearer to this insouciant, high-titted twenty-year-old beauty school dropout from Orange County who chewed strawberry bubble gum like it was her job. But I would have to stand in line, for hovering before me was Timberlake, and behind him Rag Man. And there, looming in the corner with his powerful, magnetic gaze, was Pitts.

"Ashley, my dear!" crowed Timberlake. "I'm gonna need to check your boobies! Can I see those boobies, please?"

Ashley wore a goofy tweaker's grin. "All of you guys are freaky, huh?"

"You got *that* one right, darlin'!" crowed Rag Man. He elbowed me in the solar plexus, causing me to choke. "We're professional perverts."

"Professional *perverts*? Well, if that's not the *funniest* thing I've ever heard!" She laughed loudly.

Rag Man glowed in the warmth of his success and joined in with his *haw haw*. I wondered when was the last time he'd made a twenty-year-old girl laugh out loud, laugh *with* him, include him in on the joke, make him feel like a million bucks. Ashley was sweet, I got that right off the bat. She didn't have it in her to be snobby or standoffish.

"Let me take some test shots!" cried Rag Man, caught up in the heat of the moment.

"Nah, I got bad skin!" she said.

"No!" we all cried at the same time, except for Pitts, who was still standing quietly in the corner.

"Your skin's great," I remarked casually, from my post behind Rag Man. Timberlake shook his head at me, holding his palms facing down. *Pipe down, kid. This is* my *show.*

"No, it isn't. *Drugs!*" laughed Ashley, crooking a long wrist to her hip, so her elbow stuck out, triangular and tan. "It's my own fault. But I'm getting sober, dudes!"

"Are you?" said Timberlake, politely.

"Well, from *speed!*" she cried merrily. "Just from *speed*. DK said to me, 'I don't work with speed whores.'" She giggled, highly amused at the thought. "Isn't that *funny*? That I can't be in *porn* unless I get clean?"

My wallet grew and grew, and I was getting fatter. My actual *face* was getting fat. I could buy whatever the hell I wanted now, and it showed. I took biweekly trips to Whole Foods and loaded up on the organic peanut butter–flavored goat's milk. Then I upped the ante, branching out into the more esoteric shit: flaxseed husks and lemon rinds and dehydrated beets and blue-green chlorella powders. I cornered a stoned hippie girl with hairy armpits in the Health and Beauty aisle, pressed her up against the wall, and forced her to recommend some vitamins that might calm Timberlake's frightful nervous system, bring him back to earth. Psyllium was a terrific source of fiber. Cold-milled hemp seeds provided a balanced source of omega-3s. Bioflavonoids—onions, garlic, berries—were good for musculature. Vegetarians were prone to depression.

Her hippie lips moved up and down. Dysmenorrhea was the painful discharge of menses. Hepatitis A had a long incubation period (four to six weeks). Xenoestrogens could be found in soft plastics and in pesticides. Irritated colonic mucosa led to irritable bowel syndrome.

"Quick question." Rag Man was huffing in the kitchen after his morning stroll. His breath smelled like canned pork and beans. "Either of you guys know what a *gloryhole* is?"

Timberlake shook his head without looking up. He was hunched over a paperback copy of Henry Miller's *Tropic of Cancer*, tense with concentration. He couldn't make a dent in that thing to save his life. Neither of us could. I hadn't read a book the whole summer.

"Nope," I said. "We don't know what one is."

"And we don't wanna," added Timberlake.

Rag Man belched softly and sidled over to caress my shoulders with his fatherly palm. "Sam," he said, "you know when you take a shit at a truck stop?"

"Nope."

"And there's, like, a *hole* in the side of the door?"

"Nope."

"That's a *gloryhole*!"

I gave him a noncomprehending look.

"Are you guys *slow?*" Rag Man frowned. "What the hell are you drinking, by the way?"

"Peanut butter goat's milk."

"Why's it *blue?*"

"I added some algae to it," I said, defensively.

"Well, goddammit, the *hole* . . . didn't you know, guys stick their *dicks* through it? And someone sucks on 'em!"

"Mr. Man?" said Timberlake, his interest piqued almost against his will. "What universe do you live in?"

"It's a gay thing, of course," said Rag Man. "Don't think I didn't know that. But save your jokes, gentlemen, because the visionary in me says we could bring this one over to our side."

"I don't like where this conversation is going," said Timber. "I object."

"We'll get our girls pretendin' like they need to poop," murmured Rag Man, his eyes narrowing thoughtfully, "and then all of a sudden, a big old *black wang* comes wigglin' through the hole!" Rag Man chuckled merrily, like a chubby, victorious child.

"What a hateful scatological fantasy," I said.

"*Right*," said Rag Man. "So let's *build* us one in the *garage!*"

"Are you a tiny bit gay, do you think?" said Timberlake. "Do you want to, like, explore your sexuality?"

"Look, you two," said Rag Man, holding up one pink walrus hand. He smiled wanly, not his usual style at all. I recognized it as the smile of a crafty man, a man who already knows he has won. "Pitts is behind me on this. He thinks it's a sure moneymaker. So finish drinkin' your blue milk, and put the book away. 'Cause the three of us got a job to do."

We walked out into the light of day and boarded Rag Man's rented Kia. To be annoying, Timberlake and I both sat in the backseat. "Oh, I suppose you guys think that's *funny*." Then we drove to the Home Depot in Thousand Oaks and bought a porcelain round-front 3.5-gallon twenty-four-inch dual Jet Flush with a left-handed trip lever. We also bought paint, screws, hinges, three ten-by-six-foot pasteboard panels, a black Magic Marker, and ten rolls of toilet paper.

Back home, Timber rammed the panels together. Rag Man bored a circular hole in the side of one of the walls, at crotch level. I supplied the offensive graffiti. And there we had it: a facsimile of a public restroom cubicle with dirty toilet paper trampled underfoot, where pretty girls could give unhygienic blowjobs to anonymous black dicks.

"*Nasty*," announced Rag Man, pleased at his handiwork.

"Promise me that I won't have to shoot these," said Timberlake, a desperate look on his face.

"I ain't promising nothing, city boy," laughed Rag Man, clapping his meaty hand on Timber's white neck. "We all got a job to do around here, and we need to pull our weight. Frankly, I wouldn't rock the boat right about now, if I were you—you're overpaid as it is, and if I get the notion to tell Pitts just how damn worthless you are, well, you're bound to land on your ass in the driveway with the locks changed behind you, like the redheaded stepchild you are."

"I object," mumbled Timberlake.

"That said, I'll happily take responsibility for this garage-based operation, at least to begin. Silver-tongued as I am, *haw haw*, I'll take it upon myself to introduce the ladies to the 'hole."

Finally, Rag Man was out from behind the ignominy of his editor's desk, basking in the cold light of the gloryhole, a director at last. He proved himself to be a talented piggybacker, too. After each shoot, instead of skulking off alone and forgotten, Rag Man would allow the actress to shower and dress herself, to gather her thong and whips and chains and slimy tube of personal lubricant, to say the last of her good-byes, before he'd sidle up to her and murmur into her eardrum—quite casually—"Now, do you feel like making an extra four hundred bucks today, or what?" It was only after she said yes that he would show her the toilet in the garage.

Quite the innovator, Rag Man. But the interesting thing about him was how much he *liked* the girls. Despite his braggadocio about how much he loved dirty porn, in person, Rag Man was always respectful, and he spoke to each actress with courtesy and deference. He was also totally in love with his wife and probably constitutionally incapable of cheating on her. He never made gross passes at the talent, or tried to corner them in the bathroom for blowjobs, or anything like that. But there was this *disconnect* he had when it came to evaluating their performances. He simply lived for seeing a woman choking on cock through a hole in a restroom wall. If she didn't end up upside down in a puddle of drool and her own vomit, then she hadn't "done it right." She wasn't *hardcore*.

It was weird. Maybe depressing. And when Pitts made his move on Ashley Moore, she of course quickly schlepped her belongings upstairs. My spirits fell further. Who knew where Autumn Haze had ended up, anyway? Maybe the Dumpster? Didn't matter now. Moore and Pitts fucked guiltlessly in his expensive bed.

"You know, I'm not exactly sure *why*, but I just *dig* that freakin' crazy guy!" Ashley related to me, crackling with laughter, fixing herself another delicious midnight Jim Beam and water. "Bald and proud!"

"What's so darn special about him?" I grumbled. "And, hey, I thought you were getting *sober*."

"My *nose* is getting sober," she reminded me.

"Ah, hell, we're all so full of bullshit," I sighed.

Isaac was always around to give me my out. He was working for several high-profile artists that summer, making molds and doing drawings for them in his role as a fairly high-paid artist's assistant. Like many young artists in Hollywood, he had to balance the work he did for established artists against the stuff he did on his own, as he tried to get his own career off the ground. The equation often left him exhausted, and seeing him was a healthy reminder that other life paths had their own stresses to them, too.

One night he met me for a drink in the Frolic Room. Puzzlingly, Isaac still loved bars, even though he had stopped touching alcohol. He held on tight to that club soda, and bartenders never charged him a cent.

The Frolic Room was mildly famous because Charles Bukowski supposedly used to wallow there, but it was sort of the worst bar I had ever been to. It wasn't exactly dirty enough to be interesting, wasn't lush enough to be glamorous, and the bartenders, male and female, all looked like red-faced fishermen. Pickpockets hung out in the Frolic, eyeing the drunks hungrily, feeling at home.

"So," said Isaac. "How's life in the porno lane?"

"You wouldn't believe."

"You still got that great girlfriend, right? She seemed right up your alley."

"Liz's good, yes," I said, twirling a bit on my stool. "But she doesn't understand me, I'm beginning to suspect."

"How about giving her a break?" suggested Isaac, laughing.

"Why should I?"

"You might be a hard person to date," said Isaac. "I'm just guessing."

"Because of my profession?"

"Yes," he said patiently. "Hey, over there at the end of the bar, is that a tranny? Did this place turn into a tranny bar in the last two weeks without me noticing?"

I grimaced over at the end of the bar. "Er, no. Girl, I think."

"So what is it you want Liz to *understand*, anyway?" said Isaac.

"I'm not sure, man. My overall personhood. My wry sense of humor. My daily need to see human beings gag on cock and fall over drooling. You know."

"You know what I think?" said Isaac, pointing an index finger at me gently. "You spend a lot of time disliking most people in your industry, right? But my sense is that you're *jealous* of them."

I laughed. "Why would I be jealous of *them*?" I said. "Their lives are so fucked."

"Well, for starters, you seem to envy performers for their sexual abandon, which you'd like to emulate, but won't allow yourself to."

"Tried that," I explained. "No one wants to see me naked."

Isaac tipped his chin down toward the end of the bar. "That's one *weak* excuse for a tranny, don't you think? A *true* tranny should have some star quality to her. Don't you think? This one's just totally boring."

"That's not a tranny," I repeated. "It's an actual girl. Go ahead?"

"Well, okay," Isaac said. "To compensate for your jealousy, you make fun of performers for their willingness to perform the very acts you wish you could, using your wit to portray them as fools and laggards, though obviously, not all of them are."

"Boy, you're good," I said, impressed.

"If you ask me," Isaac continued, "Liz's probably kind of weirded out by your *inconsistency*, more than anything else."

"You think so?"

"Sure. You constantly malign the 'lifers' for accepting pornography as it is—sexist, hurtful, uncreative—but you yourself vacillate wildly from indicting the business on so-called moral grounds to slavishly following its every trend, all the while reaping a consequential weekly paycheck from it."

I stared at him. "Huh."

"How could she ever know what you're thinking?" said Isaac, reasonably. "I barely know where you stand myself."

We looked at each other and shared a shrug. My gaze sort of dribbled up to the electronic lotto game that played on a small television. I followed the bouncing ball.

"Everything smells like a cigarette here," said Isaac, sniffing his club soda. "It's so disgusting."

I sighed and pushed myself off the seat, walked over to the bathroom. It was locked, so I knocked on the door. No response at all.

"It's broken, genius." A dart player sipped from his cup, then flipped his tiny javelin at the colorful board, hatefully.

"I'm confused," I admitted, returning to Isaac and settling myself on the bar stool. "I had such high hopes."

"Sure," he said. "And the slumming thing is wearing thin, I know. But dude, you're going to have to make some kind of choice sooner or later. If you refuse to commit to either camp, you're robbing yourself of any sort of continuity."

"I should quit, shouldn't I?" I said hopefully.

"What kind of question is *that*?" said Isaac, laughing. "You do what you do. Only you can say what's right."

"Jeez, what a cop-out." I sulked.

"Look, are you happy?" said Isaac. "Is this job making you happy?"

"Hell no," I said emphatically.

"Are you sure?" said Isaac, crooking an eyebrow at me.

"Goddamn it," I begged, "what kind of a cretin would actually *like* what I'm doing?"

Isaac laughed. He drank the last of his club soda, and pushed around the cubes of ice with his red straw. Carefully, he speared the chunk of lime, piercing its fibrous pulp with the straw.

"It's complicated," he said, finally.

"Thank you," I nodded. "I just . . . don't want to let go of it yet. I need a bit more time to see where it goes."

"Look, don't sell *me*," said Isaac. "Sell Liz."

"Well, maybe I will. I'll try to put it down on paper for her."

Isaac raised an eyebrow. "Seems like a complicated trick. You a good writer?"

"No," I admitted.

Safe at home, fresh from a twilight swim in my million-dollar pool, hair dripping wetly, I poised a trembling pencil in front of a lined yellow pad, counting the ways I might explain my abiding love and continuing involvement with pornography to thee, my sweet and blameless girlfriend, White Liz.

"Hi Liz! It has been several days since you've been over at our house. Any particular reason for that? I know you were bit by a spider and fear further poisoning—but are you using that as like, a *metaphor*? Ha ha! But seriously: do you feel our house is 'venomous'? I admit, Timberlake is a little hard to deal with, and ever since Rag Man constructed a cocksucking station in our garage, yeah, things have been weird. But are you implying I am the company I keep? If so, you must be racist . . ."

(Crumple)

"Now look, Liz, I gotta be honest with you. Because I really like you, and my complete honesty is what you deserve. So I'm just going to spit this out. I've become fascinated with a videotape called *Slap Happy*. I've been watching it regularly for more than two months, and for some reason, though I can't necessarily figure out *why*, I can't seem to get enough of the sight of little teenagers on their knees choking on gigantic cocks, their cheeks billowing out like ruddy sails, tears in their eyes, eyeliner raccooning, sputum spewing from their pursed lips towards the camera lens, bespattering it . . ."

(Crumple)

"Dear Liz: Having a relationship within the porn industry is tough, isn't it? Quick question: do you ever get bored with our sex life? I have to admit that sometimes I think I'm bored. Perhaps my problem is that I'm around so many other nude, oiled-up women each day. Maybe it's just a bit too tempting for me. I mean, I love *asses*, Liz. Always have. Sometimes it's hard to see all of the asses, and not try to ask if I might lick gently on one cheek? Just for one singular horny second? Hey. You know what? I swear this *just* occurred to me, but perhaps introducing another partner into our little gang of two might be invigorating for the both of us . . ."

(Crumple)

"It's not that I like *Slap Happy* so much as I am *fascinated* by it. Do you see the difference? Can you allow for that kind of hairsplitting? Perhaps, in fact, I'm watching this videotape not so much for my own sexual pleasure, you see, as for the psychological edification. Each hateful scene teems with significant questions. For example: Did porno come first, creating the hatred? Or did hatred come first, legitimizing the porn?"

(Crumple)

"I feel things radiating off of you . . . like disapproval. And I don't like it. I don't want to see myself reflected in your eyes. Lately, I'm feeling deviant. Our closeness is weirding me out. I'm a bit selfish. Alone time means a lot to me. This ain't what love's about . . ."

(Crumple)

"The more I work in the sex industry, the deeper I sink, the more and more convinced that I am—that *we* are—unearthing something valuable in the human collective unconscious. It is something deep, and ugly, and awful, but it is nonetheless *there*, and I want to know more about it. *Slap Happy* and the like are shitty, malevolent, ill-conceived films, yes: but they are *confessional*, too, and for that reason alone, they are in some small way valuable. With their unconsciously delivered paean of hate, aggression, and sexual hostility, they are clearing the air, showing us what is *sick* inside of us all, and what must be *rectified* before we can continue along a healing path. This might sound weird, Liz, but in a way, Brandon Iron is becoming a kind of hero of mine. I mean, not for the way he *acts*, but for the way he is comfortable in the disrepair of his own skin . . ."

(Crumple)

You never saw someone as happy as Domeniko when he was sticking his curved, fist-thick, yellow-black cock through a hole in a pasteboard wall.

Niko laughed softly, with his boxer shorts around his ankles, the palm of his hand on his forehead, gasping, *This is the* shit! An Asian porn actress who didn't have a name yet squatted on her knees on the other side of the gloryhole board, wearing jean shorts and a sweater pulled up over her tits. Rag Man filmed them with tireless concentration, with sweaty, old-man fascination. "*Unbelievable,*" he whispered. Reverent, caressingly, the fat man framed her tits. The back of his neck shone, greasy in the garage light.

I weaved my way out of the garage and trudged my way to the kitchen. I sighed sadly. This wasn't my house anymore.

I rang Liz. "Sweetie?" I said. "Can I come over?"

"Yeah," Liz said, thoughtfully. "That'd be nice. Let's make dinner."

I pulled the Volvo out of the driveway, carefully backing away from the battalion of expensive cars that had congregated in our circular driveway. I waited for the security gate to open for me, then sped out down the hill, escaping.

When you left our place at twilight, the traffic was always a beast. The best you were gonna do was hop on Malibu Canyon Road and inch your way up through the hills, inch along like a good little guy, hoping you didn't get *too* fucked and there were no major accidents and all the rubbernecks that came with them before you hit the 101 near Calabasas. I chugged along, trying to listen to National Public Radio, being a contributing member of society and all that crap. Before very long, I snapped it off impatiently.

When I got there, Liz wasn't home yet, so I walked over to the liquor store and got us a bottle of Jack Daniel's and a two-liter Coke. I parked myself on her stoop. Cheap night at home. Maybe we'd make pasta and turn on the TV, then I'd smoke a couple of Parliament Menthols. Boy howdy.

"Hey, beautiful," I said, when her Jaguar slowed and she got out of it. I kissed her on the cheek.

"Hey, Sam." She smiled, let her face relax, and she was beautiful, and suddenly it wasn't so bad to be at her place anymore. I could think of worse places to be.

She showered and I got the pasta going. I poured myself a nice little drink and got one ready for her. Lisa was nowhere to be seen, and that was big points as far as I was concerned. It was hot in Liz's little place, double hot in the kitchen, so I took off my shirt and looked at myself in the steel reflection of the oven. My face was distorted and my hair looked clownish. I sipped my J.D. and Coke while I stirred the pasta.

"So what's new, baby?"

Liz smiled, looking tired. "DK wants to sell me."

"*Huh?*"

"Bradley, the owner over at Deep Productions, needs a new production manager. And he wants me for the job."

"Wow! That's great! Isn't it?"

"Yeah, I guess it's okay," said Liz. "He isn't going to pay that much more than DK, but it would be a step up the ladder. The funny part of it is that DK doesn't really want to let me go, but Bradley says he'll pay him five thousand *bucks* if he gives me to him."

"Sounds like horse trading when you put it that way."

"Or slave trading." Liz tested a strand of pasta, chewing it carefully. "I guess we deserve that."

"Deep's a pretty busy company," I said. "More stress. You up to it?"

"Who cares," Liz said flatly. "I can't see doing this forever."

"Yeah, me, too," I said. Watching her carefully. "I can't see doing this forever."

We made our way around each other uneasily that night, like rat traps baited with poisoned cheese, ready to spring off at any one moment. I caught her regarding me, once, while we were watching some awful movie, but she whipped her head away immediately and stared at the screen, as if exposed.

When the movie finished, we went out on her patio to smoke. Something loomed over us, a dark shape in the sky, but neither of us could distinguish it.

"Warm out for this time of night."

Liz nodded, watching the sky.

"I'm hot-blooded," I reminded her. "Warm means a lot to me."

She said nothing.

"Hey," I said, touching her shoulder. "You wanna go inside?"

"Yeah," said Liz. "Let's go to bed."

In her bed we slid sexily over black sheets. A fan whirred over our naked bodies. The house was quiet. I traced the outline of some roses on her tattooed forearm and kissed her temple, kissed her eye-brows.

"You still mad at me?" I said.

"Never was mad at you," Liz answered, looking down at her chest.

"Yeah, you were," I said.

"I was just . . ." Liz folded her arms, and sat back. She covered her body with a pillow. It was amazing how much of her body she could cover with just one little pillow. "Well—I was worried. I don't know why."

"Do you want to talk about it?" I said.

"Sam," Liz said, and then she didn't say much else for a little while. "I just . . . I don't know where this is heading. I don't know where *I'm* heading."

"We're just hanging out," I said. "Having fun. I mean, aren't you having fun with me?"

"I don't know," Liz said. "Honestly, I mean, I *thought* I was, but sometimes I just get freaked out. I'm sorry. I don't know if it's *you*, or it's *me*, or it's being around all these creeps all day . . ."

"The creeps probably aren't helping much," I considered.

"They're not," Liz said. She caressed my face, my thigh. "I look at you, and I see *a really good guy*! I know there's a good guy down deep inside there! But sometimes I get the most fucked-up *vibes* from you."

I frowned, taking her hand from my face. "What do you mean?"

"You give off . . . a weird energy."

"What weird energy?"

"I don't *know*, Sam. It's not something I can put into words. It's like, there's this *film* around you . . ."

I groaned. "I thought I was done with hippies."

"I told you, I couldn't put it into words, okay? It's just that I feel like, I feel . . . being around all those assholes all day, doing the shitty things you do all day . . . I feel like it's maybe rubbing off on you," Liz said. She grimaced uncomfortably, then continued. "And, I don't think I like being around it."

"It doesn't turn you on?"

"What? Me feeling like you're comparing my body to the girls you shoot every day? You acting like a dick to me? Me feeling like you're *haunted*? No. It doesn't really *turn me on.*"

"But we have good chemistry."

"Sometimes," Liz agreed. "But lately I feel like . . . you're just treating me like . . . a *corpse*, or something."

"You gotta be kidding me."

"I don't *mean* like a dead body. I mean, like I'm not me. I feel like you're just fucking, basically," Liz said. "You're just . . . fucking."

I sighed, sadly. "I'm just not good at this," I said dully. "Being in a relationship. It's new to me."

"I *like* you, Sam," Liz said. "I just feel like you're *hiding* something from me. Like, your mind is double-tracking, the whole time that you're looking at me . . ."

"Well, maybe I am," I said.

"So I don't understand why you don't have the courage to just tell me what's on your mind. *Tell* me," urged Liz.

"I can't," I said.

"You can," she insisted.

"You won't like it," I said.

"How can you know," Liz said, "if you don't try me?"

"I like throat-fucking," I said.

"What?"

"I . . . I like throat-fucking," I repeated. "And sometimes I wish that when we, um, made love, you would choke on my dick."

"What the hell are you *saying* to me?" Liz asked, her face crumpling in confusion and disdain.

"You said you wanted to know what I was thinking." She stared at me, and I stammered on. "I'm *into* this thing, Liz. And I haven't been able to tell you about it, not because I've been too scared, but because the time never seemed right. But now I see that it was driving a wedge between us, and I need to be more honest . . ."

"Sam? Hold on. Are you serious? You think you need to *tell* me that you want me to suck on your dick?"

"I want you to *choke* on my dick," I clarified.

"But *why*?" Liz cried.

"I'm *interested* in it," I said stubbornly. "I feel like I want to *explore* it."

Liz stared at me sadly.

"You really want me to do this for you?"

"Please," I said. "I'll do something for you, too, if you want."

Liz shook her head. And she lowered her pillow. "I *guess* I can try."

With her small white body, Liz approached my chest. She lowered her head toward my crotch, and I felt her tongue flick on the head of my cock. I squatted lower on the bed, making an indentation on the cheap metal-spring mattress with my body weight, and my chest puffed out, and my body stiffened. My eyes combed the stucco ceiling. I concentrated on a very small cluster, some very specific dots.

"Is that good?" said Liz.

"Yeah, right, but deeper," I murmured. Gently I caressed the back of her curly red-haired head. Lovingly, I placed my right palm at the base of her skull, pulling her into me, willing her head and her mouth closer. Liz's lips opened wider to accommodate me and she gagged momentarily, an *aaaack*ing sound, and I grinned. My left hand explored her face, bashfully at first. Her lovely youthful skin, elastic and well scrubbed. I caressed her nose and tweaked it gently. Something rising in me.

I kissed her little forehead and then, with some hesitation, took her little face in my left paw, my thumb digging into her jaw, my four fingers gripping her face.

I fucked her face, hard, hearing her gasping, choking for breath. My cock grew bigger and some luminous feeling rushed up into my brain, and I held her whole head in my hand and fucked it. Faster heartbeat and sickening sounds. I fucked her face and then I took my open hand and smacked her face hard, drawing a blazing red welt on her cheek.

"What the *fuck* are you doing?" Liz screamed, pushing away from me.

"I . . . I just . . . ," I stammered.

"Get the *fuck* away from me!" she snapped. "Jesus!" There were tears in her eyes. The welt on her face glared at me.

"No," I said, "I didn't, I didn't mean to do that to you, if you didn't like, I mean, I thought you might *like* all that . . ."

Liz pushed herself off the bed, away from me; trembling, she stood between the bed and the corner wall. Her back was to me. I looked at her spine protruding, the delicate little ridges of her vertebrae. She turned around to face me, mouth tight.

"Get your clothes on," Liz said softly. "And then get the fuck out of my house."

TWENTY-ONE

Breakfast came, and we huddled around our roundtable. The heavy Malibu fog enveloped our secret mansion like an impenetrable woolpack.

"Our money's down," Pitts said, looking at the subscriber figures. "Hell, I can't figure it out. I need to get on our resellers, fast." He sipped from his coffee cup thoughtfully. "No, we need to push the envelope."

"We're here to help, man," Rag Man assured him.

There was silence at the table, until I realized some sort of response was required of me, too. "Oh yeah," I said sullenly. "Me, too."

"Something wrong?"

"Personal shit," I grumbled. "Doesn't matter. We're here for you." I nodded rather unconvincingly toward Timberlake, who, after a moment's hesitation, aped my gesture.

Pitts continued, frowning. "We're going to have to expand our platform."

"Yeah, like with the gloryhole," Rag Man said. "I'm getting some killer footage."

"No," Pitts began. "I mean, within the larger scenes themselves. My sense is that we need to get quite a bit more hardcore. I'm thinking more along the lines of—"

"A cock cruising through a wooden hole?" Timberlake asked.

"Lookahere, Red," Rag Man cried. "If you're cruising for a fight . . ."

"Guys," Pitts said. "Listen up. I want to talk to you about gapes."

Gapes were a phenomenon we all knew about in porn, but rarely spoke of. On random, terrible occasions, after a monster penis invaded a pretty girl's tiny, perfect anus, the violated orifice would, upon removal of the cock, *pause* before retracting. Standing stock-still, it would yawn blackly, like a wound. Thus, the coveted "gape."

"My *goodness!* I'm gettin' what you're thinkin'—and I *am lovin'* it!" Rag Man announced. "Ass-fuckin', in the twenty-first century! *Haw haw.*"

I groaned. "So you want us to start showing the insides of people's assholes?"

"Hey!" Rag Man said. "Don't knock it—sounds *innaresting!*"

"It sounds *gynecological.*"

"Well, according to our stats, our subscriber base likes it," Pitts said. "Gapes are a big upside."

"But why?" Timberlake said. "They're a *mistake:* a bodily dysfunction."

"Who cares?" Pitts said. "If the fans like it, we can give it to them."

"You know what *else* is good?" Rag Man said, rising suddenly, wagging a huge finger wildly at all of our faces. "You know what I've been tryin' to get goin' for *years*?"

"A liposuction?" Timberlake mumbled.

"*Ass-to-mouth!*" Rag Man cried, his eyes blazing. "Picture it: after we shove that video camera deep on in there to film *Planet of the Gapes*, our girl takes that butt-flavored dick and sucks on it like a dang *lollipop!*"

"That's great," Pitts said. "Excellent thinking."

Rag Man glowed. "That's why they pay me the *big* bucks," he bragged, sitting down with a fatty grunt, his arms folded across his chest.

"From this moment forward, I want three gapes and three ass-to-mouths, minimum, for every scene," Pitts ordered.

"Impossible," I warned. "First of all, what if the girl won't do anal?"

"Then we don't hire her."

"But," I stammered, "what if she's really pretty?"

"Well, then you could see if you can make her pussy gape," Pitts said, as kind of an afterthought. "No, never mind. I don't think people will like that as much."

"But what about . . . making it funny . . . what about . . . a story," I mumbled softly.

"Stories are all well and good, Sam. But we have to make sure we get enough hardcore footage in the bag. That's what pays our bills." He slammed his notebook shut. "Anything else? No? Good."

Rag Man rose and pip-pip-pipped his way out to his rental car, zooming off in a joyous mood to Jack in the Box. Timberlake and I strolled out to the grounds to talk strategy. Timberlake had a nearly full pack of cigarettes with him. Every now and then, he would buy a pack and then smoke about two cigarettes and get bored with them. He passed me a cigarette now, refusing to take one for himself, and

I accepted it gratefully, lighting it with one of the giant barbecue lighters that we kept on the table outside.

"Don't you sort of wish he *would* fire us, sometimes?" I said, exhaling.

"Hell no! I gotta pay off that *car*. If Pitts says bye to me, I'm history. Back to the freakin' poorhouse, probably Oakland, no less."

"Sounds awful." I shuddered. "You'd probably have to get a real job."

"Yup. When you take a second to consider the alternatives, this porno thing isn't too horrible after all."

"How's your lady with it?" I asked. "She holding tight?"

"Oh, she hates it," Timberlake answered. "But she rides in my Acura, now don't she?" He laughed that wacky laugh of his. "Wanna go take a spin? Surprise Rag Man at the Box?"

"Nah," I said sadly. "I'll pass."

"Hey, kid," said Timberlake, inspecting me more closely, "what's bugging you? You've been dragging ass all day."

"Girl problems," I said.

"*Finally*," Timberlake said. "Liz's comin' round to the *real* stud of the house." He snugged up his balls with his white-boy palm.

"I'm actually kind of bummed, guy," I snapped, "so have a little sympathy."

"Oh," Timber said. "Sorry, bro. You know, I *am* sorry." He took a moment to stare at me, then dropped his gaze. "But I mean, couldn't you *see* this coming?"

"No, I *couldn't*, actually," I said bitterly. "What are you, some kind of soothsayer?"

"You ain't such a closed book as you might like to believe," Timberlake said.

"Meaning?"

"Meaning, from this guy's front-row seat, you're starting to resemble the true porno animal," Timberlake said. "And you guys don't mate for life."

"I'm not the one. I promise you that. I came here to *change* the game, not get changed by it."

"Well, that's what you've always said. But you have to admit that lately, you've got . . . well, you've got this edge about you."

"*What* edge?"

"Don't know," Timberlake said. "Ya know? I'm just a schmuck who likes a big ass in his face. But I glance over at you sometimes, and it looks like you're watching the whole scene way more intently than anybody needs you to. You get my drift?"

"No," I said. "I don't."

"What I'm saying," Timberlake said, patiently, "is I kinda get this feeling from you that you're still deciding whether or not to go native."

"Go native?"

"You know. Join up."

I snorted. "I'm joining nothing. I'm about done here."

"*Animal*," Timberlake repeated. "Porno animal."

I walked around the big house aimlessly, killing time before my performers showed up for their shoot. This house was so sweeping, so *majestic*, and it had so many goddamn *rooms* to it that even after living in the place for more than six weeks, I hadn't really explored them all. The library, for instance, was more or less uncharted territory for me, aside from the time that Timberlake had shot a five-on-one in there with some frightening cougar that I had watched about thirty-five seconds of before fleeing. Part of the reason I never hung out in there was the fact that there were almost no books. There were about ten different leather-bound sets of encyclopedias up on the wall, and I swear there were some false books on the shelves, too, some of those cardboard jobs. It was a terrible, drafty place to be: it felt like at one point the room had been a giant garage or filling station, and they had decided to raze it and convert it to something classier in order to raise the value of the property. There were no good chairs to hang out in, or any warm, cozy desks to write your essays at. Just bullshit enormous ceilings and false yak heads extruding from the walls, with their shiny dead eyes gazing down at you.

I checked my watch glumly and wandered down to the pool. Staring down at the cold water, I considered a brisk swim. But I didn't have it in me. I just stood there, my hands stuck in the pockets of my old shorts, watching the haze part in the distance. By afternoon it would mostly burn off. That made me sad, for some reason. The haze was miserable, but I was always sad to see it go.

"What's the word?" Timber said, as he approached.

"Getting ready to film my first Gape-O-Rama, I guess."

"I just had a *great* idea for my scene," Timberlake said. "I'm gonna pretend like my girl is studying for her medical boards, right? And her lab partners just *desperately* need her to pose for a colonoscopy."

"I'm so proud of you," I murmured, my head lilting down to the grass, checkin' out those blades.

"Hey, I appreciate that, man. Now, cheer up, dude. You're going to put up something classic."

"The word is *nasty*," I said, in my best Rag Man impression.

There was nothing I wanted to do less than knock off a few gaping buttholes. But duty called, and I prepared to receive the talent. My actress turned out to be one of Spiegler's Czechs, the type you weren't so excited to greet and whisk away all for yourself. She had dried-out blond hair, a reddened face, and plenty of meat and potatoes on her bones. But what was I going to do, send her away? Instead I shoved her into the bathroom and let her get into her whore costume by herself.

Downstairs, I made a cup of black coffee and checked the age on her passport. Thirty. That was almost dead in porn years. Her name was long and complicated, but luckily she'd picked a nice, vacant sex-film moniker. She was literally calling herself "Alice."

As we waited for her to dress, a new actor named Byron Long showed up to take part. He didn't raise an eyebrow on my part, but his presence turned Rag Man into a trembling fanboy. "Well, damn if we didn't hit the big time *now*!" he whispered, awed. He sucked in all the fat of his stomach, and military-saluted our new, dreadlocked talent. "*Huge* fuckin' fan, man! This is one hell of an honor!" And I'll be damned if Byron didn't dig it. No matter the context, when someone thinks you are the tits, that's a beautiful thing. For the next several minutes, Rag Man just shook his head adoringly, and was seen to be murmuring over and over, "Byron fuckin' Long."

In all fairness, Byron was a star. And he toted around just an *immense* penis. By chance, I'd booked Sledge Hammer for the job, that gentle muscleman, and Domeniko, too. In a flash, I realized that I'd inadvertently managed to load the plate with the three hugest cocks in my bullpen, guys with penises that didn't even *connote* penises, but instead appeared to be veiny, sovereign organisms that God had gremlinized and stuck on men's bodies. When a man stopped to consider those wangs, alongside the mammoth, swelling, saline-filled fake breasts of the day, well, it gave him pause. Perhaps we were on the edge of some genetic engineering final frontier here. I wanted my grant money.

I was in a bad humor when "Alice" emerged from the bathroom, freshly douched, flushed with rouge and pancake, and it only got worse when I surveyed her more carefully. The fantasy of her body was nothing I cared very much to swim into. The performers, though, gathered around her like predictable, ravenous barracuda, swarming the day's meal. I watched them, my body slack. The man with the movie camera.

Because I couldn't bring myself to imagine a scenario, I instructed Sledge to come up with some magic.

"Let's pretend she's *hitch*hiking," said the man-child. Breathlessly, he looked to me, hopeful.

"Solid idea, Sledge," I said gently. I sent him to go get the keys to Pitts's Viper.

Alice stood out on the Malibu lawn before us. It wasn't the warmest day on record. Her hairy blond arms squeezed around her middle and she chewed her lip, nervous.

"Look," I said, "if anything feels slightly off to you, let me know." I checked my camera's lens for dried flecks of ejaculate, and spying one, I spit on the corner of my shirt and attempted to wipe it away. "I'm gonna have to go for a few gapes, but we'll try to make sure it's as painless for you as possible."

Alice just smiled at me.

"Not *my* idea, you understand—it's my boss's. As far as I can see, he's bowing to the pressures of the marketplace. But I kinda have to fall in line, if I want to preserve my own job. Do you understand?"

She grinned good-naturedly and nodded hesitantly. Alice had a nice smile, I had to admit it.

"You know," I said, walking more closely to her, "you're okay. This won't be so terrible. Listen, I'm sorry if I'm in a bad mood today. You have to understand, I do this *all* the time. I'm probably approaching some kind of overload, like that pinball machine, right? '*Tilt.*'" I shook my head, frazzled, yet amused in spite of myself. "Seriously, if we start to get on your nerves, do tell me. 'Hey, white girl,' that sort of thing. I get annoyed with that crap myself, I'll be honest. It's *childish*, don't you think?"

"Yase?" said Alice. She shook her head helplessly and hugged her arms into her belly. "But, okay, can you talk more slow? My English, not so good."

I stared at her for a few seconds despondently. "You hang in there, kiddo."

Sledge drove the Viper around the bend in the driveway, careful as could be.

"Hey baby." He opened the window and attempted a leer, but it was like a first grader leering at his mom; he could not pull this off. "Need a *ride*?"

"Oh, yase," responded Alice. And that was our scenario. I dragged out an expensive rug from the living room of the house, and we stripped the miniskirt off Alice and she lay down quietly to take the hits from Byron Long, to suck on Sledge while she was at it. I fiddled around with my camera, my finger on the tele-zoom. I rubbed my elbow against the side of my body, and their bodies went murky before me, as I wished myself somewhere else, someone else. A catcher in a big, quiet ballpark. An astronaut who loved roasted chicken. A chiropractor with a forgotten parking space.

They knocked her deeper into the earth. Domeniko caressed her lumpenproletariat breasts with nicotine-stained fingers. He bent his head to one Slavic nipple and, pursing his lips, he began to nurse. I saw bugs over in the grass jumping: little tiny guys. Byron Long was wearing Tevas and socks. The muscles of his calf twitched. Rag Man snuffled up behind me, lovin' this job. I backed away and tried to see everything. But I saw too much. I saw Liz answering phones over at DK's, rolling her pen restlessly on her desk. I saw Luiz's wife huddled over a sink in their little house, making a cup of weak tea. I saw my dad talking to a patient resting on the cushions of his couch, while another one sat in the waiting room, trolling through a *New Yorker* for the cartoons. Alice got lifted up into the doggy-style position, her butt high, and the guys all lined up to take a turn. I trudged up near to them. Sledge snuck up behind her and pumped his large hips powerfully. Alice's eyes went big. Breath escaped out from her mouth and she tried to say something, but her tiny voice was swallowed up in the schoolyard chatter. *Go white girl go white girl go!* Byron giggled. He did a little dance. *Fuckin' fine-ass white girl. Nobody told you to be that fuckin' fine.* Sledge laughed. He got tapped out by Niko. *I'm gonna get up in this motherfucker like a mechanic,* Niko said. My foot was falling asleep, so I knocked it against the ground a couple of times.

Niko got kicked out by Byron. *She got one of those asses that don't even move.* The late afternoon sun was warming my skin; it felt good on my arms and legs. *Don't rush shit, just give me your best shit.* Alice was still trying to say something, but no words came out of her working mouth. Sledge nudged Byron to the side, *my turn please huh huh.* Alice waved one hand weakly up at the air, and then the top of her head bashed against the ground and then her cheek was against it. Sledge reared back and slammed his hips forward into her like a battering ram. He performed this motion over and over: a power lifter in action. The world's strongest man.

And then Alice crumpled. She pulled her ruined womb away from Sledge Hammer.

"I cannot . . . I cannot . . . ," she gasped.

Sledge gazed down at himself remorsefully. "I . . . guess I fucked her a little bit too hard."

I watched Alice doubled over with pain for a moment, then turned my camera off. Slowly, I tiptoed over to inspect her, along with the rest of the guys. We huddled around her keeled-over body, trying to figure out the next move.

"Hey, sweetheart, are you okay?" Byron asked, in a concerned tone. "Is she breathing?"

"Alice? You breathing? She doesn't really speak English," I explained.

"Maybe we should think about getting her to a hospital," Rag Man said.

"I am fine," Alice said from the ground, grimacing. "I don't . . . go to hospital."

We watched as she staggered to her feet. Alice bit her lip, woozy from the effort, then immediately pitched back down on her bottom.

"Let me get you a water," Rag Man stammered.

"We have one right over here," Byron said.

We all tripped over ourselves to offer her a water. Sledge reached the bottles first. His outstandingly huge penis, still inflated to maximum capacity, rocketed from the center of his crotch at a rude 45-degree angle, bobbing up and down. "Here," he said softly, handing the plastic bottle to the woman who sat crumpled in a heap on the carpet before him. "This is *water*."

As Alice sipped from the bottle, Rag Man and I retreated a few steps to hide behind the Viper and talk business.

"Ya think we better quit?" Rag Man asked.

"She does look kind of broken," I admitted.

"Sledge is a huge man," Rag Man noted. "Big ol' wang."

"Yeah. Preternaturally stiff, too. They're *all* big guys. She was taking punishment in there. Something got totaled."

Rag Man rubbed his chin thoughtfully. "We can't let her go on. 'Course, at the same time, I don't see how we can really stop *here*. We only got like ten minutes in the can. No gapes or nothin'."

"I know," I said. "And what are we gonna do about paying everyone?"

"That's exactly what I was wondering." He looked at me. "Why don't you go upstairs and see what Pitts has to say about it."

I frowned. "Why don't *you* go upstairs?"

"Hell, I'm just second unit on this! *You're* the director. Don't you think you oughta step up?"

"I guess so," I admitted. "Keep an eye on that one, okay? Make sure she doesn't bleed all over the rug."

"Aye, aye," Rag Man said.

I toted my camera into the kitchen, where it was quiet and cool. A large wooden ceiling fan revolved slowly, at its lowest setting, from the ceiling. I poured myself a mineral water, then took a deep breath and ascended the white staircase up to Pitts's humble abode.

"Yes?"

"Pitts? Sam. Sorry to disturb you, man . . ."

"Not at all. Come in."

He was pecking away at his computer, wearing a pair of reading glasses. He peered at me over the top of the frames. "Hey. God, it's incredible how much time I spend in front of this thing. You'd think running a porn company would be all shits and giggles, but mostly I spend my days dealing with angry subscribers and buying banner ads. Not very glamorous, huh?"

"No, I guess not," I said. "But, hey, can I talk to you about something?"

"Yes?"

"We got a woman down. My girl's having, uh . . . some body issues."

"She shitting on you?" Pitts grinned. "Do you need a raincoat?"

"No, that I'd know how to handle. She's . . . kind of in pain. I think she got wacked too hard."

Pitts frowned. "What do you mean?"

"Sledge." *I fucked her too hard. Huh huh.* "They got overzealous, I guess. And I must have fallen asleep at the wheel."

"Oh," said Pitts. "Well, that's not good. Does it look serious?"

I frowned. "I can't really tell."

"Is she bleeding?" asked Pitts.

"No," I said. "Not yet. I asked her if she wanted to go to a hospital, but she said no."

"Probably doesn't have health insurance," Pitts explained. "Most of the foreign girls are here illegally."

We both sat there for a minute, watching each other.

"Well," I said, hopefully, "if she's not bleeding, then it's probably nothing too major."

"Right," Pitts said. "I mean, if she was *bleeding*, then we'd definitely have to take her to the hospital. I couldn't see any way around it."

"Definitely," I agreed. We both sat there nodding, for a long moment. In the Malibu distance, a coyote howled, low and mournful.

"So," I said slowly, "you want me to kill the scene?"

"Nah," said Pitts.

"I don't think she can have sex anymore today," I explained.

"Sure," Pitts said. "That's what I assumed." He turned back to his desk, slipping his reading glasses back onto his face.

"But . . . you still want me to pay her?" I asked, confused.

"Certainly," Pitts said, briskly. "Pay everybody, as usual. Do you need anything else, Sam? I should probably get back to this."

"No," I said, pursing my lips, "only—what do you want me to do about the end of the scene?"

"Just have the guys jerk off on her face," Pitts said impatiently, turning back to his computer and beginning to type. "That way, we can still use it on the site."

Evening came, and the house was quiet. All shoots were over for the day. Pitts, Timberlake, and Ashley had headed to the Malibu

Inn for dinner, drinks, and song. Rag Man was locked safely inside his room, hunched over his PC, assiduously segmenting long-form pornography into this generation's newest easily downloadable jizz-friendly Web clips. And I was lying on my bed, looking up at the ceiling.

But what if she's really hurt? I wondered. *What if something terrible happened to her insides?*

The guilt had set in a few hours after I'd sent everybody home. Now it was eating away at me. I pictured myself swooping the Volvo down in front of Spiegler's house, demanding in an outraged tone of voice to see "Alice." *Show me where she is, you bastards.* Then finding her in anguished, cold-sweat pain, like Penny in *Dirty Dancing,* and I would whisk her away to Cedars-Sinai, where a team of dedicated nurses would swab her forehead with cool rags.

Then they would turn to me. *What have you done to this poor woman?*

N-no . . . I would say, trembling with fear. *It wasn't me! It was Sledge!*

She will never be able to have children, the nurse would spit. *How could you let this happen?*

But . . . it's not my fault! It was Pitts! The gapes . . . I'm just the cameraman . . .

I sighed sadly. I would be swooping down on no one. Why should I take this Czech woman to Cedars-Sinai, anyway? She had Spiegler to take care of her. And anyway, didn't she know what she was getting into when she flew here in the first place?

A wave of peevish swill rose in my stomach, and suddenly, I was infuriated. After all, this was a nasty challenge that we'd signed up for here, and anybody too weak to stick with it was allowed to *leave.* As members of the club, we were paid a premium wage for our achievements, not because our work was *important*, but because it was *onerous*. Porn was exacting, disgusting work, but at least we could all take solace in the fact that we were living on the edge and for the *moment*.

Foul acts against humanity were videotaped carefully, then sold on street corners and in back rooms. We were the sexual garbagemen of the United Gapes of America, supplying delicious plugs of spunk to a citizenry too frightened to pursue the fantasy themselves. *Every damn day* I donned my thick-jellied yellow rubber astronaut suit to dive in and pull out another nugget of creeping doom, but was I complaining? No. Was I quitting? No! My girlfriend kicked me out of her house, and that was nothing! My own father couldn't bear to have a conversation with me without cutting it short—but that was nothing! Look at me—was I quitting?

I wasn't going to fucking quit!

I tried my hand at some occupational therapy, as it was said to ease anxiety and raise levels of self-esteem in crazy people. Cadging a bunch of neglected tools that I found in the garage, I sawed and hacked away at leftover pieces of scrap lumber, attempting to build a birdhouse. After all, fall was coming. Our feathered friends would need a place to roost. I gloved my hands, donned protective goggles. Luiz raised his weed whacker in a cautious salute. My birdhouse emerged rather irregularly, sloping forward, as if a four-year-old had made it, but nonetheless, I felt kind of elated. Within the glorious confines of my tender wooden craft box, a proper little robin baby boy might be raised.

Proudly, I looked about for a pine tree onto which I might nail my creation, when out of nowhere, a woman who looked like Tommy Lasorda with sloppy tits appeared, panting wetly.

"Sambo, I wantcha to meet my *wife!*" Rag Man said proudly, one beefy arm around his prize. "She just flew in today."

"And boy am I tired," Lady Rag Man added, dead-eyed.

I laughed politely. "I didn't know your wife was so funny."

She stared at me distrustfully. "I ain't."

Like many married couples who had grown to resemble one another in both appearance and mood, the Rags waltzed through the mansion with identical out-turned loping gaits, entering rooms and letting fly farts without ever realizing which of them had done the deed. They held hands like lovers, as Lady Rag Man wrinkled her brow suspiciously at the majestic castle. Her charisma, Frankensteinian. Luiz's dog sniffed at her ankles, then leapt away, yelping.

"She freakin' you out?" Timberlake whispered.

I nodded, too scared to speak aloud.

Bit by bit, we were force-fed the story of their romance. They had grown up in the same cornhusker town, and upon graduating from college, had gotten hitched immediately. "When you find someone who's right for ya, you go for her!" Rag Man crowed.

"Larry was very forward," Lady agreed.

"Larry?" I asked incredulously. "Tell me . . . what did *Larry* do?"

"Don't nobody up here call me that," Rag Man said hurriedly. He moved his wife's hand off his thigh and back onto her lap, whereupon she immediately placed it back on his thigh.

"But now we will," Timberlake assured him, smiling broadly. "*Larry.*"

"You're testin' me, huh, Red? Lucky for you my best girl's here, or I'd give you some kinda smack."

"Larry, I'd like to practice some gapes later. You're available, I assume?"

A normal woman would have given us a good tongue-lashing for using that kind of foul language in the house. But Lady relaxed into the land of enormous schlongs and scatological humor like she'd been born there. Though Timberlake and I attempted to persuade her otherwise, she slapped a red ball cap on her head and insisted upon shadowing us through the course of her first working day. Lady watched our scenes with splendid concentration, frowning, rarely blinking, standing about three feet from the action, licking her lips as she stared into the actresses and their spectacular tits.

"I think some of the girls might be weirded out," Timberlake mentioned to Pitts.

"So, very nicely, ask her to take a step back," Pitts said. "Not a big deal."

"But *I'm* frightened of her!" Timberlake cried. "My penis is retracting into its shell. Everyone's is."

"She's his wife," Pitts said firmly. "Make it work."

But the Rags were a hard nut. Soon I learned that they had been in a religious cult together, before the man of the house had begun tinkering with black porn. During this heady period, they had followed a guru. They had done ritualistic dances. They had enjoyed a "sexually unstructured environment."

"What the heck's that supposed to mean?" I whimpered.

"We was swingers," Rag Man whispered. "Getting buck wild. Don't tell her I told you, because she'd skin me."

Against my will, my mind flashed strobe-lit images of Lady sporting tight jeans and a cowboy hat in the jungles of Pittsburgh, getting down on her knees for a quick meal of guru cock. The image haunted me. Please just let the '70s die . . .

"And Rag Man's all *revved up* these days," I complained to Timberlake and Ashley Moore, as I attempted to prepare a mushy soup of green lentils. I consulted my recipe, frowning. "He told Byron, *git that baby-batter ready!* I mean, that's just *dumb*, right?"

"Oh, come on, they're cute," Ashley said. "I mean, still married, after all those years? And still in love? It's really rare and special."

"They're working together to craft buttbangs," Timberlake said. "That's not *cute*."

"The moment she picks up a camera and starts directing," I promised, "I am out of here."

But Lady would make partner more quickly than anyone could imagine. When a four-man in the garage brought together the tremendous talents of Tony Eveready, Domeniko, Wesley Pipes, and a long-haired, mildly handsome actor named David Steele, she was there to observe and take notes. Steele, a light-skinned, male-model type who was probably not even truly black (Egyptian?), was pleasant and polite, but radiated a sick kind of narcissism that I'd grown to associate with only the most pathological of my female stars. Still, Lady stood there watching Steele hungrily, never taking her eye off him, just mouth-breathing loudly.

Midway through the boring, workmanlike bowel movement of a scene, an argument broke out between Eveready and Steele, in reference to an accusation that Steele was trying to "bogart the pussy." Steele, unwilling to back down even in the face of the likes of the thuggish, bullying Eveready, made a grumbling remark to the tune of *Get in where you fit in, dude,* at which point Eveready told Steele to *back the fuck up, cuz,* before he murdered him with a gun. But none of that could dull the desirous embers that smoldered in Lady Rag Man's lint-colored irises. "He's *handsome,*" she gushed to me and me alone, after the scene was finished. I was packed into my special corner of the kitchen, pushed up between the broken fax machine and the ionized aluminum garbage can, trying to write my checks. "Right you are," I mumbled, zoning out on the bottles of lube, the never-ending bottles of lube.

Things were going to get worse before they got better. Feeling self-conscious about my body, I stripped naked and stood in front of a full-length mirror and regarded the insides of my thighs, which now seemed kind of bulgy. With more time to spare, I might have rustled up a quick eating disorder, but the best I could do on such short notice was immediately go find a yoga class at a strip mall near Zuma Beach. Yes, there are strip malls in Malibu; bad ones that don't have any life to them. At least the strip malls down in Koreatown and Culver City are bustling with dirt and pestilential energy. At least you can *laugh* about them. It was a terrible feeling to drive your car into one of these quiet, West LA two-story jobs and see all the red Miatas and silver Mercedes stacked up, announcing untouchable fortunes and quiet 401(k) hells.

I plucked my yoga mat from the trunk of my car and bounded up the steps into a room full of big rose-colored crystals that were also lamps and Zen fountains that peed recycled water infinitely. I paid my sixteen dollars and tried to relax into something good. But the class was packed to the gills with black-souled entertainment lawyers with frosted hair. One dude wore black biker shorts. In the mirror that lined our western wall, I could read the outline of his anus.

Somehow, my life had morphed into a slow, reflective stroll through a sewer. The human waste and vomit and semen was waist-deep. I had purchased a sweet pair of waders and a conductor's cap, but they were coming apart at the seams. Idly, I wondered why I was doing this to myself voluntarily. *Because I was good at it?*

Vinyasa flow.

Because I had no idea it would turn out like this?

Downward dog.

Because shit happened, and I had turned out to be one of the shits?

Upward-facing dog.

—

That night, Timberlake, Pitts, and Ashley headed back to the Malibu Inn to listen to a live band and suck down a few beers. They invited me to go along with them, but I said no. I returned to the dour confines of my pool-house bedroom, where I fell asleep heavily. When they came back late at night, their drunkenness woke me up.

"What's the madness all about?" I said, rubbing my eyes, as I trudged into the kitchen.

"He was *there!*" Ashley exclaimed. She washed her hands in the kitchen sink, her eyes flashing with enthusiasm.

"Who was there?"

"Emilio," Timberlake answered casually, cracking open a fresh beer. "We talked to him for a while. *Very* cool guy. He says he'll check the site."

"Aw, hell," I muttered.

"What's the matter with you, grumpy?" Ashley said, coming behind me to give me a hug. I reached behind my back to pull her tall, muscular torso closer into my body. Her small breasts felt good against my back.

"The body's not even cold in the ground," Timberlake said, clucking, "and already he needs another one."

Reluctantly, I released Ashley from my grip. "You moralistic bastard."

"You have a *girlfriend!*" he whooped.

"Liz and I are having domestic difficulties," I said.

"She's upset with you?" Ashley asked, taking a seat behind the kitchen table and tapping a cigarette out of a nearly empty pack of Marlboro Lights. She yawned.

"As it turns out, yes."

"Why?" Ashley asked absently.

"I may be a bit too porno for her."

"Too *porno?*" Timberlake said, grinning. "Sam, oh Sam. What kind of shit did you try to pull off?"

"Yeah, what'd you do?" giggled Ashley.

"I didn't do *anything*, you guys," I said. "I mean, it was like totally *harmless.*"

"Real life is not a scene," Ashley laughed.

"And real girls are not real whores," Timberlake said. "Sorry, Ashley."

"No offense taken, *dickhead.*" She smacked Timberlake on the thighs. He made to karate-chop her back.

"I just got a little too rough with her," I said. "And she wasn't exactly up for it."

Timberlake shook his head. "*Brutal*, man. Very brutal. I can see you doing that, by the way."

"You guys think I'm a whore?" Ashley said, thoughtfully. She held an unlit cigarette between her index and middle fingers.

"No," Timberlake said. "Come on, have a sense of humor. I didn't mean it like that."

"I mean, technically, I *am*, but like, so what?"

I raised my palms to her. "It's just a word."

"You guys probably think you're better than me," Ashley said. She placed her hands on her hips and approached me accusatorily. "Is Liz, like, *better* than me, because she threw you out of her house for something I let guys do to me every day?"

"No one's better than anyone," I said, soothingly.

"So *what* if I like a rough mouthfucking?"

"You . . . you like it?" I said weakly.

"I *love* it. Does that make me, as a whore, a less useful member of society? I mean, a belt wrapped around my neck turns me on—should that be made *illegal*?"

"Would you like to marry me?" I asked, approaching her with tender arms.

She sighed and pushed me away. "Dummy, Pitts is waiting for me."

"But the belt . . . wrapping around your neck?"

"He's your *boss*," she said pointedly.

"Yeah," I grumbled.

Ashley gathered up her smokes and her purse. Her heels made a clicking sound on the tile floor of the kitchen. "Good night, guys." With poise and grace, she winked at me, then walked up the stairs to her man and their wide-sprawling million-dollar bed.

Timberlake and I shrugged at each other.

"Different set of rules, huh?"

"Different strokes for different folks," he said, clapping an amiable, bony hand on my shoulder. "And so on and so on."

I just stared at my shoes, as low as I'd ever been.

"Hey, cheer up! Did I ever tell you that my mom modeled for *The Joy of Sex*?" Timberlake offered. "Yep, spread-eagled."

TWENTY-TWO

When September came, the sun was teetering on the edge of summer, so close to falling off, but there was just a little bit of goldenness left. The energy had shifted from the nervous, yellow haze of August to a sweet, rich apple glow. There was a kind of beauty in the air.

They were drinking this thing called Fiorinal. That's what I remember.

It was a clear liquid, and everyone was sipping at it, everyone being Ashley Moore, Pitts, and Timberlake. It was a late weekend morning, and we had no shoots scheduled for the day, and they were in the kitchen getting loopy, sipping this clear liquid from a cup, swooning and laughing like loons, hugging each other, getting giddy and even smoking cigarettes in the house.

"What in hell is that stuff?" I growled, edging past them to pour a late riser's bowl of cereal.

"We don't *know!*" Ashley Moore said proudly. "Come *on!* You have to drink some, too!"

"It's battery acid, we think," Timberlake said, excited. "Sammool, I want to dance with you!"

"Get your filth away from me," I said, mustering up the only dignity I had, taking my cereal into the living room, where I could munch it in front of the TV.

"Cheer up, Sam!" Pitts called. "The numbers are up! The gapes came through. It's time to celebrate! I got us tickets for a punk rock show down in San Bernardino, so get dressed, we're leaving in an hour."

"I hate punk rock," I said, scooping up a spoonful of Grape-Nuts sadly. "Thanks anyway."

"See?" Ashley Moore said. "Punk rock is bad."

"You guys are too clueless to understand," Timberlake said, looking at the end of his cigarette curiously, taking little puffs that never even got close to coming into his lungs. "You had it too easy growing up. Punk rock is the purest expression of musical angst."

"If Sam doesn't have to go, then I'm not going, either," Ashley announced.

"Bad *Religion* is going to be there," Pitts said.

"Social *Distortion*," echoed Timberlake. "You two are going to *so* wind up regretting this. The mosh pit alone is worth the price of admission."

"I don't want to be in a mosh pit," I said. "Mosh pits weren't made for people like me."

"What a puss!" Timberlake exclaimed, elatedly. "I never realized what a total puss you were until right this moment." He took another sip of Fiorinal, screwed up his face, then immediately slumped forward. "Oh, *man*, this stuff is like taking a crap right in your pants."

Pitts and Timberlake sped off in the Acura half an hour later. A short while after, Rag Man squired Lady away to a romantic seafood buffet in Santa Monica. "Buttered scallops? No?" And then Ashley Moore and I were home alone.

We trotted down to the pool. Ashley carried a full glass of Fiorinal in her left hand, jiggling, not quite walking straight in chunky clogs, on her long grasshopper legs.

We laid down towels, preferring those to the deck chairs, and cuddled on the ground, grass bunching underneath the mottled fabric. I hesitantly fingered a scar on her back. "What's this?"

"Oh," Ashley said. "I grew two inches in one summer. That's a stretch mark."

"You're tall," I remarked softly.

"No kiddin', huh?" She laughed. "Here, drink this."

I took the Fiorinal from her, but with reluctance. "God, you guys are such terrible influences." I sipped very hesitantly from the glass, then, surer it wasn't pure poison, took a deeper draft. "Not so bad."

"What did I *tell* you?" Ashley said lazily. She was chewing on her words, just the tiniest bit. Making them stretch in the sun. She lay down heavy on the large, soft towel, content and drugged, like a lean, tawny cat.

I took another small sip of the liquid, swishing it around in my mouth like Listerine before gulping it down. I checked out the blue of the horizon, and ran a hand through my hair. "So this stuff is really supposed to get you high?" I said, dubious.

"Wait on it," she murmured. "Won't be long now."

A heady little buzz started up within the minute. It was a warm crimson flush, unlike any inebriant I was used to. I bit down on my lips and tried to listen to it, nodding, laughing a little bit. Giggling, then. Toppling.

"*Seeee*," Ashley said, triumphantly.

"Goodness," I whispered, my heart beating quickly. "I may have to drink this whole thing."

Ashley turned over and gave me a scared look. "Don't, 'kay?"

"I'm just playing around," I mumbled. I ran a hand along her shoulder blades. "You have nice skin, I can massage you. I like your skin, and I can massage you if you want."

"Yeah, okay, Sam," she said. She took off her bikini top and I ran my hand over her luxurious skin. It curved into every shape I pushed it in. So moist, so silky, so athletic. So alive. So luminescent, so thick with electricity. I trailed down her spine, tickling my fingertips down an ant trail, and found her buttocks and trembling, I began to ever so lightly caress both muscular globes with the palms of my hands and in only moments, I had shivers running up both my forearms, my eyes closing. My heart beat in my head and my blood pounded. My whole mind was like: ass. My brain and my face were just white shivers, shivers and ass.

Ashley turned over lazily. "Whaaaat are you doing?" she laughed.

"Nothing," I said, kissing her. "I'm just, like, you know, getting to know you."

Giggling, she came into my grasp. Rolling on the ground, my whole mind was made to feel the weight of her, the heat of her. Her gum breath and her silken hair. Fiorinal let you breathe funny, and when I gathered her into my clutches, cloaked in God's sweet, gold, white-light night, it felt nothing like pornography; I mean, I wasn't *embittered* at all. We were trembling like two kooky fairies.

"Hey," I whispered gently, "let me fuck your mouth, 'kay?"

She nodded and she knelt on the ground and I stood up and my bathing suit was stripped to my ankles then stepped out of. In the gentle fall breeze, I was as young as I would ever be again, my skin tanned brown from a long summer.

"Go ahead—*slap* me," Ashley said, giggling. "Are you scared?"

"God, no," I said, with something like open devotion. "Watch out." And I aimed and the open palm of my hand made contact with the skin of her face. The impact produced a loud *crack!* Ashley reeled back from the force of the blow, a surprised cry escaping her. Then she opened her mouth wide, and laughing, coy, like a little girl, just kept on laughing and laughing. Soon, in amazement, I joined her. Laughing.

"Boy, that's nothing!" she bragged. "*Nothing!*"

"You think this is *funny*, huh?" I whispered. I tried a low growl at her, exploring how that felt. To growl. My blood was suddenly pounding and hot. I bit my bottom lip, in some weird version of desire and power, something high and poisonous. I tried to burn holes in her with my dangerous eyes.

"Actually," she taunted, "I think *you're* funny."

I slapped at her again, catching ear this time. She fell back, laughing, and delighted, leapt up to kiss me in the mouth. I seized her, *let me fuck you and kill you, baby*, and we both cackled and I pressed my arms around her rib cage in love and in hunger and she used her shoulders, muscular and firm, to pry herself from my grasp. Suddenly free, she yelped, giggling, and made for the pool. I dived in after her.

The cold shock of the water clawed at my heart, narrowing my lust into a kind of laser beam. And despite liking Ashley a lot moments earlier, when I was massaging her, now I just sort of wanted to chop off her head. Regaining my balance, I wriggled through the cold depths, finding her perfect body and, seizing it by the waist, I tried to pull her underneath. She gasped, fought against me, laughing and desperately begging, clawing my shoulders with pin-sharp nails.

"You fucker," she laughed. "I hate you."

"I'm crazy for you," I whispered back.

I held her tight until she ceased to struggle. I could feel her beat against me. We floated there for a moment, soft and still. She dragged her palms slowly over the thick cords of my neck, watching me, tongue touching her teeth, naughty and expectant. We kissed there slowly, her long arms looping around my neck, me supporting the soft weight of her in the water like father and daughter. Slowly, as if in benediction, I placed my two hands on her face. And slowly, with all the love inside me, I began to push her head beneath the surface of the water. She struggled against me, but I was stronger. Bubbles rose as she gradually submerged, her hair floating satin-like atop its veneer.

She stayed down there for a very long time. When she surfaced, I came to meet her and she took me into her hands, my heart hammering mightily. I was dizzy. Pulsating. And as she drew into me, onto me, she said *shh, shh,* so as to comfort me. But then I noticed that it was she who was shaking. Ashley was crying. She sobbed gracefully and soundlessly, her rib cage and stomach contracting and shaking while I held her face in my hand, gripping it, feeling her maxillary bone, the skeleton of her head, the wonder of her teeth.

I kissed her head, the top of her head, kissed her temple and her wet hair. I floated there with her until she was done.

"Hey, let me ask you something."

Ashley and I were upstairs in the shower together. Warm water was coming down on both of us and I was soaping her body, kissing the back of her neck. Some kind of romantic, postdrug, love-like feeling was seeping out of me and landing on Ashley Moore. Maybe it was misdirected emotion for Liz.

"Yeah?"

"Did you used to get slapped around when you were a kid?"

"Honestly?" She looked back at me for a second.

"Yeah, honestly."

Long pause. "Uhhmmm, yeah." Ashley pushed past me and turned off the water. Stepping out of the shower, she reached for a thick white towel. "I was always told I was a bad little girl."

"Who told you that?"

"You know . . . fucking . . . Poppy."

But then she clucked her tongue, as if to offset the seriousness of the remark. "Oh come on. I went to Catholic school. The nuns were worse. The fuckin' *nuns*, dude, with their rulers! They were hardcore."

"Did you . . . like it?"

"No," said Ashley. She took a quick look at me and dried off her right leg. Then, remembering, she reached for the other towel and handed it to me.

I dried myself off as best as I could, still standing in the shower. I paused for a long moment, then coughed awkwardly. "I'm sorry," I said. "That was . . . dumb. It's none of my business."

Ashley shrugged. "It's okay. I don't really care. Look, I don't know. I mean, you can't beat me right away, then I just get mad. But in sex I like to be told, sit the fuck down, and shut the fuck up."

I laughed. It was this relieved sound. "You're funny."

"Yeah, sure am," said Ashley, grinning. "So? What about you?"

"I'm a deviant loser," I explained. Already I was wondering: how would I tell Liz?

She smiled. "I know *that*." She neared me, her voice softening. "I mean, did you used to get whacked around a lot?"

I looked at her, honestly surprised. "I never got hit in my life."

Ashley tilted her head mildly at me, interested. "What's wrong with you, then?"

———

I was still playing my cards close to the vest with Liz. The incident by the pool with Ashley would have to remain a secret, I decided. I'd lose Liz if I told the whole truth now. As it was, she'd refused to talk to me for an entire week after the night at her house. Hell, it felt like a miracle I'd even gotten her on the line now.

"I don't know what to say, Sam," Liz said. "You fucking *hit* me."

"I'm sorry I did that," I said, chastened. "I really am sorry."

"What the hell was it all *about*?" said Liz.

"Um . . ." I hesitated. "It's really hard to put into words."

"Well, you better start trying," Liz said. I could almost hear her crossing her arms on the other end of the line. "And no bullshit, Sam."

"Liz, I can't . . . ," I groaned. There was silence on the other end. "Okay. Fine."

Another pause. "Still waiting."

"Yeah," I said, glumly. "You sure you really want to hear this?"

"*Jesus*," Liz exhaled. "You know, this is a waste of my time. So—"

"Hold on," I said. "I will try. I can't explain it, but I'll try my best, because you deserve that. Okay. Number one, I just, well, I *like* gagging. It turns me on."

"Yeah, I remember that part," Liz muttered.

"The, um, choking sounds good to me. God, this is embarrassing—do I really have to do this?"

"Just get it over with."

"It *feels* good, too."

"But *why*?" Liz said. She gave a small laugh, but it also sounded frustrated. "Why do you *like* this?"

"I don't know. I wish I knew. It's very aggressive? I'm a bully? I don't *know*."

"Try harder," Liz said.

"Well, I like the way saliva *looks* and stuff. Drool."

"Sam, that's just *gross*."

"But I can't help it that this is what I like, can I?" I said, defensively.

"Did you always like this stuff?" Liz said suspiciously.

"No," I admitted. "I just discovered it recently."

"*Porn*," she said. "It's so obvious."

"Don't be such a Republican," I said.

"No, seriously. Porn's turned you into a gross human being. And I was here to watch it happen. Gross."

"I think you're wrong, Liz," I said seriously. "People don't do things just because they watched them happen in a movie. I'm not, like, going out and *shooting* people just because I watched *Predator*." I sighed, put my feet up on the wall.

"You know, when I met you, you seemed like such a nice guy," Liz said. "That's what's *confusing* to me. Lisa says you freaked her out from the very beginning. That you had bad energy."

"Lisa was too busy grooming her mustache to think clearly."

"I never agreed with her," Liz continued, as if I hadn't spoken. "I always felt that you were this sweet guy who stumbled into the wrong job. I thought we were both on the same level—sort of working in this business temporarily, kind of as a joke, you know?"

"Exactly," I said. "That's what I *am*."

"But the other night . . . I was really caught off guard, Sam. I'm sorry I kicked you out, but I felt threatened. Now I just want to understand: why does it turn you on to see girls look like subhumans?"

"I can't explain it," I said stubbornly.

"No clue at all?"

"I like to feel . . . big."

"You like to feel powerful?"

"I like to feel *empowered*," I said. "There's a difference."

"Did you ever hit a girl before you got into porn?" Liz said.

"Well . . . no."

"Are you going to keep on hitting girls?"

"If they'll let me?" I said, miserably.

There was a long pause at the end of the line.

"You didn't respect my boundaries," Liz said.

"I know," I said. "I messed up."

"And actually, I'm not *interested* in empowering you. I like you better when you're a little bit more buttoned up, I think."

"Fine," I said, beginning to smile.

"And if you ever slap me like that again, I will rip your testicles off," Liz said. "Understood?"

"Agreed," I said.

"I don't mean to be a prude, but it disgusts me. Sorry."

"Give me another chance, Liz," I said. "Please. I'll act right."

"Well." She exhaled, mightily. "If you act *nice* and take me out to Thai food, like, *tonight,* and also try to learn how to behave around Lisa, who happens to be my best friend, then perhaps I will consider letting you sleep over again sometime soon. Okay? How does that sound to you?"

"It sounds great. I'm serious. I'm glad you reconsidered. This is all really good."

"Come on," Liz said. "Hurry up and pick me up. Maybe I'll let you spank me with a belt someday if you learn how to ask right. You sick puppy."

A strange interlude, the next two weeks. Something tight in my stomach: I had never been a liar before. My records show me that I continued to function normally, however; that I continued to work diligently in my trade, just as I always had, accruing greenbacks and karmic debt at a modest clip. A butterscotch one-namer, Mamacita, was delivered into the fold by Wesley Pipes. "There you go, Sammy," he said, nodding toward her. Mamacita smiled up at me expectantly. She was eighteen, Mexican, already built like a pear. Pipes had discovered her at a bus stop. I coughed politely. I could never have been so bold.

Ashley Moore moved out of the house. First her makeup case disappeared, then her clothes. Finally, she was gone entirely. I'd like to believe her departure was due to the hot, smoldering sensuality of our poolside soirée—*I can't go on with this charade!*—but more likely, she was just kind of ready to move on, and so was Pitts. Ashley would bunk with DK for a while until she got on her feet. Meanwhile, there was an available space in Pitts's bed, and that never lasted long. Soon, Crazy Chloe was the new chick in town.

We called her Crazy because she was one. I shot her several times, with pleasure. In one scenario, we created a "wilding," where she pretended to be a jogger. Four black men leapt down from trees and pinned her to a blanket.

Timberlake found in Crazy Chloe a goggle-eyed audience for his tales. I caught them both sitting in the gloryhole one night, sharing the toilet stall like a confession booth.

"I drove out to visit my mom a month ago," Timberlake whispered, his eyes locked on Chloe. "Took the Acura. Blew her mind."

"Right," Chloe whispered.

"It was shocking. My obese, superpsychotic mother has turned into a fat, sweet lady. She said to me on the way to an Italian buffet, 'I'm sorry about never being your mom. I was never there for you, I never supported you.'"

"People change," Chloe said sagely. She peered into Timberlake's soul. "Did you forgive her?"

"Forgive her? I felt years of angst lift off of my shoulders. *Have veal Parmesan on me, Ma!*"

Elsewhere, the porno machine moved forward, coasting on its own wretched momentum. Rag Man and Lady Rag Man strapped on their coveralls, revved up the engine. Displaying savvy I didn't think they had, they obtained the go-ahead to use the house as an after-hours "location" for scenes they themselves were bankrolling and producing. They were ready to grab a piece of the pie.

"I'm gonna sell the tapes on eBay, man," Rag Man bragged.

"Hot lesbo action," Lady added. "That's our bag."

I assisted them on a few shoots, holding down second camera for them. How could I refuse? They were the only family I had.

"I can't pay you, of course," Rag Man reminded me.

"I'm insulted you would even ask," I said evenly, taking in a deep and cleansing breath. "Remember? This is what I do."

Tony Eveready was arrested in Nevada for carting a truckload of drugs across state lines. We bailed him out. Upon his return to Malibu, I was instructed to hire Eveready as often as possible; instead of paying him, I was to subtract $400 from his now-massive debt. Family rate. It all made a kind of twisted sense. On September 20, a check was made out for $63.23 to Sav-On Pharmacy. You know what that is? That's enemas, right there. Enemas, baby wipes, and douches.

How could a man like me survive? I desperately needed to come clean to Liz; common decency demanded it. And yet, I resisted confessing. She and I dined together, shared special looks. In a way, we had never been closer. The deception added a layer of complexity; it was *adult*. We went out to a Hollywood club, met Lucky Starr there. He danced with us in the darkened club. The DJ, red-bearded, wearing a kicky little cap, was only so-so. After a while, we noticed there was hardly anyone else dancing besides us. It was this huge dance floor.

One evening, I received a bizarre, excited email from a friend of mine who was traveling through Southeast Asia:

I'm fasting, dude!

He'd landed in a health resort on a little island in the south of Thailand, where he was eating just one bowl of thin soup every day and submitting himself twice daily to hour-long colonics: one in the morning and one at night.

I'm getting clean!

Over the course of sixty minutes, he would filter ten gallons of cold water through his intestines, a gallon at a time. His belly would swell up with the water, and he would massage the length of his guts, and then, when he couldn't stand it anymore, he'd release the water, and along with it, old bits of debris that, apparently, had lined the walls of his intestines for many years. Crazy things were coming out of his body: bile, mucoid plaque, and even what looked like old bits of undigested meat. The lucky bastard.

Pitts and I were mopping up the wreckage from yet another gangbang when I introduced the idea that maybe it was time to cut the apron strings.

"I'm thinking about quitting porn," I told Pitts. "You know. Find something new."

He looked around, confused. "But we have this place booked until the end of the year."

"Let Timberlake shoot my scenes," I said, reaching down to pick up a soiled baby wipe. Wrinkling my lips with revulsion, I tossed it into the black trash bag that Pitts held open for me. "Or Rag Man. Hell, he'd love it."

"But *why*? What's the matter?" Pitts asked.

"Look, don't take this personally," I said, "but I think I need to clean out my colon."

Pitts looked at me strangely. He put the garbage bag down. "What the hell are you *talking* about?"

"I don't know," I said calmly, walking away from him a few steps. "I'm . . . considering a new way of life."

Pitts snorted. "And what's that?"

"I'd like to do something that *helps* people."

"Why don't you just volunteer at a soup kitchen?"

I laughed. "Look, this is stupid. Forget I said anything."

"Fucking really?" Pitts said. He reached into the couch, spying a mostly spent bottle of Astroglide lubricant. For a brief moment he inspected it, then dropped it into the garbage. "Well? Are you serious? Should I hire someone else?"

"I'm totally kidding around," I assured him. "I love what we do here. It's so full of mystery. I want to do it until I can't walk anymore. Until my brain fills with blood."

"Tell you what," Pitts said. "I'm going to pretend we never had this conversation." He looked at the lubed-up garbage bag, and dropped it suddenly, in disgust. "Clean up the rest of this shit by yourself."

I swept the floor, then mopped it, turning the notion over in my head. Maybe I really *could* bail. I'd feel a bit guilty about abandoning the ship, certainly, but Jesus, it was so *stupid*. "Mamacita," indeed. And that gloryhole rankled me particularly. Everyone wanted to try it. Especially the amateurs. After all, what could be easier than getting your wang sucked through a hole in a piece of wood? Even I had to admit that, jealously, I sought to take up an hour behind the wall. (But I couldn't, because only black penises are allowed in the hole.) Byron Long's cousin Darius stuck his whole small cock and tiny balls through the hole. A new girl calling herself "Mariah Cherry" hesitantly accepted them into her life. Darius strutted out into the light afterward, glowing with pride.

If I left now, I'd be giving up on my "dream." Withdrawing from the race without ever having produced the kind of cinematic masterpiece I'd planned. But brilliance had eluded me to this point. You know, maybe I *had* studied semiotics. But, like, so the fuck *what*? Making a real film took more talent than I'd figured. I suppose that I had always believed that part of it would just sort of *happen*—like I would wake up one morning to find that in my sleep, I had penned a brilliant, cutting-edge screenplay. Instead my body of work comprised a cluster of self-published, eBay-bound VHS masters and a towering pile of crude, workmanlike gangbangs. Boy howdy.

"I want out," I whispered to Timberlake one night, as we huddled on top of the brick wall that separated our compound from the outside world, watching the sky.

He sighed. "No way. Listen, I feel anxious. I need a massage like nobody's business. Samuel? Work on my neck?"

"I'm serious, I'm not *into* it anymore," I said. "I failed, man! I let it pass me by. I was out to change the game, but I didn't rise to the occasion. Now my only choice is to cut my losses. Get out while the getting's good."

"You know, in this light, you look like a really light-skinned black man," Timberlake said, studying me. "That amuses me."

"Porn was stronger than me," I said. "Wow. This is crazy. I'm really going to quit."

"And leave me all alone? You smug bastard. What are you going to do with yourself? Got any money saved up?"

"Yes. A bit."

"You are truly odd. Seriously, you're thinking about giving up this life? No more girls?"

"The girls weren't as delicious as I'd imagined them to be," I admitted. "Some things are best left to the imagination."

"You wanted the centerfold, and all you got was the staples," Timberlake said.

In the distance, there was a rustling. Some kind of meandering coyote, or a balding studio executive out for a saddened walk of shame.

"You know what porn is, man?" I said thoughtfully, picking up a pebble that lay atop the big brick wall, tossing it up and down in my hand a few times. "Porn is the embodiment of our cheesy imaginations. We dreamt up these girls with great legs and unidimensional personalities, and that's basically what we got."

"Oh, bullshit," Timberlake said pleasantly. "That makes zero sense. Don't try to philosophize, you're bad at it."

I groaned. "I hate you."

"Hey, did I tell you that I nearly had a head-on collision with Spielberg today?" Timberlake said, brightly.

"What? You're lying."

"I swear, I'm not. Steven Spielberg himself erratically fired his early-'80s, *Hart to Hart*–style Mercedes through a gas station and into my lane. Fortunately, we both swerved in the right direction. Halfway through my hateful stare, we made eye contact, and I achieved recognition."

"Well? Then what happened?"

"He flew by me, parked in front of Radio Shack, and ran in."

"But why would *Steven Spielberg* be going to *Radio Shack*?" I cried.

"He may have needed an extension cord," Timberlake said soothingly. "Maybe a calculator."

"Why are you telling me this?" I asked. "You . . . there are no words for you."

"All I'm saying, in my own little way, is that I know where you're coming from." He patted me on the arm. "I support you."

"I'm quitting," I said, picking up the pebble again and clutching it in my palm. "You just watch me."

———

Liz started working for Deep Productions. DK, heartbroken, re-fused to get a new secretary. He came over one afternoon to collect some checks for a few jobs Timberlake owed him. Ashley Moore came with him.

"*Hi,*" she said to me, giving me a little hug, and a lascivious grin. "How have *you* been?"

"Great," I said. Electricity ran through my body. "Great. Hey listen, there's this little thing I want to show you in my room. Do you have a minute?"

She came into my room and we laughed. Right away we kissed.

And then she went *I want you to choke me with the belt.* I said, *yeah!* and I got this leather belt out of my closet that I'd had forever, since high school even. It had a square metallic buckle and the leather was dark and smooth in several places where the buckle had rubbed it into a kind of permanent polish. I ran the belt under her chin and clasped it in two behind her neck and then I used it to choke her out while she gave me a blowjob. Ashley gasped and gagged. I may have slapped her once or twice. I don't recall.

But it was different this time. There was a certain pleasure in it, of course, but it also felt sort of forced. I tried to call her names, in hopes of re-creating some of our magic we'd experienced down by the pool, but neither of us took it seriously and we mostly only laughed. I fucked her face, but I think we were both feeling rushed. DK was in the living room; if we dallied, sooner or later he'd start to wonder what Ashley was up to. But mostly, it just seemed kind of rote. I looked down at her and there she was, *gaack*ing. And it just seemed so pointless. We were playing out parts in a play. We were getting attention. We were misbehaving. Sinking that ship.

Soon Ashley stood up.

"Do you want to pee on me?" she asked, carefully.

I rubbed my jaw, considering. "Yeah, sure," I said, after a second. "Why not?"

I don't remember that transaction. We walked into my bathroom, and I don't remember quite how it felt. I don't remember how the carpet felt, under my bare feet. She had all her clothes on. She'd never taken any off. She knelt and her face was over the toilet bowl. I don't remember peeing into her mouth, how it took me a moment to get started. It's weird, when you're hard: some sort of vesicle switch needs to happen. I don't remember the feeling in my stomach, like I might stop myself, or say something—except why bother? I wanted to know what it would be like. I wanted to know how it would feel.

I do remember the way her jaw hung open. Expectant, before the piss came in. She was down there, waiting for it, and there was nothing in her eyes that was really readable. She had a pretty good mask on. Ashley used happiness well, knew how to hide behind it. She was a heck of a cute girl, who still had acne, though it looked all right on her. Then I was pissing on her face and her hair. Piss was on her hair and drops were in her eyes and dripping into the toilet. I remember this really well: it felt like nothing. Like less than nothing. When I finished, she lay her head down on the toilet lid, letting it rest there. Like, relieved. And I don't remember her leaving. But she did.

On my way over to Liz's that night I picked up a bottle of bourbon. The guy behind the counter in the liquor store passed it over to me in one defeated motion. There were flecks of dried saliva at the corners of his lips. It was nearing dinnertime. Maybe he'd get a burger. Then he'd work for six more hours.

Liz buzzed me up to her place. She was happy, going on about Deep and her new office, and what it was like over there. "Bradley isn't such a bad guy, once you get used to him. He's much less sleazy than DK—he's like, almost a real businessman. He's filthy rich, drives a different Mercedes every day."

I poured myself a drink and gulped it down like a truth serum. But nothing was coming out of my mouth, so I made another one.

We moved to the couch, watched a sitcom. I can't remember what. I stared straight ahead of me. There was this feeling of ice and fear in my stomach. Liz watched the whole thing happily. During the commercial breaks, she talked about the new movies that were coming out.

When the show ended, I forced myself to speak.

"Liz . . . I . . . I have to tell you something."

That is never a good thing to hear. She looked at me fearfully.

"Someone . . . someone gave me a blowjob today."

"What?" Liz said, flinching. "Who?"

"It doesn't matter." I shook my head. "I'm sorry, seriously."

"Are you fucking kidding me?" Liz said evenly. "Sam, are you kidding around?"

"No," I said, ashamed. "I wish that I were."

Liz shook her head. Her mouth was open, and it almost looked like she was going to laugh. "Well," she said. There was a long silence, and scared, I waited for her to start to cry. If tears came, though, they didn't last for long.

"What are you thinking?" I said.

"I'm thinking, I guess we're breaking up after all," Liz said. She sounded furious. "Sweet. I'm going to be *alone* again. Wow, *thanks*, Sam. That'll be fun!"

I said nothing.

"You know, Jesus Christ," Liz snapped. "What the hell is the *matter* with you?"

"I . . . don't know."

"I *trusted* you, Sam," she said, her voice rising. "What could I have done for you that I didn't do?"

"Nothing," I said miserably. "Seriously, you did everything right."

"I'm sorry that I don't like *mouthfucking*," Liz said, angrily.

"No," I said quietly. "That wasn't it."

"Then what *was* it?" Liz said. She nudged her chin forward at me. Her eyes narrowed. I had never seen her look madder, or wiser, or more removed. "I'm listening. Tell me why you don't give a shit about me. Why you think it's cool to totally disregard my feelings. I think you owe me that much."

I racked my mind for something right to say. But I had been through this before. What in hell could I tell her? That my heart felt dead? That on Wednesday morning, I'd seen four huge black penises looming over a pale tiny woman named Bisexual Britni, who laid back on a weight bench in our home gym, waiting to be filled by them, and it had filled me with loneliness and terrible dread?

"My role models are bad?"

Liz snorted. "That is fucking weak. *God*, that is so fucking weak."

"Mental illness is contagious?" I tried.

"Yeah, well, I must have been crazy to spend this much time with you," Liz said. She pushed back against the couch in frustration, hitting a pillow with her little fist. "*Ugh!* Porn people are sleazy! I knew it in my heart! Why did I *do* this?"

I tried to think of a way to explain myself. But nothing that could be articulated in words or my dumb voice was coming to me. What, what could I say? That hitting bottom felt kinda good, now that you mention it? That after being around all these phone-sex addicts and misogynistic losers and cheap third-rate crooks for so long, I had begun to *enjoy* swimming among the diseased stream of their collective unconscious?

"I'm leaving town," I told Liz.

"Go!" she said. "I-don't-care."

"No, I mean . . . I'm quitting porn," I said bravely.

"Why would I give a shit?" she said.

"Oh," I said, stung. "No, I just thought, well, you'd be happy. You know, if you . . . cared about me."

Liz laughed. "You are out of control! Fuck! I *love* this! God, guys are always like this! You totally do whatever you want, fuck whoever you want, and then you want to 'be friends' afterwards! You are insane! Get out of here! Leave me alone! Stop fucking with my head!"

"I pissed in her mouth," I said quickly. "This afternoon."

"Sam!" Liz laughed. "I don't know how to tell you this: I think I'm over you already!"

"I wanted to see how it would feel."

"Sam?" Liz said. "You are, uh, not welcome in my house right now?"

"It was nothing special," I continued, a bit dazed, staring straight ahead of me as Liz firmly took hold of my elbow and began to guide me to the front door. "I didn't feel enlightened by it or anything."

"Sambo," Liz said, "the truly crazy thing is that I might actually like you again, someday. There's an honesty factor to you that almost outshines how completely selfish you are. But now we need to not talk to each other for like, a year or so."

"See ya, Liz," I said, waving at her. "I'm sorry. Thank you for understanding."

"Bye, Sam," Liz said, pushing me out her door. "Take care, now." And she slammed the door, refreshingly hard, in my face.

TWENTY-THREE

It was time for me to go. I had done enough. Finally, I had reached the end of my rope.

"I'm gone, I'm gone, I'm gone," I said to Pitts. "Mental health clause in my contract. Situation calls for immediate evacuation. Details to follow; and you've been great."

The Liz thing just finished me. It made me see myself in a light I couldn't ignore. More, it made me see that there actually *was* a connection between my inability to connect with her, or any of the other girlfriends I'd had, and the sex work that I'd been doing.

"I've got the house booked until the end of the *year*," Pitts protested. "I'm paying ten grand a month!"

"My karma's going black, dude," I said. "Ravens are swarming around my heart."

"You *promised*," Pitts said.

"I promised you nothing," I explained.

The team could survive without me. Nervously, I holed up in Echo Park for a couple of days, to get away from the scene of the crime. A clueless Tenzeno filled me in on the neighborhood gossip. "The lady upstairs got visited by the police . . . I think she's fencing stolen jewelry . . . her husband fought with the pet store lady, says the smell is intolerable . . . I saw him dump a bottle of Clorox bleach on their doorstep last Friday morning . . . The tamales on Sunday mornings are still happening . . . you can get them plain, or with chicken . . ." I nodded, dumbly. Keep talking. It was music to my ears.

Three days later, I tiptoed up to Malibu, began to pack my bags. Pitts crept up behind me and frightened the living shit out of me. "*Sam?*" he said with a grimace. "If you're not too busy, I'd like for you to meet Billy Watson."

"Yo," said the thick, blocky man in front of me. He was about forty years old, an immense hunk of beef. He wore a reddened, ex-ultant face and dimpled chin. He extended a giant hand for me to shake. "Pleasure."

"Bill's a buddy of mine from way back when," Pitts said. "He's been teaching English to junior high kids. But he hated that. Right, Bill?"

"Hated it," Billy said, seriously.

"I've been thinking, Bill might make a pretty decent pornographer. I'd like for you to train him."

Pitts couldn't resist staring at me balefully for a moment. To him, it was just plain *strange* that I wanted to leave. Looking back, I'm pretty sure he didn't feel rejected, or even judged. More, it confounded him, to see someone capable pass up a perfectly good opportunity to make real money.

"When Billy can do your job perfectly," Pitts finished, "then you can go."

I had little choice but to agree. Straightaway, I began to put the big man through the paces. There wasn't much to the sex business, was there? Just like anything else, it was all in the details.

"Don't bother Timberlake when he's whacking off in his room," I instructed Billy, to begin. "He likes to do it every night between about ten and eleven. It's his way of relaxing and preparing for the labors of the next day."

We strode through the hallways of the big house, our steps heavy and loud in the quiet manor. I watched Billy's big boots tread across carpets, making soft indentations into expensive fabrics.

"Avoid booking Wesley Pipes and Tony Eveready for the same job," I suggested. "Both of them talk so much, there's no room to hear what the girl has to say."

Watson nodded seriously. He was jotting notes in a small spiral-bound notebook as quickly as his huge fingers would allow him.

"Before every shoot, make sure you've got your camera charged," I said. "A pornographer without a working camera is like a soldier with no bullets. Double-check that you've got lube, towels, douches, and baby wipes in great supply, too. That should be your mantra: Lube, lube, lube."

"Lube, lube, lube," Watson chanted. A small smile was dawning on his mug. "Hey, this is fun."

"You're damn right, Bill. It is. Now: make sure you know exactly how much you're paying the girl. You don't want to get caught mid-scene in a bargaining duel. That'll kill a boner. *Never kill a boner*."

"I won't, Sam. I promise."

I sighed regally. "This isn't a difficult job. Follow your common sense, and you'll be fine. Drink a little coffee before a shoot, so you'll be alert, but not *too* much. Then you'll jabber too much. Remember: no one cares about you. All we care about is the girl. Rag Man will edit your voice out in a heartbeat, and he'll be pissed about the extra work it'll take him."

"Rag Man?" Billy said. "*The* Rag Man?"

"The genius himself," I snapped. "Pitts hasn't given you a face-to-face yet, eh? Well, I'll introduce you shortly. Please understand, you're very, very lucky to work with him right out of the box. In fact, you're incredibly fortunate to start at this level, now that I think about it. You know how *I* started out, my friend? You know what *my* introduction to porn was? Wanking myself off with a *banana* peel and then trying to make fifteen bucks off it on eBay."

"Sounds disgusting," Billy said, awed.

"That's putting it mildly. Now. Let's talk weed."

"Sure."

"All these actors smoke it, and they're going to offer it to you. Go ahead and take a little bit to be polite, and so things look interesting to you. But not *too* interesting. Don't smoke so much that you try to get *arty*. No one wants a ten-minute static shot of the side of someone's leg."

"That would be bad porn," Billy agreed.

"It would be horrible porn," said Timberlake, who joined us. "Great to meet you. I'm Timberlake. Welcome to the league. Where tig ol' bitties and tales of wonder abound."

"I'm teaching Bill about porn, Will."

"This should be amusing."

"Make sure everyone *respects* you, Bill," I said. "No one respects this character. People walk all over Timberlake, and he can't do a damn thing about it."

"He's joking, of course," Timberlake said. "The guys *adore* me."

"Of course, I'm joking," I said. "I admit, everyone likes Timberlake. He manages to put his employees at ease. So compliment your people once in a while. Let 'em know you care. After all, you're only as good as your actors. If you can't get them to produce, then you're no good. You're washed up before you start."

"Should . . . an actress be tipped?" Billy asked, tremulously.

"*Hardly,*" Timberlake laughed. "Sam? You want to handle this one, or should I?"

"If you're doing an under-three-hundred-dollars shoot, then common courtesy dictates you bump it up fifty bucks," I advised. "It's the gentlemanly way to go. But if she's up there at a thousand or more, an extra hundred is meaningless to everyone involved."

"A small gift will make a greater impact," Timberlake explained. "A book, a T-shirt. Some sort of memento. A personal touch."

We ceased moving. We stood together, our arms folded, in the living room. Divorced from the usual everyday chaos, the quiet of the house impressed me. It was a house not accustomed to silence.

"Do you guys get . . ." Billy lowered his voice to a whisper. "Well, do you guys get laid all the time?"

Timberlake and I looked at each other. "This guy's an animal," I said, finally, hooking my thumb at the 'Lake. "All the ladies want to touch his jock."

"But I never take 'em up on it," Timber said. "I'm in love."

"I sure hope I get laid once or twice," Billy confessed.

"Oh, you will. But do it the right way. No rubbing up on the talent before a shoot," I said. "That's sleazy. Word gets around. You don't want to be known as *that* guy."

"Oh, I wouldn't," Billy said hurriedly.

"Afterwards is fine," Timberlake added. "Ask to see their boobies? Totally kosher. But make sure that you've already given them the check. That way, they don't feel like they owe anything to you."

"It's not complicated, once you get the hang of it," I said to Billy. I clapped him once on the incredibly solid shoulder. His flesh felt like it was made of a sandbag. "You can do this."

Billy Watson breathed in deep and careful. "I can't wait to start."

———

I called my father, to discuss the new frontier, the open road.

"David," I said, "you're just not going to believe what I've come up with now."

"Let me sit down," he grumbled.

"Ever heard of a penile implant? I'm seriously considering getting one. Very minor operation, from what I hear . . ."

"For the love of God. *Ellen, get in here!* Your son's *completely* lost it!"

"Kidding, Dad," I said. "My Johnson's fine. Actually, it's quite large."

"What a terrible thing to joke about," he groused. "Ellen. Go away. Off the phone. Crisis averted."

"No," I said. "Actually, I'm moving on. Leaving porno."

"Excellent," my dad said, still breathing hard. "Finally, you've come to your senses."

"Yep, I'm ready to become a contributing member of society."

He coughed, perturbed, probably suspecting I was still joking. "Would you mind me asking what *led* you to this grand decision?"

"I'm just done with it, I guess."

"You should have been done with it *years* ago," he grumbled. "Never mind. What does your future hold? School, perhaps?"

"I'm thinking more in terms of *Thailand*," I said, relishing the smack of the word in my mouth. "From what I understand, there's a *fasting* program going on there. Deep in the jungle, centered around eliminating waste from your digestive tract by mechanical means. Quite expensive, of course, but very cutting-edge . . ."

"Ellen," called my dad, "I'm sorry, dear, I need you back. I'm going to faint, so you'll have to talk to your son."

"Sam," my mom said, picking up the phone, "what are you doing? Why are you torturing your father?"

"I've done nothing, Mom," I said. "I told him I was quitting porn, and he just went crazy."

"Well?" my mother asked. She waited. "Is it true?"

"It is," I said simply.

"When are you thinking about ending your job?"

"Pronto. I'm training this new guy, and when he's ready, I'm out."

"And then? What will you do then?"

"I'll leave LA, for a while at least. I just don't really want to be here anymore. I don't want to be around it."

"Feel like telling me why?"

"It just . . . well, porn wasn't what I thought it would be."

My mom sighed, then laughed. "Nothing ever is."

EPILOGUE

I'm in Thailand. I'm on a beach. And I have seventy-five boils all over my body. They're causing me an inordinate amount of pain, especially in my right armpit, where about thirteen of the worst have clustered. The sun is hotter than I'm used to, and it keeps making me sweat. Sweat drips in my eyes. I'm sweating into my eyes.

The midafternoon sun is searing into my field of vision, making it dance with neon-blue bursts. I desperately want to turn over and lie on my stomach, but a new boil has hatched up this morning, behind my right nipple, and I know that pressing upon on the newly inflamed surface of flesh with any weight at all will invoke a biblical furnace of pain so agonizingly acute that I'll be reduced to tears or, even worse, some kind of self-urination. A linen cloth lies in my little tote bag a few feet behind me, which I might simply place over my face, but just reaching for that could conceivably stir up the hornet's nest in any number of parts of my body, so I decided to simply endure it.

A breeze wafts by to cool me, but it's almost sadistically brief. I blink my eyes rapidly, trying to remember why the hell I decided to come down to the beachfront in the first place. I've been cooped up in my bamboo hut for the past five days or so, riding a wave of hunger, pain, cramping, and intense weirdness the likes of which I've never before experienced. In fact, ever since I began my colonic-cleansing fasting journey on this tiny jungle island, an hour's plane ride from the Malaysian border, I've been feeling mildly psychotic, penitent, and, because of the boils, grotesque . . . hence, the beachfront, for the normality it may dispense . . .

Two bikini-clad Swedish chicks are splashing in the water some thirty yards away from me. Both are dark-haired and both have rather tanner skins than I would have imagined for northern Europeans. They are shouting happily and constantly giggling as they splash about. Because of the distance and the language barrier and my generalized discombobulation, I can't make out what they're saying, but regardless, their body language tells all: they're happy; carefree; never had such fun. I sigh, wishing I was in the kind of shape where I could join them. I sit up to peer at them a bit more closely—in the absence of TV, one quickly learns to look for other travelers as a source of entertainment—but by chance, in doing so, I let my hand fall just above my right kneecap. Big mistake. There's a boil rising on my knee, too, and it's like being stung by a jellyfish. A wave of ice-hot pain rises in my throat and body, and doesn't recede for a full minute. Frustrated, I curse under my breath, sink back into the sand.

I'm not sure how the hell this has happened to me, but it's been five days since I've eaten solid food. Moon, the thin, friendly Thai man who supervises the wellness center's fasting program, dispenses a thin gruel each evening, but it's strictly nondelicious, consisting

exclusively of vegetable broth, lime juice, and dried cayenne pep-
per. You should see the hungry, Oliver Twist–ish looks on our faces
when we get fed: guarding our bowls carefully, so as not to spill a
single drop, we slurp each spoonful gratefully, gathering in ritualistic
communal ecstasy to listen to the truest in New Age music. Circular
swaths of incense burn continuously on wooden platforms, while the
distressed polyglot murmur of fifteen or so international fasters, hailing from France, Denmark, England, Sweden, Canada, and Israel,
interweaves with the clinking of metal spoons.

Chow's always over way too soon. Once the bowls have been collected, some of us settle down to a hammock to thumb idly through
a paperback, but most loll about on triangular mats, comparing
stories about what's recently come out of their colons. The princi-
pal topic of conversation is, quite literally, shit. Like beery vets who
prefer World War II battlefield tales over all else, we *need* to confess,
one-up, and absorb one another's intestinal horror stories. Talk of
politics, international health care, and unforeseen island gossip soon
fades into irrelevant rambles. In our little circle, we have begun to
postulate that what *others* think grotesque might in fact be subsumed
into an invigorating discussion of alternative health techniques.

Over a very short period of time, our group's developed a strong,
cultlike bond, likely due to the fact that our activities are so odd to
most that we are the only ones who can understand one another. A
tall, pretty girl named Swan, from Dallas, spends half the morning
confessing her illicit semi-escort job in Japan (she goes to dinner with
Japanese businessmen "but nothing else!") to Ed Knuth, a goofy,
dreadlocked white dude from Brooklyn who seems the manliest man
ever to put on pink yoga pants. Complicating the process emotionally
for me, I've become sort of a medical curiosity to the group, due to
my boils. No one else seems to have developed such a strong "cleansing reaction." Two Englishwomen, traveling together, both devel-

oped acne on their faces on day two, and Tomer, a shy, quiet Israeli fellow, got a quick rash on his buttocks on day three that came and went over the course of twelve hours. "I have this same rash when I am sixteen," he remembers, frowning. "Why it comes again?"

The idea behind so-called colonic cleansing is that through mechanically introducing great amounts of water into our intestines and then flushing them out, it is at least theoretically possible to be able to remove some of the accumulated organic materials that over the course of our lifetimes have come to line the walls of our intestines. To assist in this process, we're all popping a great quantity of organic dehydrated herbs, a formula developed by an American naturopath that is said to assist in the disintegration process. That's why we're not eating, too; so our organs can concentrate their energies on repairing and eliminating, rather than digesting.

Like anyone who takes part in an alternative-health regimen, I really have no idea if what we're doing is effective or useful. The lack of food, the intense Southeast Asian heat and sun, and the nearly dreamlike jungle beauty of the tiny island further confuse me. My guess is that I'm not the only one here who is feeling almost psychedelically high at many moments in the day. Yesterday, after dinner, Ed Knuth tiptoed over to me and began to massage my shoulders with no invitation and no warning. Thirty seconds later, he looked down at his own hands, like they were strangers to him, and moved away without even a word. My food-starved brain is dumping out piles of endorphins with little to no warning, and I am simply furious one moment, then absolutely compassionate the next, wanting to pet gecko lizards and adopt them as my sons and righteous heirs to my fortune. The concept of objectivity is nearly inadmissible here; and raising our minds to the task of evaluating the efficacy of this program is like asking a bunch of roving Vietnamese chimpanzees who've been sprayed down with liquid PCP if they think it's "working for them." The only thing any of us can agree on with any sort of consistency is that, without doubt, truly weird-looking stuff is coming out of our butts each and every day. And that seems to be more than enough.

I shift in the sun and, deciding finally that the heat isn't going to let up, acknowledge it's time to head back to my bunk. With no small effort, I rise to my feet, gather my bag together, and set off, moving gingerly. Soon Swan appears, looking fetching, her pupils dilated.

"Sam," Swan breathes. "*Hey*. You want to share a joint?"

"I'm in pain," I explain. "Inhaling hurts."

She just stares at me and goes, "Marijuana is a known laxative," as if that were a selling point.

For all involved, the first few days were predictably repulsive. It took a moment to gather the courage to lube up that probe with olive oil, and stick it into your own anus to receive the ten-gallon burst of creek water. But since then, since we've eased into the process, stopped eating, and let the herbs take effect, the oddest, most unpredictable stuff has begun to come out. Like fascinated amateur scientists, we all utilize colanders during the process, and even more disgustingly, Moon has gifted us each a pair of *chopsticks* to root through the accumulated detritus. Simon, an English guy in his mid-forties who's not ashamed to wear a linen sarong like a skirt, swears he's been finding pieces of white, rubbery, tire-like material in his colander, grooved in the precise S shape of his small intestine. Tomer has been using a digital camera to his advantage, snapping blurry, close-up flash pics of his bundles, bringing them back for the squealing, disgusted, giddy approbation of the group.

There's none of that viscous rubber substance to me: just miles and miles of bright green, jelly-like material. I can't figure it out for the life of me, but over the course of a few hushed conversations with

Shashi, a Reiki master and naturopath from London with beautiful glowing eyes who seems more grounded and knowledgeable than most of the rest of us (and yet, in her own way, totally insane, as if she *knows* with full calm certainty that she can cure disease with the universal-life-energy that flows from her hands), I form a theory that it's probably bile. "It's *bile*, guys," I tell the group. "From my liver."

Of course, it's a wild guess, and even if that green stuff really *is* bile, it doesn't explain in the least why I've sprouted these hellish boils. They are clustered everywhere: in my armpits, spread across my buttocks, under my nipple, and on the backs of my calves and hamstrings. Each morning I wake up with more. I can no longer sit down easily. It's challenging, in fact, to get more than an hour or so of continuous sleep. Moon himself is mystified: he's seen a pustule or so in his time, but never anyone who's harboring so goddamn *many* . . . In the evenings, after my colonic and shower, I like to stand naked in front of the small mirror in the bathroom, twisting and bending, try-ing to assess the extent of my destruction. The bumpled, red surfaces that cross my body's curves look sick and repulsive, but in that great, can't-look-away way . . . I wonder, when they eventually rise to the surface, what will I be exorcising? What will I be saying good-bye to?

Predictably, I've entertained a few thousand times the notion that I am enduring punishment for the indiscretions of the past years. Officially, I don't *believe* in that kind of mystic retribution, but with my mind the way it is now, inebriated on fasting, inundated with the pedantic New Age prattle of ten other freaks, I'm tentatively leaving it open to debate. Regardless, dealing with the intense pain is gratifying in its own way. I'm at least *dealing* with the guilt, finger-ing it, remembering my batch of regrets, even though my rational brain knows it's nonsensical to expect to atone for them.

Watching my feet, I walk down the winding path to my humble abode. For the equivalent of $2.50 a day, I've got a small little jungle shack all to myself, a modest, dingy little dwelling with a woven grass roof and the type of doors a crazed monk could kick down in a heartbeat if he had a mind to. But it's a lovely setup, high on a cliff with a small square peekaboo window from which one is free to consider the jutting rocky cliffs and aquamarine waters of the sea, and a wobbly shelf or two from which to perch your clothes and seashells and rocks and traveler perfumes and ripped books and journals and pens and expensive backpacks, already filthy from the travels.

I've even got a nice little miniature wooden porch outside my door. This morning, I lay on it for one hour while a tiny Dutch grandmother, the resident spiritual guru and white witch of the island, gave me a chakra-clarifying massage. She didn't lay hands on me once, just had me breathe through the pain, picture colors. "Inhale cleansing, white light, the color of forgiveness, peace and fire . . . Exhale brown, and black, mucus and grief . . . everything you want to get rid of . . ." Halfway through the session, the deep, constant breathing took effect like a tranquilizer dart, and I was lifted off into a cloud somewhere else, a place temporarily without pain and judgment. When the session concluded, the sweet, smiling grandmother helped me to my feet. She waited peacefully, birds chirping, her eyes closed and her wrinkled, lovely hands folded calmly in her lap, until I rummaged through my things and pulled out a quantity of Thai baht to pay her.

I open the door to my shack and sit back on my bed carefully, trying to plot out a position for reclining where my body won't scream out in pain. Horribly, I seem to have sprouted a boil next to my *spine*. The ones that rest near bony protuberances are absolutely the worst, since bones, being more or less stable, can't move, and therefore there's a kind of light pressure at every instant.

I ease myself down, wincing, and somehow find an acceptable position. I lie there for a moment, relieved. Then I curse myself: I've fucking forgotten to get my *book*. I can see it from across the room, sitting there innocently. I just lie there, for minutes on end, looking at the book. If only I had some kind of telekinetic powers . . . if only I could make it come to me by the force of *Reiki* . . .

I sigh, then heave myself forward to a sitting position. Shaking my head, I decide to get the hell out of here. I couldn't read now, anyway; I don't have the concentration for it. Nor can I sleep. I've got four hours to kill until my evening colonic; it seems an interminable, boundless stretch of time. Then I remember: there's an afternoon yoga class at the wellness center that could occupy a couple of hours. Though I won't be able to do most of the postures, maybe I could participate in the breathing . . . maybe, I reason, if I could get the endorphins flowing, I could start to feel like some kind of human . . .

Slowly, I put on a new pair of fisherman's pants, change my shirt, find a few baht to contribute to the class fee. Closing the door of the shack softly behind me, I begin to wind my way through the hilly, tropical jungle path of the island. The air is humid and alive with the sounds of small insects. Small trees sprout from the mountainous surfaces, making good handholds on some of the steeper inclines and more precipitous declines. The path evolves from dirt into rocky, slick stone surfaces, where it behooves the traveler not to step falsely: one misstep could land him hundreds of feet down below, with a broken ankle, arm, or worse . . .

I am sweating through my thin cotton shirt by the time I arrive at the center's curious outdoor yoga platform, netted against the buzz of tropical insects. There is a small spigot before the entrance. Turning on the water, I place my hands under the coursing stream, and I scrub them back and forth until the dirt dissolves from across my knuckles and the sand escapes from under my nails. A handful of water gets splashed across my face. Liquid courses off my eyebrows and nose, runs onto the collar of my shirt. I grin, wet-faced, feeling better, more refreshed.

I step into the shala and grab a mat, staking out a spot in the middle of the floor. Going into a gentle warm-up, I bend forward, my head lowering toward my knees, my spine lengthening and unwinding under me. My navel draws in, and my hips tilt slightly forward. There's a loosening in the backs of my thighs, a pleasant stretching accompanied by a minor release in my lower back. This is a good place to hang out, so I just stay right there, and try to breathe.

More people pull into the room — Knuth, Swan, Shashi, Simon, Bug, a severe-looking Frenchwoman who works on documentaries for the Discovery Channel — and I catch the buzz of conversation in the room, mixing with the familiar sounds of modern-day yoga practice. The fibers of a spandex legging being snapped; a boy's beard rubbing against the stone floor; a middle-aged woman wondering aloud about cucumber water. *Seriously, is that* good? I pull myself deeper into my stretch, angling my neck slowly from side to side, letting my head go heavy and full.

Eventually the volume drops and a palpable silence fills the room, a sure sign that our teacher's here. I raise my head rather awkwardly to get a look. She's fairly young, serious-looking, and not anyone I've seen before.

"Alison," a woman greets her.

"Hi," she says pleasantly, walking to the front of the room, where she places a large cloth bag on the ground. She surveys the class for a moment, then lowers her head, opening the bag, beginning to rummage in it.

I rise up and down on my toes a few times, trying to warm up my ankles. It's a little painful. I've grown weak over the past few days. There's something to that, though: to feeling weak, to feeling vulnerable. I try to explore it. I press my palms together in front of my chest, forming an upside-down V, and take some larger breaths tentatively, my rib cage expanding as full as it can go. The boils, for now, at least, aren't plaguing me.

As I hold my posture, Alison sets up her yoga mat, begins a few preliminary stretches herself. She sits down, folds her legs in front of her, and hugs one to her chest. She's very pretty. Dark hair, sinewy arms, a mystical angel-wing tattoo covering each shoulder blade. As I'm checking her out furtively, she raises her head and looks directly at me. She catches my eye.

It's like everything else stops. Rushes. Freezes. My body gets cold.

Alison is sitting there with her leg pressed to her breasts, her knee in one hand, and I am standing, with my palms pressed against each other, trying to breathe, wondering about the night's next ridiculous colonic . . . but we are gazing directly into each other's face for a very long moment, making the kind of eye contact that human beings who don't know one another can almost never sustain. My lip trembles, suddenly.

I wonder for a second just what the hell she's doing. She's looking deeply at me, not smiling. And, in a terrible rush, it comes to me. She knows who I am. Alison must have had some connection to the Los Angeles porn scene: maybe she had a boyfriend who watched a lot of movies. Maybe she'd even had a friend in the business, one who did her six scenes, before moving on.

Or maybe, God help me, she'd worked *herself*. It wasn't likely, but it was damn well possible that she knew what it was like to do the deed on camera, feel the heady rush of a big paycheck for a quick, cheap debauch. Maybe she'd posed in front of an Internet camera, took Web chats from grinning, horny guys she secretly wanted to punch in the stomach; maybe she'd met Brandon Iron or Byron Long, knew what *Slap Happy* was, had someone else waste the money she'd earned with her pound of flesh.

I just stand there, gulping, without moving, continuing to stare at Alison's face for what seems like a very long time. *There's no way,* I think. *She's no porno girl. I'm making way too much out of this — chalk it up to temporary fast-induced psychosis. Then again . . . maybe she was just one of these healers who* knew *stuff.* I can't get the thought out of my head: maybe she could see inside of me, she could see what was draining out of me during this week of intense purging, see the blackness, the stuff I'd done wrong, all the guilt I'd been holding inside. I know it doesn't make sense, it *can't* make sense — she can't know this, she *can't* know what I've done — but I fear it nonetheless. I tremble, shaking. Tears rush into my eyes, blurring my vision. I want to move on . . . get out of here . . .

Finally, Alison stops looking at me. She lets go of her leg and breaks her gaze. She stands, bending her knees, and breathes in a long, cleansing breath. She smiles, addresses the class. "Everyone ready to begin?" she asks. We all nod, say yes. And then, as if nothing at all had passed between us, Alison walks to the front of the room and begins to teach.

It's evening. In the room where I receive my colonics, it's dark and cool. I lie back on the wooden board, looking up at the ceiling. A speaker coming from the upper left corner of the room is softly leaking sounds of Sade. A pyramid of green incense is burning. The tube is inside me. Inhaling deeply, I steady myself, then release the catch. Water flows swiftly down from the large container hanging from the ceiling, passing through the piping, and ripples into me. A half gallon of water slowly tumbles its way into my rectum, swirling gradually up into my large intestine. My stomach swells unexpectedly as I massage the water through me.

I was twenty-three years old when I found porno. I was a child.

I won't sit here and pretend I never loved it. I did. I won't pretend I never exulted in the excitement, never died of laughter or shivered in the giddy light of degeneracy. But neither will I hold on to porn forever.

I lived inside of porno, day in and day out. I picked out the high heels in the bathroom, smelled the perfume. I fingered the g-strings, stared at the soft downy arm hair of teenage women who were working for the attention, for spurious fame. I huddled in a clutch with my strong actors, clung to the majesty of their cocks like they were my own. And despite what I might have said at various moments, it was never just about the money. I thought you could disappear into porn, climb a ladder into the act of it and the heat of it, watch, wide-eyed, and stick yourself in for a quick taste. But it was so hard to climb out without blood on your hands. In the end, I didn't leave because porn was simple, or stupid. I left because my own actions while inside it presented me with a vision of myself that I didn't much like or respect.

Porn aged me. It aged me in dog years. My eyes have seen the gloryholes, far too many to forget. But I try not to let it define me. The real story is now. The real story is *always* now.

Outside, there's the friendly murmur of indistinct chatter. I gaze down, observe my swollen stomach. It's distended, crying out for release. I hear a gurgle deep within—a thoroughly humble and humorous sound. With a gasp, unable to hold my ground any longer, I release the water, let go of my bowels, and it all flows out from within me. I laugh, a desperate, relieved, dying sort of sound. I stare up at the ceiling, breathing, smelling the pungent reek of what's come out of me.

ACKNOWLEDGMENTS

If this addendum appears rather too expansive at first glance, well, I apologize. But the truth is, writing this book took awhile, and in order to complete the job, I greatly needed the help of many friends, family members, and colleagues. It's my sincere hope that the number of salutes included here doesn't in any way diminish the specific gratitude I feel toward each one of you.

Mom and Dad, I love you guys deeply. It might not have been your most cherished dream to have your son become a pornographer, but you stepped up and dealt with the shock admirably. Thank you for engaging with me honestly every step of the way. I cannot express how much it meant that you accepted me, trusted my judgment, and let me know that you were on my side.

My early readers were crucial: Ruby May, Jen Collins, Mark Allen, Bryan Bell, Ben Holt, Kevin Murphy, Rebecca Stern, Raafi Rivero, and Anna Welch got pages flung at them along the way, and their enthusiasm got me through dark spots. Josh Lefkowitz (Whutsiznaim), David Gueringer, Sam Cooper, Stephani Norwood, Warren Frazier, Grace Krilanovich, Ben Westhoff, Andy Isaacson, Amir Flesher, Adi Flesher, and Jean-Paul Travers swooped down and read the whole goddamn thing. These charitable friends gently helped me understand which chapters I was meant to salvage, and which I'd need to axe violently, then walk away . . .

Reilly Brennan, Anna Tes, Nate Luzod, and particularly Shane Mahoney deserve special thanks for their incredible work in publicizing an earlier, self-published version of this book. I'm also grateful to my agent, Ryan Harbage, for doing a superlative job in representing me, and for going to the mat for me when it counted most.

Jon Wagner and Tony Cokes inspired me with their teaching. Jason Kasarda kept me laughing all the way, every day.

It's been a thrill to work with the Simon & Schuster team. Giant thanks to Jen Bergstrom for bringing me into the fold; to Jen Robinson for getting the word out; and to Michael Nagin for a great cover. Extra-special thanks to Emilia Pisani for her invaluable assistance in the editing process. And to Jeremie Ruby-Strauss, my talented editor-at-large, thanks for taking a chance on me when no one else would. I'm grateful.

Willie Timberlake gets a big-time tip of the hat here, for allowing me to reprint several large portions verbatim from the many letters he sent me over the years. These were wild epistles, from a strange and talented brain. In fact, T, your stuff was so good, and reeked so deeply of the real you, that I couldn't resist snatching quite a few key phrases and putting them in your mouth. *I have three pairs of slacks suitable for work. Only one of them has cum stains on them.* Well, me too, Will. Me too. I'll await your upcoming book with great anticipation. I sense it will be clever, disgusting, relentless, and wise: just like you.

My single greatest nod is owed to Julian Hoeber. Not only did he read every word in this book at least twice, he talked me through nearly every major structural decision. He spent hours on the phone convincing me that I had no choice but to write this book truthfully—which of course meant delving into all the embarrassing stuff I wanted so badly to forget. Without Julian, I would have quit; in fact, I might well not have started. That I made it to this point at all is testament to his considerable skills as a remarkably lucid thinker and generous friend.

And finally, I owe a considerable debt to the people I met at every step along the way in the sex industry. Thank you for taking me in, allowing me to see your lives, and making me one of you. In retrospect, it was all a bit much . . . but I still wouldn't change a thing.